PENGUIN CLASSICS

HEROIDES

PUBLIUS OVIDIUS NASO was born in 43 BC at Sulmo (Sulmona) in central Italy and educated at Rome, where his studies were concentrated in the law and rhetoric. While such a background prepared him for a public career, he also devoted himself to poetry. His first published work was *Amores*, a collection of short love poems; this was followed by *Heroides*, verse-letters, *Ars Amatoria*, a handbook on love, *Remedia Amoris* and *Metamorphoses*. By about AD 8 he had become a prominent literary figure in Rome. However, in the same year he was banished to Tomis, on the Black Sea. It is generally thought that the reasons for his exile include the contents of the *Ars Amatoria*, which greatly angered Augustus. He continued to write, notably *Tristia* and *Epistulae ex Ponto*, and always spoke longingly of Rome. He died, still in exile, in AD 17.

HAROLD ISBELL graduated from Loras College, Iowa, in 1959. He took his MA in 1962 at the University of Notre Dame, later joining the university's faculty in the Program of Liberal Studies. Prior to 1972 he was Writer in Residence, Director of the Writing Program, and most recently held the position of Associate Professor of English at St Mary's College at Notre Dame. From 1972 until 1983 he was an officer and a director of the Continental Bank and Trust Company in Salt Lake City. Over the years he has served on the boards of directors of one school, two ballet companies and a publishing house. At present he is retired and living in San Francisco, California. His poems, reviews and essays have been published in various places, and he is also the editor and translator of *The Last Poets of Imperial Rome*, which has appeared in Penguin Classics.

OVID

Heroides

Translated with Introductions and Notes by
HAROLD ISBELL

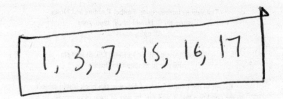

PENGUIN BOOKS

PENGUIN BOOKS

Published by the Penguin Group
Penguin Books Ltd, 80 Strand, London WC2R ORL, England
Penguin Group (USA) Inc., 375 Hudson Street, New York, New York 10014, USA
Penguin Books Australia Ltd, 250 Camberwell Road, Camberwell, Victoria 3124, Australia
Penguin Books Canada Ltd, 10 Alcorn Avenue, Toronto, Ontario, Canada M4V 3B2
Penguin Books India (P) Ltd, 11 Community Centre, Panchsheel Park, New Delhi – 110 017, India
Penguin Group (NZ), cnr Airborne and Rosedale Roads, Albany, Auckland 1310, New Zealand
Penguin Books (South Africa) (Pty) Ltd, 24 Sturdee Avenue, Rosebank 2196, South Africa

Penguin Books Ltd, Registered Offices: 80 Strand, London WC2R ORL, England

www.penguin.com

First published 1990
Reprinted with a new Chronology, Further Reading and corrections 2004

026

Translation, Introductions, Further Reading and Notes
copyright © Harold Isbell, 1990, 2004
All rights reserved

Printed in Great Britain by Clays Ltd, St Ives plc
Filmset in Monophoto Bembo

ISBN-13: 978-0-14-042355-6

www.greenpenguin.co.uk

Contents

Contents

Introduction

Publius Ovidius Naso was born in 43 BC, and died in AD 17. He was educated in Rome where his studies were concentrated in the law and rhetoric. While such a background prepared him for a public career he also devoted himself to poetry. By about AD 8, he had become a prominent literary figure in Rome. That year he was banished to Tomis, a dismal provincial town on the Black Sea. The reasons for the exile are thought to be twofold, with general agreement that the contents of the *Ars Amatoria* as well as some other unspecified fault had greatly angered Augustus.

Ovid was a prolific writer who produced a number of long works that were widely read in his own day and in the centuries after his death. He devoted much of his poetic career to the subject of love and its effects. It is evident that Ovid sought immortal fame by abandoning the epic style of Virgil and devoting himself to a celebration of human experience. In all his works he explores human emotion, its causes and effects. Though writing in the period following the great achievements of Virgil and Horace, Ovid displayed a level of competence that is in no way diminished by comparison with the competence and accomplishment of his forebears. He did not follow in the footsteps of his immediate precedessors except to demonstrate his own richly independent genius. It should be noted that any attempt to establish a chronology of composition for the extant works of Ovid is certain to be frustrated. Though a consensus seems to have arisen among scholars, any evidence is necessarily fragmentary and too often inconclusive. For the most part it is possible to place various works sequentially in the chronology but at many points the placement becomes a matter of conjecture.

If it can be said that the *Heroides* as a unified work has a common subject matter, it is very simply the tension that exists between what is desired and what is possible within the context of love and erotic desire. Though this tension between what is wanted and what can actually be achieved is in every case doomed to be frustrated, each letter defines and describes the amorous experience in terms that are unique to the circumstances of its writer.

It is significant for an understanding of this work that one should be attentive to the narrative style. A narrator writing in the first person or epistolary style is necessarily confined; the narrative flows out of an individual experience with all its sensory and imaginative limitations. The progress of each letter, then, necessarily moves in ways that indicate the state of mind of the fictive character writing it. In every case the letter is the product of a mind which has come to some critical juncture. As the letter develops out of the uncertainty, even the terror, of crisis we perceive the mind's expression as reflecting the mind's distracted condition. While such a notion may seem a commonplace observation, it is essential to any understanding of Ovid's accomplishment.

Very simply put, Ovid is not so much telling a story as he is fleshing out the bare bones of another author's minor character to reveal a depth and profundity of personality not inconsistent with the character we already know from other reading. The subject of Ovid's sources can be confusing and complex in the extreme. One consideration, however, is important. In selecting the materials to be used Ovid ranged widely through the works available in his day. As well as a deep knowledge of Homer, he also shows a great familiarity with Greek and Roman drama and literature. Ovid has always been famous for his ability to use and manipulate mythological material, and he also displays a working knowledge of geography and astronomy. Clearly Ovid was a man of substantial learning who was able to adapt this to serve the task at hand.

Throughout the work there is a recurring concern with obligations and duties. But it is only seldom that any of Ovid's characters find themselves torn between their obvious obligation to an existing contract of marriage and their desire for immediate gratification. The resolution of such a conflict takes a variety of forms but they are all, for the most part, rationalizations which insist that the ardour of passion has created its own obligation – or necessity – which now must be honoured. In the hands of these characters stability becomes a movable thing indeed. There is a recurring motif of legalism through many of the letters. There is talk of lawyers and suits, of what is owed and what is expected. Where the usual understanding of marriage has been that of a binding contract publicly executed before witnesses, there is now a strong attempt to apply the same form to desire and infatuation.

The experience of love is a very complex emotional phenomenon. Love exists in many forms and it can be both rational and irrational, with every possible degree of difference between the two. While an ideal love might find the lover wishing for that which is best for the beloved, the love which is revealed in these letters is never totally altruistic but is always egoistic to some degree. Even when the writer of a letter wished for the beloved to be preserved from harm, the unstated premise always remains that the safety of the beloved must be maintained so that the lover can continue to possess the loved one. Out of this pattern Ovid develops the rich and pervasive ironies that are central to each letter.

The ethical vision revealed in these letters is quite at odds with any usual understanding of ethics and ethical norms. In almost every imaginable way Ovid sets his characters against the accepted standards of public morality. That the behaviour here revealed might have a very strong feeling of realism about it only emphasizes that public morality and private behaviour are quite frequently at odds, not only for these fictional characters, but also for Ovid and his contemporaries, as well as for us.

The *Heroides* begins with the good wife, Penelope, writing to her husband, the long-absent Ulysses. For Penelope the absence of Ulysses is not a simple thing easily described, because she lacks definite information. Without doubt Ulysses remained true to his intention that he should return from Troy to Ithaca. However, there were also the long delays, delays which he might have prevented. While duty continued to call the absent husband, just as powerful were the calls to pleasure and adventure that Ulysses never hesitated to indulge. While Ulysses certainly saw his various adventures as necessarily dictated by the circumstances in which he and his men found themselves, Penelope shrewdly suspects that the necessity might have been less urgent. Through all this, however, Penelope remained not only faithful but single-minded in her devotion to Ulysses.

It is quite obvious that Penelope could have concluded that Ulysses was indeed dead or at least lost to her. At such a juncture she could have made for herself a marriage on terms that would be at least as desirable as those of her marriage to Ulysses. This, however, she chose not to do. Why did she remain faithful to Ulysses? Was it that she wanted to be in the position of returning his kingdom to him or was it that she feared his anger at the time of his return? Whatever the reasons might have been, the fact is that this first letter is the one which most exemplifies an altruistic love. Written within the context of a marriage contract that she is desperately trying to maintain, it affirms a degree of virtue and probity that is matched only in the letter of Laodamia (XIII). However, the virtue demonstrated by Penelope is that of an older woman who might well have sought amorous adventures in the long absence of her husband. The love of Laodamia for Protesilaus is very much more erotic, so that Laodamia has little or no incentive to choose between lovers. She desires only her absent Protesilaus and that he should be preserved in safety for her. The fidelity of Laodamia has not been tested by the passage of time and the onset of other passion. The fidelity of Penelope, however, has been tested and has not been found wanting.

An important consideration in reading these letters is the attention given by the fictional authors to the twin phenomena of death and separation. Many of these characters openly discuss the likelihood of their own suicide if in fact the separation they now address does not come to some satisfactory resolution. On the other hand there is often a strongly expressed fear that the beloved to whom the letter is addressed might die or come to serious harm before a return can be effected. It is a commonplace of modern criticism that Ovid always displays a very acute understanding of the workings of the human mind. Certainly this observation is true in relation to the *Heroides*. A number of the writers observe that their love is coloured by fear. It is interesting to look closely at the fear which is here being described.

Earlier, mention was made of the distinction between altruistic love, in which the lover's sole object is the good of the beloved, and egoistic love, in which the lover's sole object is the good of himself or herself. An examination of these two definitions will very quickly show that the likelihood of an entirely altruistic or generous love is quite remote while the likelihood of a totally egoistic or selfish love is only somewhat more likely. While it could be argued that either extreme on this continuum is behaviour that displays a severe pathology and therefore is seldom found, it is also obvious that for most people the experience of love is a mixture of the two characteristics.

The letters of the *Heroides* present this dichotomy in a rich variety of ways. Many of the letters – and the sources from which they are derived – reveal a personality that is deficient in one way or another. On the other hand we must observe that very few, if any, personalities in either life or fiction are able to function consistently to produce an optimally good life. I would suggest that it is a personality which exhibits both good and evil that is most interesting for an audience and most typical of the people with whom we, the readers, live and work.

A few of the characters in these letters are quite evil; one thinks at once of Phaedra and Medea. Yet even here, particularly in the case of Medea, the evil is not entirely unalloyed. Medea does briefly reveal herself as a pitiful person able to be concerned for those around her and who profoundly regrets the actions she must take in retaliation for the great wrong that has been done to her. For others the evil is more subtle, revealing itself as a failure to know and to understand, a failure to be wise, an ignorance which is – in the eye of the reader – at least partially culpable. At this point one must think of Paris. Perhaps the greatest number of the characters are in error because they have chosen to be ignorant. The most pervasive ignorance in the letters, however, is the almost universal wish to equate the ardour of a personal passion with permission – even a mandate – to pursue the passion.

The literary device most commonly employed by Ovid is irony. The epistolary style of narration, using the first person throughout, greatly facilitates this because it permits a pervasive failure to perceive any larger reality within which an action can have meaning or significance. Another and very important aspect of this irony is that the reader in every instance is almost certain to know the outcome of the story, an outcome which the writer cannot know at the time the letter is written and one which it seems the writer is never able to foresee with sufficient clarity to alter a course of action.

Another source of irony is to be found in the fact that every lover is writing out of a desire for union with the beloved, a union which it is hoped will result in stability and permanence. While this is the stated desire of the writer, it is the reader's universal experience that nothing in this life can be static. The irony arises with the reader's realization that the only stability free of change is to be found in the death of either one or the other or both parties. While love causes one to desire the unchanging fulfilment of love, it is only in death that anything can be said to be free of change.

This apparently impossible paradox is addressed in letter XIII, Laodamia to Protesilaus. These two had been married only a little while when Protesilaus was summoned by Ulysses to join the Greek forces being marshalled by Menelaus. Laodamia grieves that her husband set sail on the first good wind and also that, having left Phylace, he and his ships have been detained at Aulis. She urges him to prosecute the war so that peace may quickly be won and he can return to her. At the same time she knows of an oracle which prophesies the death of the first Greek to set foot on Trojan soil. Though it must seem improbable that this one man out of so many should be the one to die in this way, the reader already knows that in fact Protesilaus will impetuously jump from his ship and soon enough become the first Greek casualty.

While Laodamia is being most conventional in her plea that Protesilaus hurry home to her, the fact is that even if he survived the war he would not be free to return until the war had ended. By urging him to hurry she is unwittingly urging him to his death. It seems that she recognizes this, yet she cannot believe that he will be the first to die. Though she warns him about the prophecy, she also urges him to return quickly, and thus she reduces the prophecy to a playful banter. By this transformation she ultimately denies its import. The irony resides in the fact that while she cannot know for a certainty what will come to pass, the reader knows all too well what will happen.

Laodamia ends her letter before she knows of her husband's death. But the myth proceeds beyond the letter's end. In the myth Laodamia does finally learn that Protesilaus has died. The gods take pity on her terrible grief and permit Protesilaus to leave the Underworld for three hours. At the end of this time Laodamia is so unwilling to be separated from him that she commits suicide so that they will at least be together in death. At such a juncture the reader might well wonder if Laodamia has accomplished much more than a cessation of pain. But if the separation of the lover and the beloved is the ultimate pain, then the cessation of that pain, whether by a reunion or by mutual death, is a good thing.

Throughout these letters there are recurring patterns of imagery which have the effect of uniting the letters into a whole and also serve to place the *Heroides* within the tradition of erotic poetry. Two of these images are fire and arrows. By now it is a cliché to refer to the experience of being in love as being on fire or being pierced by an arrow. Perhaps the expression was a cliché in the time of Ovid as well. However, the fact that the symbol has been used for many centuries does not alter the fact that it continues to be a powerful and compelling description of a person's state of mind.

The image of fire is central to the myth of Paris. Ovid's audience would remember that Hecuba, near the end of her pregnancy, dreamed that she was giving birth to a blazing ember which very quickly spread its flames to the city of Troy. Priam's advisers saw the ember as a representation of the child about to be born. The baby was left exposed on a hillside, but as so often happens, it was secretly rescued and grew to manhood. In his letter (XVI) Paris shows that he is familiar with the story. Though he identifies the blazing ember with his own person, he understands the prophecy as a symbolic statement, assuming that it refers to him blazing with the flames of love. He utterly fails to understand the identification as a literal statement of the fate of Troy. And by this failure to understand it seems that Paris – at least as he is here depicted by Ovid – seems convinced that what he will bring back to Troy is the intensity of his love in the person of Helen, his beloved. This profound failure to understand has cataclysmic consequences. Many of these letters take their origin and point of departure from some aspect of the Trojan War, and many of the characters – like Paris – will find themselves in a conflagration that is nothing more or less than the ardour of love set within the destruction of country, of family, and of personal position.

Similarly the arrow is a pervasive image, echoing as it does the iconography commonly associated with Cupid and the experience of love. But the arrow, like fire, also carries the suggestion of rapacious violence. In each case the effect of fire or an arrow is one of the greatest and most destructive aggression. Again and again we see the horrific consequences of love unleashed. While every character embraces love without reservation, the reader must always confront the ruin following from such an act.

It is instructive to consider Ovid's use of myth, the material which came to him from the literary and religious past of Greece and Rome. Ovid's ability to bring myth into his work has, through the centuries, dazzled and confused his readers. While a diligent reader of the *Heroides* can trace and elucidate the various myths that are cited or to which Ovid alludes, a few at least will be either so obscure as to defy explanation or will obviously refer to works no longer extant.

The mythological apparatus must never be seen as an exercise in pedantry. On the contrary, a very good case can always be made for the totally appropriate placement of each mythological element in the *Heroides*. An extreme example of this can be found in the double epistles of Acontius and Cydippe (XX and XXI). The first letter, by Acontius, outlines the plot and sets it within a religious context. Acontius has found a most attractive young woman at the shrine of Diana on Delos. To catch her attention and win her affection he rolls into her path an apple on which he has incised the words of an oath. Cydippe is given the apple by her nurse who urges her to read. Without thinking, the girl obeys and speaks aloud the words of an oath in which she seems to call on Diana to witness her determination to marry Acontius.

Cydippe falls ill. Already betrothed to an anonymous youth chosen by her father, she does not have the strength to be married. Acontius argues that her infirmity is the result of breaking an oath to Diana; Cydippe argues that an oath to be valid requires an informed consent which she never gave. It soon becomes obvious that Cydippe's illness is caused not by the anger of Diana but by the fact that she suddenly finds herself ambivalent and more than a little interested in the attentions of Acontius. In this letter the myth becomes a vehicle by which Acontius can pursue his desire while Cydippe very nicely argues that Acontius' case has no merit. At the very end of her letter the myth has been abandoned as she realizes that she is drawn to whatever attractive qualities she begins to perceive in Acontius. Acontius' approaching victory is not something given him by a goddess but is brought about by the way in which he has managed to attract the attention of Cydippe. In other words, Acontius is about to have Cydippe because he has presented himself as a possibly attractive object.

Another significant and important myth that reverberates throughout the *Heroides* is the Judgement of Paris. The myth is first mentioned by Oenone in her letter to Paris (V). According to the myth, the wedding of Peleus and the goddess Thetis was attended by all the gods and goddesses except Eris, or Strife. To revenge herself on both

gods and men Eris threw into the party a golden apple inscribed with
the words, 'For the fairest'. Three goddesses, Aphrodite, Athena and
Hera, all of great beauty, each assumed that of course the bauble
must be meant for her. An argument broke out and Zeus, to bring
peace to the wedding party, sent the three in the company of Hermes
to Paris who would presumably be able adequately to judge feminine
beauty. Each of the goddesses offered Paris a bribe: Hera pledged
that if chosen she would render all the world subject to the rule of
Paris; Athena, that she would guarantee that Paris would always be
victorious in war; Aphrodite, the goddess of love, that she would
give Paris the love of the world's most beautiful woman, Helen.
Paris lost no time in determining that the beauty of Aphrodite was
pre-eminent. With that Paris – and Troy – secured the protection and
patronage of Aphrodite while Hera and Athena gave their favour to
Greece. The effects of the choice were disastrous.

With the release of Strife into the affairs of gods and men, the
Trojan War followed. But where the war in all its complexity would
require much more than a decade to come to an end, this very simple
myth summarized the entire history. While the fact of a Trojan
débâcle and a Greek victory might be virtually inexplicable, this
myth provided an explanation.

Myth and mythology are not normative values in the Heroides;
rather they are used to describe, to summarize, to provide paradigms
that elucidate but never shape the characters given to us. Myth and
religion do not direct the action of these letters; rather they describe
the action either as it has been carried out or as it is about to be
carried out.

It is quite obvious that the Heroides as we have it today exists in
two parts. The first fifteen letters were written at a relatively early
point in Ovid's career and were probably published after the first
edition of the Amores but before a second, revised and expanded,
edition of that work. The last six letters of the Heroides (XVI–XXI)
probably date from the time of the Fasti. Though we have virtually
nothing beyond internal evidence to provide any dating of these
works it quickly becomes clear that the final six letters, the so-called
double letters, are of a markedly different style, and the characters
are treated quite differently from those of the first fifteen letters.

Henricus Dörrie, however, in his recent edition of the text, separates the fifteenth letter – Sappho to Phaon – from its usual place in the sequence and places it after the text in an appendix. It seems, by now, that scholarly opinion is nearly unanimous in seeing this letter as of genuine authenticity despite the uncertainties which surround its manuscript tradition. The issue, as it is raised by Dörrie, concerns the question of whether or not this letter is to be included in an edition of the *Heroides*.

It seems sufficient to say that the letter's characters – the poet Sappho and the absent Phaon – are not found in mythology and therefore do not belong with those of the preceding fourteen letters. It may well be that in his lifetime Ovid published an edition of the *Heroides* which did not contain this letter. However, we must recognize the fact that this letter not only exists in the manuscript tradition but is said by various ancient authors to be listed among the others of the *Heroides*. It also seems quite accurate to assert that at this time there is no textual study which questions its Ovidian authenticity. Certainly it must be noted that in the *Amores* (II.18, lines 19–34) Ovid makes clear and unequivocal reference to the subject of this letter as well as to those of Penelope (*Heroides*, I), Phyllis (II), Oenone (V), Canace (XI), Hypsipyle (VI), perhaps Medea (XII), Phaedra (IV), Ariadne (X), and Dido (VII). A careful survey and analysis of the issue of this letter's authenticity and its place in the canon can be found in Jacobson, *Ovid's Heroides*.[1]

It seems, however, that a critical comment more germane to the fact at hand is that this fifteenth letter is different in kind from either those that preceded it or those that follow. This is worth consideration. The fifteenth letter gives us a writer who is more nearly a historical figure than any other character in the *Heroides*. In addition, Sappho is a woman of relatively low birth who is writing to a man of even lower status. We know nothing of Phaon except that he is an exceptionally attractive man who has been at one time the lover of Sappho and who was employed as a boatman. While the question of homosexual attraction has at least been hinted at in some of the other earlier letters, this letter addresses the issue directly.

Of the early letters all are written by women and all, with the exception of Sappho's, are written by figures found in classical myth. In every case these early letters are written by women to lovers who are now for a rich variety of reasons absent and whose absence may well be permanent. Some of these women are quite helpless when confronted by such a situation, while others fairly bristle with threats of either suicidal or homicidal destruction. Most write out of an erotic experience fully consummated and in many cases with off-spring near at hand. Only one – Phaedra – writes in the hope of first enticing, then seducing, an aloof and virginal young man. In almost every case – perhaps with the exception of Penelope – the burden of a deeply erotic desire argues against the restrictions placed on the individual by the norms of society.

The last six letters (the double letters), though obviously written within the constraints of the first-person narrative, display significant differences when compared with the first fifteen letters. In the three sets of double letters the initial letter is written by a male lover and the second is the woman's reply. In itself this structural change represents a significant departure from the earlier letters. The differences, however, are greater than this most obvious one.

In all the earlier letters the absent male figure is portrayed as a rather simple character uncomplicated by considerations of any aspect of his lover's personality or circumstances. The one characteristic these fifteen men have in common is that they are unfeeling and unconcerned. In a close reading of each letter we notice, especially in the first fifteen, a posture of supplication which views the absent male object of the letter as a being of great and even god-like power. At the same time the heroine realizes that the man who exercises such power over her fortunes and her feelings has already revealed himself as un-god-like and inhuman in his treatment of her.

In the last letters this typology is entirely reversed. Each of the three correspondences is initiated by the male figure who wishes to overcome some obstacle that presently hinders his amorous pursuit of the object of his desire. In the case of Paris the obstacle, as he sees it, is the commitment of Helen to an existing contract of marriage. In the case of Leander it is an ill-defined shyness that requires him to swim secretly to Hero and thus places him at the mercy of the elements. For Acontius it is the fact that Cydippe not only does not know him and hence cannot love him but that she also is betrothed to another.

The letters of each of these three men are written with an air of secrecy which suggests that something improper or even illicit is being attempted. Certainly for Paris and Acontius this is true. For Hero, however, the secrecy is of another character. It would appear that the correspondence of Hero reflects a shyness before another kind of perceived impropriety. Because they live on opposite sides of the Hellespont they almost certainly represent different cultures. Presumably each is the offspring of a family of prominence, if not of royal status. In an environment of marriages arranged for dynastic reasons quite independent of love and affection, it is entirely probable that the respective families would either oppose or prevent such a liaison. Interestingly, it is Leander and Hero's nurse who argue that they must maintain secrecy. Hero, on the other hand, would be quite content to have Leander with her for any length of time. The plot line is not unfamiliar. One need only think of *Romeo and Juliet* and *West Side Story* to know that such a conflict has a perennial interest.

The absent men of the first fifteen letters are presented as flat and uncomplicated and those men of the last six present themselves as driven by an overriding passion. Throughout these twenty-one letters it is the men who injure by their various defects and deficiencies. Though Hippolytus (IV) is an exception to this, Phaedra certainly argues that he does her great injury by refusing to acknowledge her overtures. Whether or not this is actually true of the character is beside the point because all we have here is the character as the work presents him. In the double letters, particularly those of Helen and Cydippe, it is the woman who recognizes the difficulties which will follow from the correspondence. However, these women also examine the difficulties and finally find a way to acquiesce in the proposal. Whether the acquiescence represents a denial of their own circumstances or a solution of the problem is a question never addressed.

There is another important distinction between the single and the double letters. That is, in the first fifteen letters the pleasures of love have already been tasted, either in fact or, as in the case of Phaedra (IV), in the imagination and the writer of the letter now has nothing but the bitterness of love denied. In the last six letters, on the other hand, the tone is one of hope and optimism, where the possibility of love has only been suggested or, for Leander, too briefly enjoyed, and is yet to be experienced in its fullness.

The *Heroides* is a varied work. While the similarities and unities from letter to letter are striking and even at times quite obvious, it is still difficult to identify precisely a type of these letters. Because they were written over a period of time and because they include plots and characters of the widest diversity, they are, paradoxically, as much united in their variety as in their sameness.

The one quality which runs through all is the irony with which every situation, every expectation, every setting for action is viewed. What is most desired, a stable and consistent enjoyment of love, is in fact uniformly denied. At the same time the ethical and legal norms of appropriate behaviour are everywhere shown to be less than satisfactory because they frustrate the reasonable expectations of joy and happiness. While the reader is never far removed from public morality, the reality here described is action taken in private which attacks both the public morality and those who subscribe to its strictures. It would seem that Ovid does not so much undermine the laws as demonstrate that the law is honoured more in the breach than in the observance.

The form in which I have cast my translation requires some comment. All the letters are translated into an English syllabic couplet, in which the lines are of alternating length with eleven syllables in the first and nine syllables in the following line. The concluding couplet of each letter is set in lines each containing twelve syllables. Beyond this simple quantitative consideration I have made no attempt to use a form based either on accent or on rhyme that has any relation to Ovid's own scheme. In Ovid, the couplet structure is basic to the style of the poem. It is important, I believe, to duplicate that structure in a translation because the flow of Ovid's writing, the pattern of his expression, is so precisely fitted to the couplet form. For me the goal was an English translation that captured at least some of the form as well as as much of the substance as possible. Because this correspondence is invariably less than perfect, the reader must endure the treason worked by the translator on the original.

For my work with the text of Ovid I have relied on two recent editions: that of Dörrie[2] and of Showerman.[3] For a critical analysis of the entire work I have been greatly dependent on Howard Jacobson, *Ovid's Heroides*.[4] My only regret is that Professor Jacobson has treated only the first fifteen letters of the *Heroides*. Another work of great value to the student is the essay by W. S. Anderson, 'The *Heroides*'.[5] A new and valuable departure in the method and style of Ovidian criticism is to be found in Florence Verducci, *Ovid's Toyshop of the Heart*.[6] Beyond these works the literature is indeed vast. Several of my favourites are H. Fränkel, *Ovid: A Poet between Two Worlds*,[7] E. K. Rand, *Ovid and his Influence*[8] and L. P. Wilkinson, *Ovid Surveyed*.[9] A very useful and illuminating understanding of the place of women in that Roman society which was the first audience of the *Heroides* can be found in the work of Mary Lefkowitz and particularly in her two books, *Women in Greece and Rome*[10] and *Women in Greek Myth*.[11] Her recent essay, 'Feminist Myths and Greek Mythology', is most instructive.[12]

I do hope that this translation will make available to the interested reader a work that has been a perennial favourite since the death of Ovid. Perhaps it will even encourage others to study what I regard as a most fascinating work of imaginative literature. Surely the last word has not been written on that art so slow to learn, the art of love.

It was my former teacher, Paul Beichner, CSC, the Chaucer scholar, who chanced the remark more than twenty-five years ago as we walked to lunch that the *Heroides* needed another translation. For this I am grateful.

Finally I write remembering two men who lived variously as scholars and my colleagues, but always as my friends: Patrick Miles Sweeney and Vincent Louis Heinrichs.

NOTES

1. Howard Jacobson, *Ovid's Heroides* (Princeton: Princeton University Press, 1974).

2. Henricus Dörrie, *P. Ovidii Nasonis Epistulae Heroidum* (Berolini et Novae Eboraci: Walter de Gruyter, 1971).

3. Grant Showerman, ed. and trans., *Ovid in Six Volumes*, volume I: *Heroides and Amores*, (Cambridge and London: Harvard University Press, 1977), pages 1–311. Second edition, revised by G. P. Goold.

4. ibid.

5. W. S. Anderson, 'The *Heroides*', in *Ovid*, ed. J. W. Binns (London and Boston: Routledge & Kegan Paul, 1973), pp. 49–83.

6. Florence Verducci, *Ovid's Toyshop of the Heart: Epistulae Heroidum* (Princeton: Princeton University Press, 1985).

7. Hermann Fränkel, *Ovid: A Poet between Two Worlds*, Sather Classical Lectures, University of California, vol. 18 (Berkeley and Los Angeles: University of California Press, 1945).

8. E. K. Rand, *Ovid and his Influence* (New York: Longmans, Green & Co., 1925).

9. L. P. Wilkinson, *Ovid Surveyed: An Abridgement for the General Reader of 'Ovid Recalled'* (Cambridge: Cambridge University Press, 1962).

10. Mary R. Lefkowitz and Maureen B. Fant, *Women in Greece and Rome* (Toronto and Sarasota: Samuel-Stevens, 1977).

11. Mary R. Lefkowitz, *Women in Greek Myth* (Baltimore: Johns Hopkins University Press, 1986).

12. Mary R. Lefkowitz, 'Feminist Myths and Greek Mythology', *The Times Literary Supplement*, no. 4451 (July 22–28, 1988) pages 804 and 808.

Chronology

_____

(Many of the dates, especially the publication dates for Ovid's works, are approximate and controversial.)

BC

43 *20 March*: Ovid born at Sulmo.

31 *2 September*: Battle of Actium; Octavian defeats Antony and Cleopatra.

28 Propertius 1.

27 Octavian becomes Princeps and Augustus.

25 Tibullus 1.

23 Horace *Odes* 1–3.

22 Propertius 2–3.

20 Ovid publishes the first edition of the *Amores*.

19 *21 September*: Virgil dies; his virtually finished *Aeneid* is published soon after.

   Death of Tibullus; his second book is probably published post-humously.

16 Propertius 4. Propertius publishes no more, and the date of his death is unknown.

15 Ovid publishes the first collection of the *Heroides*, letters from heroines.

10 Ovid publishes the second edition of the *Amores* sometime around here. He then probably goes on to write a first version of the *Ars Amatoria*, in two books.

8 *27 November*: Horace dies.

2 By now Ovid has almost certainly written his (now lost) tragedy, *Medea*; he embarks on a process of revising his elegiac works, adding a third book to a revised *Ars Amatoria*, publishing the *Remedia Amoris*, and adding the double epistles to the *Heroides*. After this process is complete (by ?AD 2), he is embarked on the *Fasti* and *Metamorphoses*.

AD

8 Ovid is relegated (in effect, exiled) to the Black Sea town of Tomis. His *Metamorphoses* is virtually complete and the *Fasti* half finished. He continues to work on the *Fasti* intermittently in exile, but never completes it.

9–12 Ovid composes the *Tristia* and the *Ibis*.

13 *Ex Ponto* 1–3 published.

14 *9 August*: Augustus dies. His adopted stepson, Tiberius, becomes emperor.

17 Ovid dies in exile. *Ex Ponto* 4 is published posthumously.

Further Reading

Since the publication of this translation in 1990, a number of scholars have addressed the critical and scholarly understanding of the *Heroides*. The following recently published titles are not meant to be exclusive, rather they should be seen as indicators of what is available.

Brill's Companion to Ovid, ed. Barbara Weiden Boyd (Leiden and Boston, MA, 2002).

Hagedorn, Suzanne C., *Abandoned Women: Rewriting the Classics in Dante, Boccaccio, & Chaucer* (Ann Arbor, MI, 2004).

Lindheim, Sara H., *Mail and Female: Epistolary Narrative and Desire in Ovid's Heroides* (Madison, WI, 2003).

Spentzou, Efrossini, *Readers and Writers in Ovid's Heroides: Transgressions of Genre and Gender* (Oxford and New York, 1997).

I: Penelope to Ulysses

Of all the stories and characters taken by Ovid from the epics of Homer, the story of Penelope and Odysseus must have been one of the most familiar to a Roman audience in the time of Augustus. Penelope writes this letter just after Telemachus has returned from his trip to Pylos where he sought information and advice from Nestor. As she writes, Penelope gives every indication that she knows well the details of the Trojan War. For the purposes of the fiction which Ovid is here creating she is familiar with this from listening to the many accounts by returning men – but men from Argolis, not from Ithaca, because the Ithacan forces under the command of Ulysses have not yet returned – as well as from whatever Telemachus might have learned on his travels. It is significant that Penelope writes this letter out of a deep suspicion that Ulysses is detained not merely by adverse winds and seas but also by his own dalliance with other women. In this suspicion, of course, she is entirely correct because Homer is careful to tell us that Ulysses did in fact linger with both Calypso and Circe for many years.

Penelope has been injured and she does not hesitate to berate Ulysses for that injury, an injury which might have been prevented, or so she guesses, had he only wished. The divine enmity which is delaying Ulysses seems not to be known to Penelope. Still, it must be noted that Ulysses has not always conducted himself with the prudence and care that might be expected of a man with serious obligations in other places.

Penelope complains at the depredations visited upon her by the many suitors who have gathered about her house in the prolonged absence of her husband. That they should do so is not surprising, since the kingdom of Ulysses was rich; to marry his widow would be to take possession of this kingdom and to accede to Ulysses' throne. In this, Penelope must be seen as a woman of very great power because she has the ability to make any of these suitors incomparably rich and powerful.

While Penelope can be seen as a veritable paradigm of virtue, a model beyond compare, Ovid also takes pains to show another side to her wifely virtue. At turns in this letter she is angry, fearful and anxious. Finally she preserves herself and Ulysses – surely a good thing – by deceiving the suitors in her assertion of a wife's obligation. The wifely paradigm of unreal proportion thus becomes once again a human being in whom the forces of good and evil struggle for supremacy but achieve only an uneasy truce.

The Penelope of Ovid is unlike that of Homer. In Homer, Penelope is not a well-developed character. She is, after all, not central to the action of the *Odyssey*. Here, however, she is not only the narrator but also the subject of her own narrative. All else becomes secondary to Penelope and the world which she creates as her habitat. That the names of these two literary characters, one Homeric, one Ovidian, are the same must not blind us to the fact that in these two works they are quite different.

The Penelope of the *Odyssey* never shines an unfavourable light on Ulysses. But then, Homer's Penelope can hardly be said to define any reality in which she exists. Homer's Penelope achieves her ends not so much by asserting herself as by proceeding indirectly, even by passivity. If the Penelope of Homer is the conventional wife to such a degree that she can become an exemplar, then Ovid's Penelope is unconventional, and though she is successful in her aims she gives new meaning to the notion of fidelity.

This new Penelope not only has the temerity to question the honour of Ulysses, she also does not hesitate to speak of her loss, her deprivation, her danger, even suggesting that the travails of Ulysses are diminished by comparison with her suffering. The Penelope of the *Heroides* – quite unlike that of the *Odyssey* – asserts that she, rather than Ulysses, is primarily and most properly worthy of sympathy and compassion. Finally, Penelope sees the events of the Trojan War as being her quite specific injury.

The importance of all this is not the portrait of Ulysses that we are given, but the fact that this portrait comes to us from the hand of Penelope. While we might be inclined to think Penelope a woman of great nobility, even heroic, in point of fact she is entirely susceptible to the most ordinary human passions. Penelope in the *Heroides* lacks regal dignity and in this respect she is exactly as Ovid intended her to be.

Penelope to the tardy Ulysses:
    do not answer these lines, but come, for
Troy is dead and the daughters of Greece rejoice.
    But all of Troy and Priam himself
are not worth the price I've paid for victory.[1]
    How often I have wished that Paris
had drowned before he reached our welcoming shores.
    If he had died I would not have been
compelled now to sleep alone in my cold bed
    complaining always of the tiresome
prospect of endless nights and days spent working
    like a poor widow at my tedious loom.
Imagining hazards more awful than real,
    love has always been tempered by fear:
I was sure it was you the Trojans attacked
    and the name of Hector made me pale;
if someone told the tale of Antilochus
    I dreamed of you dead as he had died;
if they sang of the death of Menoetius' son,
    slain in armour not his own, I wept,
because even clever tricks had failed; when they
    told the tale of Tlepolemus' death
I saw you die the death of that great warrior,
    drenching the Lycian's spear with warm blood.[2]
No matter which Greek died, their names could have been
    the same, my loving heart became ice.
But the god of chastity heard my prayer;
    Troy is a ruin and you are safe.
Our gods have seen the gold of Troy, our altars
    smoke with sacrifice, our men are home:
a wife gives thanks for her husband's return; he
    tells of fate and the conquest of Troy.
Older men and young girls marvel in silence;
    the wife cherishes his every word.

While they eat one will dip his finger in wine
    and trace on the board a map of Troy,
being careful to point out all the landmarks—
    both Sigeum and the Simois,
Priam's palace, all the places where such fierce
    battles were fought between the armies,
the two tents of Achilles and Ulysses
    and the path made by Hector's body.[3]
I sent Telemachus searching for you and
    he returned with much information.
When he came to Nestor's palace he was met
    and told of all your wonderful deeds.[4]
He told me the tales of Rhesus and Dolon,
    one died asleep, the other by guile.[5]
Yours was the courage, while forgetting your own,
    that let you set your stealthy feet where
the Thracian camp was pitched for the night and you
    could slaughter so many so quickly
with only one man to help. You were careful,
    I'm sure, always to think first of me!
Until I learned of your return to the lines
    with the horses of Ismarus my
heart could not stop leaping with fear at the fall
    of each word while that story was told.[6]
But what is all of this worth to me if Troy
    has been conquered by your arms, its walls
reduced to level ground? Pergama, I fear,
    was defeated for other women,
for me it still thrives.[7] I am not changed because
    I go on alone without my lord.
Fields of grain grow on the site of Troy, the soil
    has been sweetened by Phrygian blood
while ploughs drawn peacefully by captive oxen
    turn up the bones of buried heroes
and ruined palaces are covered by vines.
    You are a victor but I am here
alone while you loiter in some foreign place.
    Whoever comes to our shore must hear
my questions until he thinks I am crazy;

4

then I give him letters meant for you.
I sent word to Nestor at Pylos but he
    had no certain knowledge of your fate;
nor have the Spartans said anything useful.
    Where are you now, where do you delay?
If only the walls of Troy still stood and I
    had not prayed for early victory,
at least I would know the place where you fought and
    I would be afraid only of war;
then my sorrow would be that of many wives
    but as it is now I am alone.
Though no one has told me what things I should fear,
    it seems that everything frightens me.
I consider the perils of land and sea
    and wonder which has caused your delay.
But while I worry alone at home, perhaps
    it is only love that detains you:
be sure that I know how fickle men can be.
    Perhaps you describe me as simple,
and fit only for keeping your royal house,
    but I pray that I am mistaken,
that my charge is as slight as a fitful breeze,
    that you do not choose to stay away.
Here at home my father, Icarius, begs
    me to abandon my widow's bed.
He scolds me and says I am foolish to wait.
    But I am Penelope and I
am Ulysses' wife. My father knows this and
    he is less insistent than he was.
I am sure that he has watched me with care and
    is moved by my faith and chastity.
I have been your wife and yours I shall remain.
    But suitors besiege me in your house.
Men from Dulichium and Samos, even
    Zacynthus, gather about the door.[8]
Here in your hall they are the new masters and
    no man dares rebuke them. Should I tell
how Pisander, Polybus, and cruel Medon
    grow fat on the wealth won by your blood;

and how the grasping hands of Eurymachus
    and Antinous are never at rest?[9]
My heart is torn open, your riches wasted.
    But shame is added to this ruin
when your servants Melanthius and Irus
    bring in flocks of sheep to be slaughtered.[10]
We three – old Laertes, young Telemachus
    and a wife with no strength – cannot fight.
When I sent our son to Pylos these men tried
    to prevent his trip but he escaped.
I pray that he lives long, that he be the one
    to close our eyes in the peace of death.
We three have the aid of only three servants:
    two herdsmen and your very old nurse.[11]
Laertes cannot raise the royal sceptre,
    he is old and much too weak to fight.
Nor am I, a woman, strong enough to drive
    these villains out of your kingly hall.
Telemachus will become a man like you
    but first he needs a good man's training
that one day he too will be a man and have
    the strength that is proper to a man.
You can be sure that none of these men gives him
    the least example in manly ways.
You are my refuge and my home, my husband.
    Have a father's concern for your son;
let us see a son's concern for your father
    who waits now for you to close his eyes.
Just remember, I was a young girl when you left;
if you came at once you would find an old woman.

NOTES

1. At the time of the Trojan War, Priam was King of Troy. He was the father of many very distinguished children, including Hector, Cassandra and Paris. For a more complete discussion of the family of Priam, see PARIS in Appendix 1: Principal Characters.

2. Antilochus was one of the sons of Nestor and Eurydice. As a young man he was among the many contenders for the hand of Helen. When the Greek forces arrived at Troy, Antilochus distinguished himself as being not only one of the youngest but also one of the bravest of the Greeks. In the funeral games which were held after the death of Hector, Antilochus used trickery to defeat Menelaus for second place in the chariot races. After the event, however, he did disclose his action with an apology to Menelaus and an offer to give up his prize. Later in the war, he was killed by the Ethopian, Memnon.

Menoetius was the father of Patroclus. As a boy, or a very young man, Patroclus became the attendant and friend of Achilles. Though this is not directly stated in the *Iliad*, there is a long-standing tradition that Patroclus and Achilles were lovers. When Achilles was summoned to join the Greek forces at Troy, Patroclus made the journey with Achilles. Patroclus fought alongside Achilles until Achilles, his pride injured, withdrew from combat. While Achilles was sulking in his tent Patroclus realized that the Trojans were causing serious damage to the Greek position. He sought from Achilles permission to return to battle but he dressed himself in Achilles' armour and bore the latter's weapons. In this guise and mistaken for Achilles, he routed the Trojan forces and was for a time victorious. Finally, however, he was slain by Hector. After much difficulty, the Greeks were able to secure his naked body and they withdrew with it to their lines. Achilles, deeply grieved at the loss of his friend, refused to permit the rites of burial until he had avenged the death of Patroclus. This he did and the funeral occurred with the slaughter of twelve Trojan men over the body of Patroclus. Penelope here is very much concerned that Patroclus had been unable to survive by utilizing deceit. Clearly, her fear is that Ulysses, who is known for his skill at using deceits, might also fail to survive. See ACHILLES in Appendix 1: Principal Characters.

Tlepolemus was the King of Rhodes. He took nine ships of men and supplies to Troy, where he died in hand-to-hand combat with Sarpedon, King of Lycia, a Trojan ally.

3. Sigeum was a town in the vicinity of Troy. The Simois is a river flowing into the river Scamander near the city of Troy.

Hector was the oldest of Priam's sons. From the outset of the Trojan War, he led the Trojan army into battle and for most of the war effectively prevented a Greek victory. When Achilles returned to battle he and Hector met in hand-to-hand combat on the plain before the gates of Troy. Achilles gravely wounded Hector who, as he died, prophesied the speedy death of Achilles. Seeking revenge for the many men who had been killed by Hector, Achilles tied the hero's body to his chariot and dragged it three times round the walls of Troy as he made his way to the coast.

7

4. Nestor, King of Pylos, went to Troy with ninety ships when he was already a very old man. Upon his return to his home he regained his kingdom without strife. He was widely regarded in the Greek world as a man of great wisdom whose advice was actively and often sought on many different matters. When Penelope sends Telemachus to Nestor in search of information about the fate of Ulysses, she is not merely seeking to know the whereabouts of her missing husband, she is also hoping that Nestor can provide the boy with manly advice and counsel.

5. The story of the night-time foray into the Thracian camp – the Thracians were allies of Troy – is found in the *Iliad*, X. In this story Rhesus was a Thracian king who was killed by Ulysses, and Diomedes the 'one man' who went with Ulysses. Dolon was a Trojan spy apprehended and killed during that night raid.

6. Ismarus is a mountain in southern Thrace. The horses that belonged to Rhesus came from this place. Clearly, Penelope's assertion that Ulysses thought always of her while engaged in this noctural adventure is ironic in the extreme.

7. Pergama was the central fortification, the citadel around which the city of Troy was built.

8. Dulichium is an island in the Ionian Sea and in antiquity was thought to have been a part of the kingdom of Ulysses. Samos is an island off the coast of Asia Minor, not far from Ephesus. Zacynthus is an island in the Ionian Sea, just off the coast of Elis. These three are all in the vicinity of Ithaca. Penelope is making an extremely important point concerning the future of the House of Laertes. That is, without Ulysses to assert his regal prerogatives, the dynasty will be overthrown by one of the many suitors who have come to Ithaca from all parts of the kingdom.

9. Pisander and Polybus would be killed as Ulysses and Telemachus attacked the suitors. While Medon is here called 'cruel', in point of fact in the *Odyssey* his life is spared by Ulysses when Telemachus requests it. While Ovid and his readers would have known the outcome of the story, in fact Penelope as she writes this could not have foreseen the consequences of Ulysses' return. As the story is told in the *Odyssey*, Antinous was the first to die when Ulysses and Telemachus charged the banqueting hall. After the death of Antinous, Ulysses revealed himself to the suitors, and Eurymachus tried to lay the blame for all the waste and depredation on the dead man. When Ulysses refused to be placated, Eurymachus rallied the suitors to resist the attack. Enraged by this, Ulysses shot a second arrow and killed Eurymachus so swiftly that his body fell across his place at the table.

10. Melanthius was the goatherd who attempted to help the suitors by bringing a great armload of armour and weapons. Ulysses sent Eumaius, the

swineherd, and Philotes, the cowherd, to apprehend Melanthius as he rummaged in the cache of weapons. Ulysses, after they had captured the goatherd, commanded Eumaius and Philotes to bind his hands and feet behind his body and tie him to a pillar near the beams at the top of the hall, where he was left to die in agony. In the *Odyssey* Irus is the name given to a beggar at the house of Ulysses. Here, Ovid makes Irus one of the household servants.

11. These three are Eumaius, the swineherd, Philotes, the cowherd, and the old nurse Euryclia, who at the return of Ulysses recognized him in his disguise by a scar which he had had since boyhood.

II: Phyllis to Demophoon

In many ways Phyllis is very much more typical of the heroines of the *Heroides* than Penelope. The events which precipitate this letter are quite simple and all too familiar: Demophoon arrives, falls in love, takes every aid and succour and then hurries away on urgent business leaving behind the most extravagant promises to return – promises which, as the letter reveals, are not likely to be honoured. The story has been told with only minor variations many times throughout all of literature.

In her narrative Phyllis has every opportunity for rage, not to mention threats of revenge. Yet throughout she forgoes this entirely predictable response to the great wrong done her by Demophoon. In this she remains an entirely sympathetic and even pitiable character, a victim violated as much by her own goodness as by the careless deceit of Demophoon. The letter as written by Phyllis is almost a stereotypical presentation of a host sharing literally everything with an ungrateful and avaricious guest. That the host here is actually a woman only compounds the outrage perpetrated by Demophoon. In the usual order a woman could reasonably expect that the transfer of her possessions and the loss of her virginity to a man within the context of a loving trust would secure for her a stable and lasting marriage. Phyllis, however, has been loved and left.

But the transgression of Demophoon is not merely against ordinary decency. Phyllis is a princess, the daughter of a rich and powerful king, and on her actions depend the lives and fortunes of her subjects. In introducing dynastic considerations of the utmost gravity Phyllis becomes very much more than a woman realizing to her shame that she has indulged in a foolish affair. As she writes this letter Phyllis is at last convinced that though she has – at least by her own lights – loved well, she has in fact loved most unwisely because she failed to recognize the possible consequences. Yet as she here presents herself as a simple woman swept off her feet by an experienced man of the world, the reader cannot help remembering that love is blind.

The fault is not, however, entirely that of Demophoon. His deceit has its counterpart in the eagerness of Phyllis to be deceived and finally to deceive herself. By the end of the letter, as she recognizes the horror of her folly, she is reduced to the absurdity of finding the world of nature, the wind and the waves, agents of trust and security. Indeed she finds them the agents of beneficent deities, while humankind, especially Demophoon and her own subjects, are traitors to her needs and desires.

If Phyllis can be said to have a dominant vice, it is the vice of a credulity too easily adopted. She has not merely loved unwisely, she has in fact contrived her own downfall. The predictable treachery of Demophoon has been matched by her own foolish generosity.

Phyllis sends her complaint to Demophoon:
    you have not kept your promise to me.
I welcomed you to the shores of Rhodope
    and when you left your pledge was precise:
you would come when the moon's horns grew
   together.[1]
    Since then the moon has grown full four times.
When will the tides bring a ship from Attica?
    Counting days is a lover's business:
if you counted out the days like I, you would
    see that my complaint comes none too soon.
I still have just a little hope left, for we
    believe slowly when belief brings pain.
I have deceived myself by defending you;
    I could not think you had injured me.
How often when the wind was good I have tried
    to see the sails of your ship coming;
I have cursed Theseus, because I thought that he
    kept you from your intended voyage;
there have been times when I thought your ship was
  wrecked
    and you were drowned in the raging waves.

With prayer and incense I have beseeched our gods
    that you might be hurried on to me.
When the wind blows and the sky is good, I think
    if he is well he is coming now.
You swore by the gods to come again to me
    but even they have not brought you back.
It is quite clear to me now, not even love
    will move your ship, you delay too long.
When you left this port you unfurled your white sails
    and the wind blew your promise away.
I have not seen your sails again since that day;
    the promise you made has not been kept.
Tell me what have I done? I loved unwisely,
    my crime was simple: I wanted you.
My fall becomes its own reward, I am left
    with nothing more than your faithlessness.
You swore that we two were bound to each other
    but where now are those bonds that held us?
You put your right hand into mine and called on
    the living gods to witness your pledge;
we stood betrothed and Hymen's bond was given
    by you to guarantee our marriage.[2]
You swore fidelity by the raging sea
    over which you freely come and go,
by your grandfather – unless he too is one
    of your lies – who calms the sailor's way;
by Venus and those weapons that wound me now,
    the one the bow, the other the torch;
by Juno who guards the marriage bed and by
    the mystic rites of the torchbearer.[3]
If these injured gods desired their just revenge
    even your life could not be enough.
Like a mad woman I believed your speeches,
    I took your word and rebuilt your ships;
I gave you beams and planks of seasoned timber
    and oars to rush you away from me.
My pain is caused by weapons that I gave you.
    I believed your many begging words;
at last your family's great names convinced me

and I even believed in your tears.
But perhaps even tears can be taught to lie
    and flow whenever they are required.
I also trusted the gods by whom you swore;
    but why did you pledge so many times?
Any one of those pledges, even the least,
    would have been enough to trap my heart.
I have not regretted that I gave you aid;
    but my kindness should have ended there:
my welcome included myself and my bed,
    I pressed my body to yours; the night
before should have been the last night of my life.
    I should have been dead before you came.
But I hoped for better things, things I deserved:
    hope that rests in what is owed is just.
Remaining innocent, I would have received
    the proper reward for my goodness.
I was tricked by your words. Your glory is cheap,
    my trust deserved consideration,
I loved you as a woman loves. This will be
    the only thing remembered of you.
When men read the mighty deeds of the heroes
    they will read about Demophoon.
You might be a hero: let your statue stand
    with those of the sons of Aegeus.[4]
Your father will be first with his great deeds carved
    in white marble, followed by Sciron,
stern Procrustes, the mixed bull and man, Sinis,
    Thebes vanquished, the Centaurs defeated,
Pluto's kingdom assaulted – all will be there
    but last of all these, the inscription
carved beneath your statue will tell your story:
    'By tricks he stole love from his hostess.'[5]
Of all your father's great and wonderful deeds,
    you remember nothing more, it seems,
than his abandonment of a bride from Crete.[6]
    The only deed that causes him shame,
that is the one action you seem to admire;
    you have made yourself heir to his sin,

you take to yourself the shame of his deceit.
    Ariadne has a fine lord now,
without my envy, she drives a harnessed team
    of fine tigers before her high chariot;
but the men I rejected will not return
    because rumour has announced to all
the men of this country that I have preferred
    to take the offer of some stranger.
The opinion they hold is simple to state:
    'If her preference now is for the
Athenian wit, then let her go to Athens
    and let her seek the learning she wants;
another can be found easily enough
    to rule here in armed and warlike Thrace.
What has happened proves that she is more than wise.'[7]
    Anyone who thinks the deed is wrong
because of its result ought to be condemned,
    for if our waters should foam beneath
the insistence of your mighty oars, then they
    will say I planned well and I will have
their undying loyalty for the wisdom
    that saved myself and my countrymen.
That is all impossible. You will never
    sleep in my bed or bathe in our surf.
It is my fate that I have been found unwise
    and without the counsel of wisdom.
I cannot lose sight of the day you sailed off.
    Your ships were waiting on the waters
of my harbour, ready to leave, and you closed
    your arms around me putting your lips
on mine mingling tears and lingering kisses;
    a whispered pledge of undying love,
you cursed the breeze that played in your sails. Your last
    words were even shouted in the wind:
'Phyllis, do not forget that I will return.'
    Is it your sails that keep you away?
Obviously, you had no plan to return.
    Do you think I will sit here and wait
even though your mind is already made up?

But I cannot help waiting for you.
Though you are tardy, return to the woman
    who loves you more than anyone else.
Why should I beg? You have taken another
    by now, you have forgotten Phyllis;
hers now is the love that once you gave to me,
    by now, you have forgotten my name.
If you ever want to know about Phyllis,
    she, when you were nearly dead, rescued
you from the raging sea, she opened her port
    to you and your ships, she gave the wealth
of royal Thrace. She welcomed you and she gave
    freely and without the least regret
the priceless gift a maiden gives only once.
    The land of Lycurgus was too large,
she made it a part of her dowry; your hands
    deceitfully accepted all things given
that seemed of even the slightest worth.[8]
    Finding you without riches I gave
a king's estate, from Rhodope to Haemus,
    through which the swift river Hebrus flows.[9]
And my innocence also I gave as you
    undid the ties of my chastity.
This bridal was witnessed by Tisiphone
    shrieking her horrid hymns while a bird
that avoids the day's light sang her dismal song
    and throughout the ceremony small
serpents coiled around the neck of Allecto
    and the lights were torches from a tomb.[10]
Though my soul is heavy I climb on the rocks
    and along the thickly grown shoreline
wherever the ocean spreads itself; whether
    the soil is loosened in the warm sun
or whether the cold constellations glisten,
    I survey the straits: whenever sails
appear from far away I pray that they be
    gods bringing an answer to my prayers.
I run to the beach and stand there. As the sails
    come nearer, I grow weaker and soon

I fall backward fainting in my servant's arms.

    The bay is shaped like a bow pulled back,
its horns rising up out of the sea in cliffs.

    I want to drown myself in that place,
and I will if you are not faithful to me.

    The currents will carry me to you
and your eyes will see my unburied body.

    If you were hard as iron still you would
be driven to say, 'Not in this way, Phyllis,

    should you have followed me to this place.'
I long for poison; I wish that I could plunge

    a sword in my heart so that my blood
could be poured out and my life would be finished.

    Since you placed your arms about my neck
I should gladly tie a noose about it now.

    In choosing death, I will not delay.
You will be the cause of my dying; my tomb

    will have the following inscription:
'Demophoon killed Phyllis: a guest, he stole love

and by his theft caused the death that came from her
    hand.'

NOTES

1. Mount Rhodope is a range of mountains in western Thrace. Phyllis is saying that he promised to return when the moon had come round to the full, or within the period of one month.

2. Hymen, or Hymenaeus, was the patron god of marriage.

3. Poseidon was a god associated with the sea, with earthquakes and with horses. His son by Aethra was Theseus, who was the father of Demophoon: hence he is 'your grandfather'. Venus was a goddess of fertility, Juno the goddess of marriage and the wife of Jupiter. Cupid was often represented pictorially with at least one torch as a symbol of the ardour of carnal love and desire. Cupid is also often shown armed with a bow and arrows. In this passage, Ovid seems to suggest that a female torchbearer – either Demeter or Hecate – is also present.

4. See the entries for THESEUS, MEDEA and ARIADNE in Appendix 1: Principal Characters.

5. Sciron was a son of Poseidon. He was a brigand who robbed travellers as they passed by his lair. After robbing them, he compelled his victims to wash his feet; while they were doing this he kicked them over a cliff where they fell to the beach below and were eaten by a giant sea-turtle. Sciron was killed by Theseus.

Procrustes was the nickname (it means 'stretcher') of a man who lived near Eleusis. He was so called because he would invite travellers to spend the night with him and if they did not fit the bed which he provided he either cut off parts of their bodies or would stretch them out until they fitted it exactly. Theseus turned the tables on Procrustes by showing him the same hospitality.

The Minotaur, 'mixed bull and man', was killed by Theseus with the aid of Ariadne.

Sinis was an outlaw who killed his victims by tying them by the arm and leg of one side to a bent-over pine tree, while the arm and leg of the opposite side were tied to another arched pine tree. When the cords holding the pine trees in position were cut, the poor victim would either be flung to his death or torn apart by the rebounding trees. Sinis was killed by Theseus in the same way.

The great accomplishments of Theseus continue to be listed. In the conquest of Thebes by the seven heroes (as told by Aeschylus in *Seven Against Thebes*), it was Theseus who arranged for the burial of the seven. In middle age Theseus and Pirithous, King of the Lapiths, became close friends. Pirithous invited Theseus to his wedding, to which he also invited the centaurs. In the battle that broke out, Theseus assisted in the defeat of the centaurs. In another account, Theseus and Pirithous vowed that they would help one another find brides. Pirithous decided that he would abduct Persephone, Queen of the Underworld. Nothing could have been more dangerous. Because of their oath, Theseus went with Pirithous to the Underworld where, having arrived, they found themselves unable to leave. According to the story, Heracles, in the Underworld on another mission, was able to take Theseus back to the light of day, but failed to save Pirithous.

Clearly Theseus was of great heroic stature, and in this passage Phyllis lists some of his more obvious accomplishments. It is significant that she specifically mentions three men – Sciron, Procrustes and Sinis – who had seriously violated the laws of ordinary hospitality and trust so that each received a just and appropriate punishment at the hands of Theseus.

6. In his many adventures in the ancient world of the Mediterranean Theseus eventually came to Crete, where he fell in love with Ariadne, the daughter of King Minos. With Ariadne's help Theseus was able to enter the labyrinth, kill the Minotaur and make his escape. Ariadne then went with Theseus and was abandoned by him on the island of Dia, the modern Naxos.

Ariadne, who had given everything she held dear to fulfil her love for Theseus, was eventually married to another. Though this spouse is identified differently in the various accounts, the context here suggests that it was Ariadne who was eventually married to Bacchus, or Dionysus as he was known to the Greeks.

7. It would seem that Phyllis herself is very conscious that she cannot go on ruling Thrace, but must – by marrying – provide the country with a king.

8. Though very little is known of Phyllis, Ovid seems to suggest that her patrimony included lands in addition to what was usually thought of as Thrace. The significant fact is that she gave Demophoon gifts of inestimable value.

9. Rhodope and Haemus are two mountain ranges in Thrace. The lowland between the two ranges is drained by the Hebrus.

10. Tisiphone and Allecto are two of the Erinyes, or Furies, whose mission was to punish those who had injured their own kin. Most particularly, they avenged parents who had been wronged – even murdered – by their own children. Phyllis suggests that by submitting to the seductive attractions of Theseus she has betrayed her family and hence is deserving of punishment by the Furies.

III: Briseis to Achilles

The character of Briseis is derived by Ovid from the *Iliad*. In that source, however, the character of Briseis is scarcely developed and she is little more than a pivot around which the fabled wrath of Achilles is developed. While she may have been loved by Achilles in Homer's account, we should also note that for him the loss of Briseis must surely have been perceived as an insult of the gravest proportions. We know very little about Briseis and the charms she might have had in the eyes of Achilles; we only know that upon losing her Achilles retired from combat to his tent. In the *Heroides*, Briseis becomes a woman richly endowed with human feeling who grieves that she has not been reunited with the man she loves, who fears that she will be supplanted by another, and who must now find her future life with those who destroyed her homeland, her family and her heritage.

For Briseis the attraction identified as love is dangerously close to the fear of abandonment. She does not object so much to captivity as to the uncertainty and instability that it has brought into her life. In this, Briseis echoes a theme which permeates the *Heroides*: the lover and the beloved both seek to bring into their lives a degree of permanence and changelessness that in reality is nearly impossible of attainment.

But the situation of Briseis is still more tenuous. She is not only a pawn in a mysterious game being played out by characters superior to her in every way but she is also a barbarian. Achilles is a Greek and Briseis is not. Whatever difference there may be between the two, this is the single most important one. As a barbarian, as a captive, as a woman, Briseis finds her ability to bargain and to plead weakening with each turn of events. Not only is it a man's world, it is a Greek world, and she has no rights to assert. Her only salvation lies in her ability to be loved by Achilles and for her this can happen only in a passive fashion. The fact remains that for all Briseis' humanity, which Ovid develops so well, her fate is that she remains no more than an item of exchange between two very powerful men. For Briseis to refer to the costly gifts sent by Agamemnon to appease Achilles as her dowry only heightens the cruel irony which has become the tone of her life. She enters the story as a chattel and that status is never altered. The only change is that she is now revealed as a person deeply injured and with little hope of relief.

The relationship as defined by Briseis is not simply that of two lovers made equal by the intensity of their affection. While Briseis certainly loves Achilles, his love is never defined, except tangentially: its lack seems to be reflected by the emissaries. Briseis constantly tempers her appeal to Achilles, begging his forbearance in a way that makes the reader suspect that Achilles might well have no desire for her. At the same time she never denies that Achilles has been, quite literally, her lord and master. His dominance did not arise out of her love for him – it is not something that she gave freely. Rather he is dominant because he was first her master and she was his slave. The bonds of love only followed the initial bonds of defeat and captivity. The irony of her situation is only heightened in the reader's mind by the fact that the ordinary language of erotic literature refers to the experience of love as a kind of slavery, a kind of captivity.

Indeed, Briseis lost her humanity in the destruction of Lyrnessus and the slaughter of her family, becoming at best only a body and at worst simply an object. In every sense of the word, she is now a chattel. It would seem that she interprets her position as fulfilling the erotic needs of either Achilles or Agamemnon, but she is virtually uncomprehending before the very real possibility that her situation is created by something that has to do with matters of rank and importance.

Finally the reader must realize that the overriding emotion in Briseis is not jealousy of the woman given to Achilles as wife or of the captive girls given as concubines, nor is it anger that she has been replaced by these others. Briseis has seen her world of comfort and security destroyed, and she now fears that something of the sort might happen again. It is the fear of desertion that colours and shapes her life and provides the context within which this letter is written.

The words you read come from stolen Briseis,
    an alien who has learned some Greek.
A few of these lines are blurred by falling tears,
    tears which are as heavy as my words.
If it is right to complain, my lover and
    lord, I complain. Not through your fault was
I claimed by Agamemnon but you failed me
    by too easily giving me up
when that angry king's harsh demand came to you.[1]
    Eurybates and Talthybius came
for me and you obeyed with no reluctance.[2]
    Each one glancing at the other's face
wondered in silence if we were still lovers.
    You could not refuse, but you might have
eased my pain with only a little delay.
    Without a kiss, you let me leave you.
I could not stop my tears, I pulled at my hair,
    and I returned to captivity.
I wish I could elude my guards after dark
    but someone would catch this timid girl;
a Trojan patrol might find me and give me
    to a woman of Priam's family.
Perhaps you did not resist Agamemnon
    because resistance could not succeed.
Even so, many nights have passed and still you
    have not demanded that I return.
Perhaps I left because you had no choice; still,
    all these nights I am away and you
have not demanded that I return to you.
    Your delay and anger fade slowly.
Menoetius' son whispered 'Why do you weep?
    In a little while you will be back.'[3]
Not only have you failed to demand me back,
    you now oppose my return to you.
Come now, Achilles, earn the name others have
    given you, be an anxious lover.
The sons of Amyntor and Telamon came –
    one related by blood, the other
a comrade – with Ulysses, Laertes' son.[4]

With them I was to return to you.
Begging you to relent, they came to announce
    the apology of the great king.
Many fine gifts magnified their little prayer:
    twenty bright vessels of hammered bronze
with seven tripods equal in weight and craft,
    ten talents of gold and twelve horses
that were quite accustomed to winning races.
    But you did not need his final gift:
many young girls of stunning beauty taken
    when Lesbos fell. And in addition,
you were offered a bride, though you have no need:
    one of the three daughters of Agamemnon.[5]
All this you might well have paid for my return;
    but you refused both the gift and me.
What act of mine has cheapened me in your eyes?
    Where is your careless love gone to now?
Perhaps a dismal lot still crushes the sad
    and I will not find a sweeter time.
Your brave men levelled the walls of Lyrnessus.
    I who was part of my father's land
have seen my dearest relatives lying dead:
    the sons of my mother, three brothers,
comrades in life, are today comrades in death;
    my husband writhed in the bloody dirt,
his body heaving as he lay on the ground.
    Though I lost so many dear to me
my loss was eased by loving you as brother,
    as my husband, and as my master.
By your mother's divinity, you swore that
    I was better a captive than free.
Now I come to you again with a dowry
    but you refuse both me and the wealth.
Not only that, they tell me that when dawn breaks
    you will unfurl your sails and leave me.
I fainted when I heard the awful story.
    To whom will I be left when you go?
Who will comfort me when I am left alone?
    May lightning strike or the earth swallow

me before the sea foams with your oars leaving
    me farther and farther behind you.
If you must go, I will not burden your ships,
    I follow as captive, not as wife.
My fingers know the art of working with wool.
    You will take a beautiful bride, one
like Thetis, worthy of Peleus, and so
    should you marry; I will be a slave
spinning out my day's work until the distaff
    once full of new wool grows thin as threads
are drawn out from it. But only one thing, please:
    do not let your bride be harsh with me –
for I fear that she will not be kind to me –
    do not let her tear at my hair while
you watch and remember that once I was yours.
    I fear nothing so much as the fear
that I will be left here behind when you sail.
    Agamemnon's anger has vanished
and Greece is at your feet; at last all has been
    subdued by you except your anger.
Why does Hector harass the Greek lines? Take up
    your bright armour – but take me back first –
and the god, Mars, will help you to victory.[6]
    I caused your wrath, I can easily end it.
It would not be shameful to yield my prayer:
    Meleager's wife roused him to fight.
The tale is one I have heard, you know it well:
    A mother cursed her son for killing
her brothers, but then war came and he refused
    to fight in defence of his country.
Only his wife could change his mind.[7] I envy
    her: I have wasted my words on you,
yet I am not angry. Though called to your bed,
    I have not presumed to be your wife.
Some woman once called me 'mistress'. I replied,
    'That name adds to the shame of slavery.'
I swear this oath. By the bones of my husband
    which, though scarcely buried, are sacred;
by the souls of my three brothers, now my gods,

23

who bravely died when their country died;
by your head and mine which we laid side by side
    and by your sword which my family knew:
I swear that the Mycenaean king has shared
    no couch with me. If I lie, leave me.
If I asked you to swear a similar oath –
    'Bravest one, swear that you have tasted
no joys except the joy you have known with me' –
    you would refuse. The Greeks think you mourn,
but you are making music and a gentle
    maiden holds you in her warm embrace.
Why won't you fight? Because to fight is a risk
    while a lyre and Venus at night bring
delight. It is safer to lie on your couch
    holding some girl close to you, plucking
at the Thracian lyre, rather than taking
    into your hands the massive shield and
the sharpened spear, and putting upon your hair
    the weight of a helmet made for war.[8]
Once great deeds rather than safety pleased you most
    and the glory of battle was sweet.
Was this merely a trick to win me captive
    when you won the glory of my land?
By the gods, it cannot be. May the great spear
    from Pelion fly to Hector's side.[9]
Send me, O Greeks: let me present your message
    to my lord. I will achieve more than
Phoenix, more than Ulysses, more than Ajax;
    I will mingle your words with kisses.
You will remember when my arms touch your neck;
    the sight of my breasts will stir your heart.
Though cruel and more savage than your mother's
    waves,
    my tears and my silence will crush you.
Be decent toward me, brave Achilles, do not
    torture poor Briseis with delay.
With me in your tent you can take up arms and
    make your father in his old age proud.
Take me back, return to the battlefield and

one day Pyrrhus will wish for your luck.[10]
But if love has turned to weariness, kill me
    rather than make me live without you.
But your deeds have already done this to me:
    my skin is old, my colour is gone;
my trust in you is the one hope I retain.
    When that goes, I will join my family,
my brothers and husband, and I will leave you
    with the shame that you left me to die.
Why should I wait for you to tell me to die?
    Draw your sword, plunge it into my flesh,
I have blood that will pour out of my pierced breast,
    let me be struck down by the weapon
which should have killed the son of Atreus if
    the goddess had not prevented it.[11]
But save my life, it is the gift you gave me.
    What I received when you conquered me
give me again, I ask you now, in friendship.
    Troy has many for you to slaughter,
your sword is ready, its victims are waiting:
    destroy them, they are your enemy.
But I beg you, whether you decide to remain
or leave, be my lord, command that I go to you.

NOTES

1. Agamemnon was a king of Mycenae, and leader of the Greek forces at Troy. He and his brother Menelaus were the sons of Atreus and hence were known as the Atreidae.

2. Eurybates and Talthybius were the two most prominent heralds in the Greek forces. Eurybates, a big man with curly hair and a dark complexion, was especially valued by Ulysses for his ready wit and mental acuity. Talthybius seems to have won the dubious distinction of always being the one called upon to carry some disagreeable message which was, invariably, against his own better judgement.

3. Patroclus, the close friend of Achilles, was the son of Menoetius.

4. Phoenix was the son of Amyntor, Ajax the son of Telamon. This delegation was deliberately chosen to include some of the most respected and

eminent men in the Greek army. Telamon was the brother of Peleus, the father of Achilles, so that Ajax and Achilles were cousins.

5. It is interesting to compare this passage with the corresponding text in the *Iliad*, IX.122–47. After offering material things of very great value, Agamemnon also pledges numerous women. In addition to the seven beautiful women taken at the fall of Lesbos, Agamemnon also promises that twenty of the most beautiful Trojan women will be given to Achilles after Troy has fallen. And finally, he pledges one of his daughters as wife to Achilles.

6. Mars was the Roman god of war and farming. He is usually associated with the Greek god, Ares. Mars was the father of Romulus and Remus, the founders of Rome.

7. Meleager was the son of Oeneus and Althaea. At his birth the three Fates – Clotho, Lachesis and Atropos – appeared suddenly in the chamber where the birth had taken place. According to Clotho and Lachesis, the child would lead a life of nobility and bravery. Atropos, however, pointed to a blazing log in the fireplace and prophesied that the infant would die the instant the wood turned to ashes. The child's mother leapt out of her bed, took the wood from the fire, extinguished the blaze and put it in a safe hiding-place.

As the child grew, he exhibited the nobility and the bravery prophesied for him. The end of Meleager's life is told in two very different versions, one by Homer in the *Iliad*, Book IX, and the other by Ovid in the *Metamorphoses*, Book VIII. In this passage Briseis is referring to the Homeric version. According to this account, Meleager took part in the great Calydonian boar hunt, killed the boar and received the animal's hide as his trophy. A battle then broke out between the Calydonians and their neighbours, the Curetes. So long as Meleager fought with the Calydonians they were victorious. Unfortunately, he killed several of his mother's brothers, the sons of Thestius. In her anger Althaea cursed him. Enraged by this, Meleager refused to fight. The tide of battle then turned against the Calydonians. Meleager only relented when his wife, Cleopatra, urged him to return to the fight. There is also a reference to Meleager in *Heroides*, XX.

8. Orpheus, the great player of the lyre, was a Thracian by birth. The shield, the spear and the helmet are probably an oblique reference to an alternative tale of the early manhood of Achilles. In this account, it was prophesied that Troy would never be defeated without the help of Achilles. At his mother's insistence Achilles was dressed as a girl, renamed Pyrrha, and raised by Lycomedes with her daughters on the island of Scyros. However, Ulysses came in search of the boy because it was known that only he could ensure the conquest of Troy. Ulysses, always skilled at disguises, whether fabricating his own or piercing those of others, laid out various articles of feminine

charm along with a spear and a shield. While the girls – and Achilles disguised as Pyrrha – were looking through the collection, Ulysses had a trumpet blown as if to signal an imminent attack. At once, Achilles stripped himself, took up the spear and the shield, and made himself ready for battle. Upon being found out, Achilles then very willingly joined the Greek forces and went off on the great expedition to Troy.

9. A reference to the fact that Achilles was reared on Mount Pelion, along with several other Greek princes, by the centaur, Chiron. Hector, the son of King Priam of Troy, was the leader of the Trojan forces and the foremost of their warriors.

10. Pyrrhus, sometimes called Neoptolemus, was the son of Achilles by Deidamia.

11. Agamemnon could have been attacked by Achilles, but Thetis, the mother of Achilles, prevented any violence.

I V: Phaedra to Hippolytus

The story of Phaedra and Hippolytus has been told in a number of accounts throughout antiquity and in later years. Because the story seems to have a perennial attraction we can only assume that it strikes a chord in its many successive audiences.

As Phaedra begins this letter – curiously enough, she writes to Hippolytus while he is living under the same roof – it seems at first that she is a girl or young woman enjoying a liaison with a boy or young man of her own age. Because the reader certainly knows the myth both in its beginning and in its end, this self-deception must heighten the interest of the story. Only later in the letter, long after the reader has come to such a realization, does Phaedra reveal her perception of the situation as it really is: that she is an older woman – if not middle-aged – seeking a young and attractive lover to replace her unsatisfactory husband.

In this vein Phaedra makes the rather startling assertion that until she became enamoured of Hippolytus she had never before known love. This would seem to imply that she has loved neither Theseus nor any man before him. Phaedra appears to suggest that her failure to experience love prior to this has left her with a kind of virginity, or perhaps purity, which she can now offer to Hippolytus.

However, Phaedra's love for Hippolytus can be seen in an entirely different light. Because of the injury done by Theseus to her family, the house of Minos, Phaedra could well be embarking on this affair to exact from Theseus a kind of revenge. Towards the end of the letter Phaedra refers to the Minotaur as her half-brother and finally she wishes Hippolytus well by praying that the nymphs give him flowing water to drink! In these two separate passages Phaedra anticipates if only by suggestion the means by which Hippolytus will die.

The possibility of reading this as a revenge can be carried a step further when we remember that Hippolytus would normally be heir

28

to the vast possessions of Theseus. By disrupting this transmittal of property, Phaedra has in her hands the means of allowing her own sons to inherit and so of redressing the injury done by Theseus to her and the house of Minos. It is tempting to read the myths of Theseus and Minos as a quasi-historical account of two rival commercial ventures. By killing the Minotaur and surviving the test imposed by Minos, Theseus has lived to preserve his possessions from Minos' grasping hands. If Phaedra can turn the estate of Theseus from his first-born, Hippolytus, to her own children, then she will have transferred to the descendants of Minos the property of a hated rival. This would in itself be no small victory.

But whatever might be said about possible motivations for the behaviour of Phaedra, the fact remains that she and Hippolytus are stepmother and stepson and she has became infatuated by the physical charms of her husband's son. An already illicit relationship becomes very much more serious because it is not merely adulterous but also incestuous. Early in the letter Phaedra outlines many of the characteristics of what would one day be called courtly love: first and foremost, the love must be clandestine; the love must be between persons of approximately equal social rank; and the love must also be adulterous. However, there is little if any indication that the love can or should have even the slightest taint of incest.

In this fourth letter of the *Heroides*, Ovid – in the character of Phaedra – introduces the idea of love as a deified personification. While the Romans often identified Cupid with the proper name Amor, it is used here to heighten the purported helplessness of Phaedra before the harsh demands of her passion. Similarly Hippolytus is presented here as rejecting Phaedra's advances because of his dedication to Diana. For the first time in the *Heroides* the blind impetuosity of love, as well as its rejection, are attributed to the actions of deities beyond the control of the characters involved.

Almost every critic of the *Heroides* has noted the rhetorical qualities of the work. Here, especially, we see the play of rhetoric as almost a definition of the term: the fourth of the *Heroides* is an elaborately persuasive document. Phaedra uses every possible argument to persuade Hippolytus to accede to her request. She insists that her infatuation is innocent, even girlish; she points out that because they live in the same house no one will notice their transgression, if indeed it is a transgression; and she attempts to counter nearly every objection

that Hippolytus might raise. Yet one objection she cannot address:
that he might find her unattractive, not merely because of her
marital situation but more importantly because of her age. The
comic possibilities inherent in a relationship between lovers of a
wide disparity in years are many. But not every older woman can
successively seduce every younger man on whom she sets her
eye, even if her argument is beyond reproach. In the last analysis
seduction is accomplished not by reason but by infatuation. With-
out mutual attraction the finest rhetoric will not accomplish this
goal.

A girl from Crete sends her greeting to a man
    who is the son of an Amazon.
This maiden wishes for him the good fortune
    she lacks unless he gives it to her.
Whatever words are here, read on to the end.
    How could reading this letter hurt you?
Indeed, my words might even give you pleasure.
    These letters carry my secret thoughts
over land and sea; even enemies read
    letters another enemy sends.
Three times have I tried to speak with you, three times
    my tongue has stuck in my mouth, three times
the sound of my voice has been stopped at my lips.
    If Love is joined with modesty then
love should never be deprived of modesty.
    Modesty is shy but Love is bold;
it is Love that commands me to write to you
    because modesty made me silent.
Whatever Love commands must not be ignored.
    The gods, the lords of all, are themselves
subject to Love's command. Could I disobey?
    When I was so confused Love said, 'Write.
Though made of iron, he will surely give his hand.'
    Love will aid me: while warming my bones
with fire may he turn your heart to heed my prayers.
    You may inquire, but I tell you now:

I will not basely forsake my marriage vows;
    my name is free from all infamy.
Because it has come late, love has come deeper.
    I am on fire with love within me;
my breast is burned by an invisible wound.
    As a young steer is chafed by the yoke
and a colt barely endures the first bridle,
    so has my heart rebelled against love.
This heavy load does not rest well on my soul.
    When the art is learned in youth, a first
love is simple; but love that comes after youth
    always burns with a harsher passion.
I offer you a purity long preserved;
    let us both be equal in our guilt.
Fruit picked from a heavy branch is good, the first
    rose pinched by a slender nail is best.
But even if the innocent purity
    in which I have always lived my life
were to be stained by this unaccustomed sin,
    I would regard this fortune that burns
me with such flames a kindly fortune. Base love
    is worse than love merely forbidden.
If Juno gave me her brother and husband,
    Jove, I would prefer Hippolytus.[1]
Now, incredibly, I turn to strange pastimes:
    I want to be among the wild beasts.
Delia, who is known to all for her bow,
    is mine; like you, I have chosen her.[2]
I take my pleasure in the forest driving
    deer to the net and urging my hounds
over the hills. I hurl the quivering spear
    and I rest my body in the grass.
I drive a chariot around the dusty track
    and twist the bit in the horse's mouth.
At other times I am swept up like the mad
    screaming disciples of Bacchus who
are driven by their god's frenzy or like those
    who worship on the ridge of Ida
rattling drums and snares or like those possessed and

31

given up to the sacred madness
brought by half-divine dryads and fauns with horns.[3]
  When the madness leaves me I return
and others tell me what I was; in my heart
  I know I have been possessed by love.
Perhaps I am paying a debt to Venus
  for the favours my family enjoyed:
Jove founded our line by loving Europa –
  he came to her disguised as a bull;
Pasiphae, my mother, was raped by a bull
  by whom she bore her burden of shame.
Aegeus' lying son used the helpful thread
  my sister gave and escaped the maze.
I too, a child of Minos, must be subject
  to the same law that rules my family.
It is our common fate that one house took us –
  your great beauty has conquered my heart,
your father captured the heart of my sister.[4]
  Theseus and his son together
have been the destruction of we two sisters:
  you could erect a double trophy.
Once when I went to Ceres' Eleusis –
  the soil of Crete should have held me back –
you pleased me most though you had pleased me
  before.[5]
  Dressed in white with flowers in your hair,
your sun-tanned cheeks were coloured by modesty.
  It was then that love pierced my body.
Some would have called you stern; I saw only strength.
  Get rid of these men who look like girls;
men who are truly men are more than handsome.
  That frown, the hair that falls where it must,
the light dust on your splendid face, suit you well.
  I admire you when you rein in the
stubborn necks of your high-spirited horses,
  forcing a turn in a slight circle.[6]
I admire your arm whether it hurls a lance
  or grasps the iron-headed hunting spear.
There is no more for me to say except that

32

whatever you do delights my eyes.
Exhaust your harshness there in the wilderness;
    do not wage a campaign against me.
You live the chastity of Diana while
    you pilfer what is owed to Venus.
Something which never takes rest will not endure.
    Rest repairs the limbs and renews strength.
If the bow is never relaxed it will lose
    the tension that makes it a bow; you
would do well to imitate the weapons of
    Diana while you follow her lead.
Indeed, Cephalus was a mighty hunter,
    and many beasts fell beneath his spear
to the ground, yet he did no harm in yielding
    himself to enjoy Aurora's love.[7]
Many times that goddess shrewdly went to him
    leaving behind her aged husband;
and Venus, too, often reclined with the son
    of Cinyras by a holly oak.
Moreover, Oeneus' son blazed with love
    for Atalanta of Maenalus –
he gave her the wild beast's pelt to be a pledge
    of his love for her.[8] We too can be
counted as lovers like these. If one removes
    love, your forest is only rustic.
I will come to you, I fear neither the cliffs
    nor the slashing tusks of the wild boar.
There is a slender isthmus which hears throughout
    its length and breadth the roar of two seas.
In that place, land of Troezen, Pittheus'
    kingdom, a place dearer now to me
than my native land, we together can dwell.[9]
    Neptune's heroic son is absent
now, detained by his dearest friend, Pirithous.
    Theseus, we must conclude, loves him
more than he loves Phaedra; loves him more than he
    loves you, his son.[10] But that is not all.
We have both been deeply hurt by Theseus.
    With his club he crushed my brother's bones

and scattered them over the soil; then he left
    my sister helpless with the wild beasts.
Your mother was a most courageous warrior
    and worthy to bear such a strong son.
Where is she? She is dead, speared by Theseus.[11]
    Even such a promising baby
as you were was not enough to save her life.
    I ask you, why did they not marry?
Why, unless perhaps he feared you as rival.
    He sired brothers but took them from me,
raising them in his own way to be his heirs.
    I wish my breast which has injured you
so greatly, fairest man, had been torn open.
    Go now, pay your respects to the bed
which your father denies by his wicked deeds.
    If I seem a stepmother who would
lie with her husband's son, ignore such silly
    words. Such virtue was out of date in
Saturn's reign and it died in the next age when
    Jove decreed that virtue was pleasure.[12]
Because Jove made his sister his wife the gods
    have come to see that nothing is wrong.[13]
The only enduring contract is that which
    is preserved by the chains of Venus.
Do not worry that our love must be concealed,
    only ask the help of Venus and
she will hide us in the mantle of kinship;
    we will be praised for our embraces
and I will seem to be a good stepmother.
    The same roof will always shelter us:
no austere husband's gate will need unbolting
    in the dark of night, no guard must be
evaded, all doors will always be open.
    No one will question your presence here.
You have kissed me in public, this will not change;
    even on my couch you will be safe:
indeed, your fault will earn you the highest praise.
    Hurry, do not delay, tie our bond
together now, I shall pray that love will spare

you all the bitterness I must feel.
Though I am proud, I can bend my knee in prayer.
    But where now is pride, my high-flown words?
All are fallen. I was determined – if love
    can determine anything – to fight
long rather than be conquered, but I confess
    I am overcome. I beseech you,
I extend to you a queen's regal arms, let
    me only clasp your knees. Love does not
care for what is proper, modesty has fled
    the field of battle and its standards.
If this letter offends you, give me pardon;
    let your hard heart grow softer for me.
My father is Minos who governs the seas,
    my ancestor hurls the lightning and
my grandfather drives his gleaming chariot through
    the day wearing a crown of sunlight.[14]
Nobility lies underneath love. Pity
    my family, if you cannot spare me.
Jove's island, Crete, is a part of my dowry;
    each one in my court can be your slave.
Cruel man, change your mind: my mother made a bull
    desire her; are you fiercer than that?
By Venus, who is closest to me, spare me.
    May your love never be rejected,
may the nimble goddess guard you in the glades,
    may the forests give you beasts to kill,
may your friends be satyrs and the mountain gods,
    may your flying spear pierce the wild boar,
may the nymphs – though I hear you despise women –
    relieve your thirst with flowing water.
I mingle my prayer with weeping: you are reading
    my words; I beg you, try to imagine my tears.

NOTES

1. Jove or Jupiter (the Greek Zeus) was the king of the gods. Juno (the Greek Hera) was his sister and his wife and thus queen of the gods. Ovid is

here indulging in a little irony because Hera was notoriously jealous of the many liaisons of Zeus. In other words, it is extremely unlikely that Juno might ever look with benevolence on an alliance between Jove and Phaedra, but even if it were to be, Phaedra would reject Jove in favour of Hippolytus.

2. The name Delia is sometimes given to Diana in a poetic context. The term is derived from the place of her birth, the island of Delos. More often she is called 'the Delian'. It is important to note that Phaedra is invoking the patronage of the virgin deity Diana (often identified with the Greek Artemis), who was known as the goddess of the hunt and of wild places as well as of childbirth. However, it is unlikely that Phaedra could have also invoked the virginity which was the common characteristic of the followers of Diana.

3. This is a reference to the maenads, female followers of Dionysus (the Roman Bacchus or Liber). Wherever the god went, in heaven or on earth, he was followed by satyrs and maenads. The maenads were known for their ritual orgies in which they were often joined by women from the surrounding country. Needless to say, such participation by local women caused great consternation among their men, whether fathers, brothers, husbands or lovers.

Phaedra is asking for the protection of Diana and at the same time asserting that she is experiencing a Bacchic or Dionysian madness.

According to Showerman (op. cit., see note 3, page xx), the reference to the worshippers on Mount Ida suggests the followers of Cybele, who was usually taken to be the mother of all the gods. Strictly speaking, she was not a member of the Greek pantheon, but appears in the various religions that were located on the mainland to the east of Greece.

The nymphs were lesser female deities found in some particular place or object, or even in some natural phenomenon. Dryads were tree-nymphs found principally in oak trees. Nymphs were generally thought to be possessed of an aggressive sexuality which was enhanced by their own beauty and attractiveness to men. Fauns or satyrs were lesser male deities usually represented pictorially with some combination of horses' tails, upright ears, small horns and goats' legs and hooves. To emphasize their masculinity, they were often drawn with erect penises or at least very prominent genitalia. The satyrs' principal occupation was the pursuit of nymphs.

The point of these references to Diana, the maenads, the followers of Cybele, the dryads and the fauns is that Phaedra has found herself pursuing quite uncharacteristic activities. By implication, the explanation for such behaviour is that she has fallen in love.

4. While it might be debated whether the divine gifts showered on the family of Phaedra were indeed favours, Phaedra does allude to her genealogy. It is important to remember here that the house of Aegus was involved with the house of Minos repeatedly and in various generations. For a detailed

account of Theseus and the house of Minos, see THESEUS and ARIADNE in Appendix 1: Principal Characters.

5. Eleusis was an Attic city not far from the Isthmus of Corinth. In ancient times it became sacred to Ceres (the Greek Demeter). According to the myth, in the time of Theseus Eleusis was governed jointly with Athens.

6. Hippolytus, as his name suggests, was renowned for his skill in breeding and training horses. This would be in keeping with his devotion to Diana.

7. In various accounts, there are actually two characters known as Cephalus. In this passage Ovid blends the two into one. First, Cephalus was a king of Athens with two divine gifts: a hound that always caught its prey and a great spear that never missed its target. While hunting one day Cephalus saw something stir in the underbrush, threw his spear and to his horror realized that he had struck his beloved wife Procris. The second Cephalus was the son of Hermes. As he grew to manhood, his great beauty caught the eye of Eos, goddess of the dawn (the Roman Aurora), who abducted him and by him bore Phaethon, who was in turn abducted by Aphrodite and made the guardian of her shrine. That Phaedra should refer to this myth is ironic because it suggests something of what she is experiencing at the hands of Hippolytus.

8. While Aurora was enamoured of Cephalus, she was also the wife of the aged Tithonus. Presumably he was too old to give her adequate sexual satisfaction, so she found her pleasure with Cephalus.

Cinyras was King of Cyprus and the father of Adonis. Here too is a considerable irony because Adonis was the offspring of an incestuous union of Cinyras and his daughter Myrrha.

The son of Oeneus was Meleager, who fell in love with Atalanta and as a token of his love gave her the hide of the Calydonian boar which he had killed. There is further reference to this myth in letters III and XX.

9. Pittheus was the grandfather of Theseus, and it was at his court at Troezen that Theseus spent the first sixteen years of his life. Some years after this, Theseus sent his son Hippolytus to Troezen with the idea that the boy would one day inherit the kingdom of Pittheus.

10. Neptune was the god of the sea whom the Romans associated with the Greek god, Poseidon. The father of Theseus was either Poseidon or Aegeus, and Theseus seemed to prefer the former. However, by emphasizing the heroism of Theseus in this context, Phaedra is once more indulging her taste for irony. The suggestion that Theseus loves Pirithous more than he loves his wife can also be taken as an aspersion on Theseus' manliness. Pirithous was King of the Lapiths.

11. Theseus, after killing the Minotaur (which would have been Phaedra's half-brother, since it was the offspring of her mother Pasiphaë and the bull

sent by Poseidon), did crush the monster's bones and scatter them over the soil of Crete. After the death of the Minotaur, Theseus took Ariadne aboard his ship but then abandoned her before returning to Athens (see ARIADNE in Appendix 1: Principal Characters). The myth of Ariadne is developed at greater length in letter X.

The mother of Hippolytus was the Amazon Hippolyte (also known as Antiope), who died in Athens after appearing at the wedding of Theseus and Phaedra and threatening to kill all the assembled company. By some accounts she died in the mêlée that broke out at the wedding; others say that she died in hand-to-hand combat with Theseus. However, it is strange that Phaedra should here invoke some sort of piety unless it is to be assumed that in her desperation she is quite irrational.

12. This is a reference to the development of divine morality as the heavens passed from the era of Saturn to that of Jove. For the Romans, the era of Saturn was generally thought to have been a golden age.

13. Cronos, the King of the Titans whom the Romans identified with Saturn, took Rhea, his sister, to be his wife. Cronos was warned that one of his children would overthrow him. To prevent this, as Rhea bore each of their offspring Cronos ate the infant. However, the youngest, Zeus, was hidden away by Rhea and her mother Ge. In time, Zeus grew to manhood and rescued his siblings from the body of their father. The young gods then defeated Cronos. Zeus also took Hera, his sister, as his wife.

14. The ancestry Phaedra recalls is impressive. The name of Minos, like that of Theseus, figures prominently in the ancient world. Though the name is to be found in many mythical accounts, it seems reasonable to assume that the maritime hegemony centred at Knossos in Crete reflected the prestige and power of Minos.

Jove was always the pre-eminent god of the sky and all the phenomena associated with it. One of his many titles was Thunderer, and it was well known that he commonly punished transgressions by striking the miscreant with a lightning bolt.

The sun-god was Helios, the father of Pasiphaë and thus Phaedra's grandfather.

V: Oenone to Paris

The opening lines of this letter are curiously abrupt. But it is not difficult to imagine the character of Paris as Oenone imagines him to be: so infatuated by Helen that he might even allow her to censor his mail; so terrified of retribution from Menelaus and his Greek allies that he must fear any letter. Such a reading would border on the ridiculous until we remember that Paris could well be described as a man with more beauty than sense – a man, moreover, of less than heroic courage. It would seem that as Oenone begins to write this letter she is writing out of a very strongly imagined situation. She has already given much time to achieving an understanding of the present condition of Paris and she quite literally begins her letter in mid thought.

But the argument of Oenone that she was only a simple nymph who was in every way loyal to Paris is greatly undermined when she talks of her amorous adventures with various deities of whom Apollo himself was one. Though she insists that Paris should have remained faithful to her, she scarcely presents herself as a woman of unblemished and uncompromising virtue.

Oenone tries to present herself as simple even to the point of passivity in the face of the momentous events which have swirled up about her. This, however, is not an entirely accurate description. The opening lines of the letter read like the cut and thrust of a dagger. If Oenone chooses not to avail herself of the usual devices by which an injured woman quenches her anger, she does not hesitate to pick and probe at the supposed – and generally accepted – weaknesses of Paris. He appears as weakly credulous, particularly in her account of the Judgement of Paris as he himself told it to her. While she recognizes that the whole story borders on the unbelievable, she accepts it so that she can in fact use it as a way to impugn his good sense.

Oenone appears to take up contradictory positions in her attempt to define her new relationship with Paris. Though she is terrified by the outcome of his choice of Venus as the most beautiful, she is more concerned with the prospect of disaster than she is with the possibility that she may be supplanted in the affections of Paris. She seems to believe that she can remain Paris' wife even when he has secured the love of Helen.

Oenone reveals herself as a rustic caught up in what she perceives — by the prophecy of Cassandra — to be a disaster. As she looks back with great longing to the pastoral idyll that was her life with Paris, she has little real desire to move beyond it. Though she sees herself as worthy of a nation's regalia, she really wants nothing so much as life as it once was, an impossible dream. She utters no curses and wishes for no disasters, but she accepts the prophecies of Cassandra as true and finds no alternative but to wait until they are fulfilled in their most awful detail.

Will you read? Does your new wife forbid? Read on,
    no Mycenaean has written this.
Rather, Oenone the fountain-nymph, well known
    in the Phrygian woods, writes these words
and complains of the way you — my very own,
    if only you will permit — treat her.
What god opposes my desires? Is there some
    guilt that will not let me be your own?
If one must suffer, one should suffer calmly;
    but undeserved pain is much more sad.
You were a nobody when you married me;
    I was the daughter of a great stream.
You are one of the sons of Priam now, but
    then — with all respect — you were a slave;
you were held a captive and I was a nymph,
    but I was content to marry you.
With our flocks we took our rest beneath the trees
    on couches of fallen leaves and grass.
Often we laid together on hay or straw
    in a hut that kept the frost away.
Who led you into the mountain ranges where

40

your quarry was hiding, who showed you
the den where the wild beast hides her new-born cubs?
    Many times have I hunted with you.
I have helped you place the hunter's wide-meshed nets;
    Many times have I led the swift hounds
over the ridges and cliffs after wild game
    You carved my name on beech trees and I
can read there 'Oenone', product of your hand.
    As those trees grow the words likewise grow.
Grow high and straight so that everyone will know
    my name and the honour that is mine.
May that poplar growing beside a stream live
    on with lines carved by your eager hand:
'If Paris rejects Oenone and still lives,
    let the Xanthus flow back to its spring.'
Xanthus, hurry backward; you must turn, waters,
    flow back to the springs from which you came.[1]
Oenone has been spurned but Paris still breathes:
    the Xanthus must turn back to its source.
My doom began, this awful storm of changed love,
    when Venus and Juno and unarmed
Minerva, though she is more beautiful armed,
    came to ask that you judge their beauty.[2]
Choosing one, you lost the other two. My heart
    raced and a chill tore at my cold bones
when you told me this story. I sought advice –
    I was afraid – from the old and wise.
All agreed with my fears, there could be no doubt,
    it was clear some evil threatened me.
Firs were cut and hewn, a new fleet was readied
    and ships were launched on the deep blue waves.
Your tears fell when you left, do not deny them.
    Victims of grief, we wept together;
your arms held me closer than a clinging vine
    holds the elm. The wind was right but you
insisted that it was not – your comrades smiled –
    and you returned to kiss me again.
It seemed that your tongue could never say, 'Farewell.'
    A light breeze rippled the idle sails

41

on the rigid mast, the oars made the sea white.
      My eyes followed your departing ship
and tears fell down from my cheeks to the dry sand.
      I prayed that you might return swiftly
and I begged the daughters of Nereus to
      hurry you: it would be my ruin.[3]
I knew that prayer could accomplish your return,
      but instead my prayers helped a rival.
A great rock looks down on the ocean; the waves
      break at its base, it is a mountain.
From its peak I was the first to see your sails;
      my first desire was to rush to you.
Patient, I waited, and soon I saw something
      purple in the bow. I was worried:
you had never worn such a colour before.
      The breeze quickened, the ship came to shore.
My heart shivered when I saw a woman's face;
      this was not enough – why did I stay?
I must have been mad – you held her in your arms.
      I tore the clothes away from my breasts
and beat my hands against my flesh; my long nails
      tore at my tear-stained cheeks and my cries
filled Ida's holy land with their sad lament:
      I took my grief to the barren rocks.
So may Helen grieve and so may she lament
      when she is deserted by her love.
The pain I endure was brought by her and she
      should suffer then as I suffer now.
It seems your taste has turned to women who leave
      husbands to follow you on the sea.
When you were only a poor shepherd you were
      content with no one but me, your wife.
I am not impressed by your wealth, nor am I
      touched by the thought of your great palace,
nor have I the least desire to become one
      of the many wives of Priam's sons;
Priam could not scorn a nymph as his son's wife
      and proud Hecuba would hardly need
to hide her relationship with me. I am

42

worthy of becoming and I wish
to be the wife of a powerful man; my
    hands would be a sceptre's ornament.
Do not scorn me because we lay on beech boughs;
    I should have a purple marriage-bed.
My love will not injure you: it brings no ships
    to punish you, it conceives no wars.
But that runaway daughter of Tyndareus
    carried a proud dowry to your bed –
an armed enemy demanding her return.
    Should you give her up to the Danai?[4]
Ask Hector, your brother, ask Deïphobus
    and Polydamas; seek the advice
of sombre Antenor, try to determine
    what Priam himself would urge on you.[5]
These are old men whose long lives give them wisdom.
    It is a sad start that lets you prize
a stolen woman more than your native land.
    Your position is awkward with shame;
her lord is a just man seeking what is his.
    If you are wise, you must not suppose
that she will remain always faithful to you;
    like the son of Atreus who cries
out at the corruption of his marriage-bed
    and suffers a wound from a wife who
gave her love to another, you will suffer.[6]
    Wounded virtue is never restored,
it remains always lost. Does she burn with love?
    She loved Menelaus the same way.
He lies in a deserted bed, so shall you.
    You and he alike are trusting fools.
Happy Andromache, Hector is faithful.
    Why could you not be like your brother?[7]
But you are lighter than dry leaves drifting on
    a fitful breeze, you are even less
than the smallest tip of a spear of grain dried
    in the insistent warmth of the sun.
Your sister saw this, I recall: with her long
    hair undone, she sang to me: 'What have you done?

Why scatter seed over sand? You are ploughing
    with oxen but they do nothing for
a Greek heifer is coming to bring ruin
        to your country, your house and yourself.
Keep her far off, the Greek heifer is coming.
        Sink that unclean ship while there is time;
it is heavy with the weight of Trojan blood.'⁸
        Her loud voice could not be mistaken
and the words ran madly together until
        her maids took the deranged girl away.
My golden hair stood on end and now I know
        the truth of her words: the heifer feeds
in pastures that once were mine; though beautiful
        she lives in adultery, having
abandoned the gods of her marriage contract,
        a stranger has made her his captive.
Theseus – someone of that name – stole her away
        from her father's house.⁹ Should we assume
that a lusty young man would have returned her
        still a virgin? How do I know this?
Love taught me. Perhaps you call this violence
        and in this way cover her crime, but
one stolen so often must encourage theft.
        Although Oenone herself remains
still chaste, she could have been false to her husband
        as her husband has been false to her.
The satyrs, a nimble and carefree crowd, sought
        me out as I lay hiding in the
secret dens of the woods. And Faunus also
        came for me in the rocky cliffs of Ida
with pine boughs braided in the horns of his head.
        Faithful Tros, Troy's builder, once loved me
and the secrets of his gifts ran through my hands.
        We wrestled together for the prize
of my virginity; I pulled at his hair
        and scratched his face with my fingernails.
I did not want gems and gold for my disgrace,
        my native gifts were used first in shame.
But he healed my torn body and injured pride;

he quickly turned my shame to honour.[10]
Every helpful herb and every healing root,
     wherever it grows, is known to me.[11]
But herbs and roots will not cure the wounds of love;
     I am skilled but still I am helpless.
The cure that neither the good earth nor a god
     can give, you alone can give to me.
You are my hope, I deserve your aid: pity
     this miserable maiden. My love
for you has not brought an army of Greeks and
     I do not come in bloodied armour.
But yours I am, as yours I was when we were young;
     let me be yours again and always. Hear my prayer.

NOTES

1. The river Xanthus was in the vicinity of Troy. In antiquity it was also known as the Scamander, and today is the Menderes.

2. Venus was the Roman goddess of love and corresponded to the Greek goddess Aphrodite. Juno (the Greek Hera) was the Roman goddess of marriage and the wife of Jupiter. The story to which Oenone here refers is known as the Judgement of Paris (see letter XVI and PARIS in Appendix 1: Principal Characters).

3. Nereus was a god of the sea, and he was of considerable importance until the advent of Poseidon. He was the father of the nereids, fifty sea-nymphs. Oenone, of course, was ruined when Paris returned to Troy with Helen.

4. The Danai were the Greeks, who were sometimes known as the sons of Danaus, an ancient King of Argos.

5. Hector and Deïphobus were sons of Priam and brothers of Paris. Polydamas was a close friend of Hector. Polydamas was most notable for his consistently wise advice. Unfortunately, however, more often than not Hector ignored the advice of his friend. Antenor, a member of Priam's council, was one of the most respected and trustworthy of the elders of Troy.

6. Menelaus, the husband of Helen, was the son of Atreus. He and his brother Agamemnon, and their respective families, were commonly known as the Atreidae.

7. Andromache was the wife of Hector. Hector and Andromache were often cited as models of conjugal fidelity and happiness.

8. This refers to the prophecies of Cassandra, the sister of Paris. It was her fate to speak the truth but always to be disregarded.

9. Because Helen was so incomparably beautiful, her hand was actively sought by very many young men. At one point Theseus kidnapped her. However, Helen's twin brothers, Castor and Pollux, the Dioscuri, led an army to rescue her.

10. Faunus was a Roman god often associated with the Greek god Pan. He was a deity of the woods and fields whose special care was for the fecundity of crops, herds and flocks. In this he was a patron of the husband-man. Tros was an ancient king who gave his name to Troy.

11. Oenone was said to have learned the arts of prophecy, as well as of medicine and healing with herbs, from Rhea, daughter of Uranus and mother of Zeus.

VI: Hypsipyle to Jason

Unlike many of the other heroines, Hypsipyle does not adopt a subservient attitude towards Jason. Though she has been loved and left, she is still Queen of Lemnos and the leader of those women who sought their freedom by slaughtering their oppressors, the men of Lemnos. In writing this letter Hypsipyle is clearly torn between an aggressive and dominant attitude and that of a woman who has fallen in love with a man who came to her island and fathered two sons. It must be noted that Ovid has very clearly presented a character with all the potential for deep conflict.

Hypsipyle first argues that she is at least worthy of a letter. This simple assertion bears further examination. After killing their men, the women of Lemnos could hardly be expected to rush quickly into new alliances. While Hypsipyle and her sisters might well have wanted children, these could have been fathered by the Argonauts without the entanglement of love. But Hypsipyle at least has fallen in love and now wishes reunion with her beloved. Ironically, when she could have accepted the favours of Jason and then summarily dismissed him or even killed him, she did neither; now she is left with the pain of his faithlessness.

While Hypsipyle scorns the barbarous ancestry and actions of Medea, she herself is capable of the same kind of violence. Her frustration in being deprived not only of her lover but also of her victim becomes obvious when she lays an elaborate curse on Medea. While she might suppose that Jason has been seduced by Medea, she and the reader must know that Jason has hardly shown himself to be a paragon of virtue. Certainly the reader who knows the outcome of Jason's affair with Medea will not be surprised that Jason now shows so little regard for Hypsipyle (see JASON and MEDEA in Appendix I: Principal Characters).

Hypsipyle in attempting to conquer Jason and receive his love has herself been conquered and has lost what she now most desires. This is crucial to an understanding of her character. In the beginning of the letter her attitude is almost one of annoyance – 'Why did rumour bring the news rather / than letters from you?' She then becomes progressively more angry and more vengeful until at the end she pronounces a truly terrible curse. Through all this, her accusations of infidelity are countered by her assertion that he is the victim – almost innocent – of the evil charms and potions of Medea. This ambivalence is interesting because it suggests the same frame of mind in which Hypsipyle and her comrades destroyed their men. The triangle of Jason and these two violent women is a nice study. In the eyes of Hypsipyle, Jason is being victimized by Medea in much the same way as she herself might have victimized him had she so chosen. Having won her love and trust he has managed to escape her wrath and now she has become the victim.

Your keel is said to be safe in Thessaly
    and you are rich with the golden fleece.[1]
As much as I can I applaud your safety,
    though the message should have come from you.
If you wished to hurry to my side, the winds
    might have forced you to another route
away from the kingdoms I have promised you,
    but a letter does not need the wind.
Hypsipyle deserved at least a greeting.
    Why did rumour bring the news rather
than letters from you? I heard the whole story –
    you yoked the bulls of Mars to a plough
and scattered seeds that grew a harvest of men
    who died without feeling your hand's thrust.
I heard about the watchful dragon guarding
    the spoil of the ram, the golden fleece,
which was so boldly stolen. If only I
    could tell the doubters, 'He wrote this with
his own hand,' I would be proud. But why complain
    that my lord is slow? If I am yours
I have been treated with every indulgence.
    But I have also heard that you keep

48

some barbarian poisoner to share the bed
    that once you promised me in marriage.[2]
Love makes me jealous and forces my belief;
    I hope these rumours can be denied.
A Thessalian arrives from Haemonia and
    almost before he touches my sill
I say, 'Tell me about my lord, Aeson's son.'[3]
    Standing in chagrin, he cannot speak.
He looks away, I leap to my feet, tearing
    the garments from my breast. 'Does he live?
Or must I also die?' 'Alive,' he answers.
    But love is also afraid: I make him swear;
with a god as witness I hardly believe.
    I become calm and ask him of you.
He tells about Mars' oxen with brazen feet,
    how they ploughed, the serpent's teeth scattered,
like seed in the dirt, of men bearing weapons
    suddenly sprung up out of the land,
earth-born men, killed in battle with other men,
    living their lives in only one day.
He tells about the dragon overcome and
    again I ask if you live because
hope and fear cause trust and doubt to alternate.
    As he tells each episode to us
excitement hurries his speech on until he
    reveals the injuries you have done.
Where is your promised fidelity? Where are
    the marriage oath, the torches that might
better be used now to light my funeral pyre?
    Our marriage was public; Juno was
summoned there to join us as was Hymen too,
    his temples adorned with hanging wreaths.
But dismal, bloodstained Erinys rather than
    Juno or Hymen walked before me
in procession bearing the unlucky torch.[4]
    What concern were the sons of Minyas
or pines from the hills of Dodona to me?[5]
    Tiphys the helmsman, why could you care
at all for anything of my native land?[6]

We have no ram with resplendent fleece
nor was Lemnos the realm of old Aeëtes.
　　At first, before my fate led me on,
I wanted to drive the strangers out with my
　　　　army of women, for we know all too well
how to conquer men. I should have let
　　troops so brave defend my good judgement.
I saved that man with my city, I took him
　　under my roof and into my heart:
you stayed for two summers and two winters and
　　when the third harvest came you contrived
a reason to sail away from us. With tears
　　you spoke: 'Hypsipyle, I am torn
from you, but that fate grant my return, I am
　　yours as I leave and will always be.
May what I leave heavy in your belly grow
　　that we together may nurture it.'
Thus you spoke, with tears flowing down your false
　　face.
　　　　Weeping, you could not speak, you must leave.
You were the last to board the Argo. It flies
　　on, sails billowing, the dark blue waves
pour out from your departing keel. You look back
　　to me; from a high tower that stands
so that from every side the shore can be seen
　　I look out to sea. There, high above
the shore, I watch your sails grow smaller, my face
　　and bosom wet with tears that sharpen
my vision and soothe my troubled heart. My fear
　　for your safety was mingled with prayers
and innocent vows that now I must observe.
　　　　Shall I deny these vows because she,
Medea, enjoys their fruit? Shall I go on
　　praying for your safe return to her?
This makes me sick; my heart seethes with rage and love
　　mixed in me; shall I bring sacrifice
to the holy places because Jason lives
　　though he is no longer mine? Must some
victim die because a loss has come to me?

I was never secure, and I feared
your father would choose for you a bride from Greece.
    I never feared a barbarian slut.
The wound that I feel now has not come to me
    from the place I had thought it would come.
Neither with the beauty of her face nor with
    a woman's charm has she won, instead
she won you with enchanting words and the herbs
    she harvests with a magical knife.
Indeed, she could draw the moon out of its course,
    she could hide the horses of the sun
in darkness, she could stop the flowing of streams;
    bringing life to the trees and the rocks,
she causes them to move about the country.
    So often she prowls among the tombs
with her garments undone and her hair flowing;
    she gathers bones from warm funeral pyres,
she curses the absent to their doom; she makes
    figures of wax and drives needles through
their unlucky hearts; more is better not known.
    Love is won by virtue and beauty,
it cannot be found in the juices of herbs.
    Can you embrace a woman like this?
Can you be alone with her and still not fear,
    enjoying the sleep of the still night?
She must have forced you to do these awful things:
    like those bulls, you wear her heavy yoke,
and like the dragon, you too have been subdued.
    Her name will be written with your deeds;
the wife's exploits will hide the husband's glory.
    Someone loyal to Pelias could well
attribute your mighty deeds to her poisons.
    He could say, 'This splendid fleece of gold
was taken from the Phrixian ram not by
    the son of Aeson, but by a maid,
a Phasian girl, Aeëtes' daughter.' Go now,
    ask Alcimede; seek her advice;
nor does your father approve your choice, he sees
    your bride coming from the frozen north.[7]

Let her find herself another man, one from
        the banks of the Tanais, or from
the Scythian swamps or even one from Phasis.[8]
        Fickle son of Aeson, you are less
certain than a breeze in the spring; why did you
        take from your words the weight of your pledge?
You left here mine, but mine you have not returned.
        But if you could be returned to me
I would be your mate as I was when you left.
        If you can be moved by noble birth:
I am daughter to Thoas, Bacchus was my
        grandfather and his bride with her crown
of stars outshines the lesser constellations.[9]
        Lemnos is mine to give as dowry,
a rich land and me also you will receive
        along with the vassals of this land.
By now the gift you left in me has been born.
        Rejoice, Jason, rejoice for us both.
My labour was sweet because it caused the birth
        of a precious gift I had from you.
But now it is my turn to rejoice because
        our love has been favoured by divine
Lucina with two children, a promise for
        us both.[10] They resemble only you,
but their innocence is quite without deceit.
        I very nearly sent them to you
as ambassadors with Medea's servants
        but remembering her cruelty
I was turned away from that path for I feared
        Medea, a stepmother whose hands
are well made to commit any evil act.
        There is no crime she could not commit;
if she could tear her brother limb from limb and
        scatter his bleeding flesh on the earth,
could I expect her to honour my pledges?
        She is what she is, and you are mad,
made senseless by foreign poisons. Is it she
        for whom you left Hypsipyle and
your wedding bed? While the bond that made me yours

and made you mine was given chastely,
She is yours in shame. She betrayed her father
 while I saved Thoas; she left Colchis
while I remain here on this island, Lemnos.
  But if sin means more than piety
and if she won you with a dowry of crime,
 then I ask, does anything matter?
That crime once done by the women of Lemnos,
 Jason, is one that I must condemn
rather than admire; but passion drives the weak
 to arm themselves and seek their revenge.
Now, how would it have been if driven off course
 by storms you had entered my harbour
as you should have done, but with your companion?
 I would have met you with our infants –
you must have wished that the earth could swallow you—
 with what expression would you have gazed
on your children, how could you have looked at me?
  What death would you deserve as reward
for such infidelity? You however
 would have been welcomed into safety
not because you deserved it, but because I
 would choose to be merciful to you.
But as for your woman, I myself would have
 splashed my face with her blood and also
your face, that she stole with her vile arts. I would
 have been Medea for Medea.
If the just Jupiter above notices
 my prayers, may the woman who usurped
my marriage-bed suffer the fate I endure
 at her hands. As I am alone, wife
and mother of two, may she also one day
 lose both her husband and her children.
May she keep nothing of stolen goods for long,
 may she wander always an exile;
seeking safety and refuge in all the world.
  A wretched sister to her brother,
pitiless daughter to a wretched father;
 may her children and her husband know

the bitterness these others have had from her.
    When she despairs of finding shelter
by land or sea, let her fly; but may she go
    poor, without hope, bloodied by her crimes.
I, Thoas' daughter, cheated of my husband, pray
this for you: live now together, cursed in your bed.[11]

NOTES

1. Hypsipyle's letter to Jason opens at the point at which she has learned of his safe return to the city of Iolcus. From Hypsipyle's island of Lemnos Jason travelled to Corinth, and Medea; from there he went – with Medea – to Colchis, where he captured the golden fleece. Then he and Medea, with the crew of Argonauts and the golden fleece, returned to Thessaly. Medea will be the heroine of letter XII.

2. This is a reference to Medea.

3. That is, a traveller coming from the land in which Jason lives would naturally have news of Jason and his affairs.

4. Juno and Hymen were the Roman god and goddess of marriage.
Erinys was a Fury, one of the avenging spirits. Generally, Furies were believed to punish those who had caused injury to members of their own families; they often visited retribution on children who had killed either mother or father. It is interesting to note that Hypsipyle did not in fact permit the death of her father when the women of Lemnos killed their men. Perhaps the suggestion here is that Hypsipyle could just as well have killed her father, for she is still being punished as though she had done so.

5. At least one account of the Argonauts suggests that they were descendants of Minyas. This, however, is unlikely since it would appear that only Jason was descended from Minyas. Minyas himself is not a clear figure. He is variously said to be the son of Poseidon or Aeolus, or of Chryses, a Boeotian king.

6. Tiphys, a Boeotian by birth, was the helmsman of the *Argo*. He saw to the launching of the ship and then had the responsibility of steering it safely through many dangers until his death.

7. Alcimede was the mother of Jason. She killed herself when her husband, Aeson, was forced by Pelias to commit suicide. If Jason is to consult Alcimede, he must either seek her through an oracle or go to the Underworld to find her.

8. The Tanais is the modern river Don. Scythia was a region that lay approximately north and north-east of the Black Sea. The Phasis is a river in

the vicinity of Colchis, the homeland of Medea, which flows into the Black Sea. Phasis, like many place-names in the ancient world, though belonging properly to the river also came to be applied to the surrounding countryside. The point is that all three of these regions are outside the familiar world of Hypsipyle and Jason. Hypsipyle is repeating the argument that Medea is a woman of barbarian origins and should therefore find herself a man who is also a barbarian.

9. The Roman god Bacchus corresponds to the Greek god Dionysus. The bride of Dionysus was Ariadne, daughter of King Minos of Crete. She was taken from Crete by Theseus but later abandoned by him. Dionysus found her in her distress, gave her a crown of seven stars, and made her his wife. After her death the stars were returned to the heavens. Ariadne is the heroine of letter X which is addressed to Theseus. See ARIADNE and THESEUS in Appendix 1: Principal Characters.

10. Lucina was the Roman goddess of childbirth. Sometimes, however, the name of Lucina is joined to that of Juno or Diana.

11. This curse will, in large measure, come to pass when Medea writes her letter to Jason (XII).

VII: Dido to Aeneas

Any discussion of this seventh letter must recognize its strong relationship to various sections of Virgil's *Aeneid*, most particularly the fourth book. A problem does arise, however, in such a comparison because the narrative style of the two works is profoundly different. To place side by side a character who is revealed by a third person narrator extrinsic to the action of the narrative and one who is speaking in the first person in the epistolary style is to take the risk of comparing characters who are almost entirely different. Such a discussion requires that the reader first examine the character of the narrator so that one can understand the character being presented.

A literary work is first and foremost only that. In this case the literary work is a 'fiction', a thing which has been made, which has as its goal the telling of a story. That we are given certain specific pieces of information is something determined solely by the author. In the case of the *Aeneid* the author stands at one remove from his characters because those characters are given to us by a narrator who is in turn created by the author. In the *Heroides* the writer of the letter is the immediate creation of the author and as such immediately begins to reveal herself as she perceives herself to be. Here it is Dido whose interests and welfare are at issue, and it is Dido who describes for us the character of Aeneas and that divine mission which seems such a burden to his conscience and such a perplexity to her.

For Dido the only appropriate goal for Aeneas is that he should remain in Carthage as her husband and king. For the Roman audience, then, the accepted story of Aeneas and his divine mission as it has been worked out by Virgil is put in a new perspective by Ovid's Carthaginian siren. I use the term quite deliberately because I think that there is here a parallel between the epic of Aeneas and the epic of Ulysses. For both – and this must be the understanding of both the Roman and the Greek audience – the hero properly belongs at the end of his quest. For both heroes there is a strongly persuasive call to something else, something that will frustrate the larger plan by inserting an easier though less desirable goal.

Ovid's Dido is not an inferior – and less successful – copy of Virgil's. This cannot be over-emphasized. Where the reader finds Ovid's Dido deficient it can well be imagined that these deficiencies are also repellent to Aeneas. This discussion becomes especially pointed because the primary source for Ovid's Dido is accessible to us. However, the proximity of the *Aeneid* to the *Heroides* was even more obvious to the Roman audience because Virgil, who enjoyed the gracious, though perhaps somewhat self-serving, patronage of Augustus, was a very real personage in the affairs of the day.

Of course it cannot be denied that the conservatism of Augustus, his desire to restore to the state and its subjects the virtues of an earlier age, must have struck Ovid as some kind of regressive nostalgia. That Augustus died in the imperial purple while Ovid's life ended in dismal exile should tell us something of the successes and failures of each.

It might be an interesting exercise to read this seventh of the *Heroides* as though we knew nothing of Virgil, as though the *Aeneid* had never been written, as though this letter and its author were Ovid's sole invention. In such a context Dido's endless attempts at persuasion and Aeneas' apparent determination to be off on other business would be little more than that. Not unlike other figures in the *Heroides* Dido has given Aeneas everything as a sign of her love and he has given her little beyond the possibility of an unborn child and the certainty of a Trojan knife. At that the story becomes another account of a woman's foolish credulity before a less than scrupulous man bent on self-aggrandizement.

But such is not the case. This letter exists in a context that is social and political as well as literary. Ovid's letter and its writer are not so much better or worse than their obvious source as they are different. Perhaps, at root, the difference is that which obtains between elegy and epic.

And so, at fate's call, the white swan lets himself
down in the water-soaked grasses by

the Meander's shoreline to sing his last song;
    but I will not hope to move your heart
with my prayer because the god opposes me.[1]
    After the loss of all that is mine,
good name, chastity of both body and soul,
    a loss of words is not important.
But I ask again: are you still determined
    to abandon me to misery
and permit both your ships and your promises
    to sail from this shore on the same wind?
Aeneas, are you still determined to leave
    both your mooring and your solemn pledge
to seek a kingdom in remote Italy,
    a place whose shores you have never seen?
Aren't you impressed by the new walls of Carthage
    and the sceptre I've placed in your hand?
You have rejected what is done and insist
    on pursuing some unfinished work.
I have given you a kingdom; still you seek,
    through all the world, a land of your own.
Let us suppose you find the country you seek:
    who would give it to you? Is there one
man who would trust a foreigner in his fields?
    You must win another Dido's love,
you must give pledges to some other woman
    and I know you will again be false.
How do you hope to found another city
    like this so that you in a tower
can observe a people that belongs to you?
    If all your wishes were granted now,
without any further delay, could you find
    a wife who will love you as I have loved you?
Like devout incense thrown on smoking altars,
    like wax torches tipped with sulphur, I
am burning with love: all day long and all night,
    I desire nothing but Aeneas.
But Aeneas is not grateful; he rejects
    my care for him. If I had no love
for him he could go and I would be willing.

But no matter how bad he might think
I am, I can never say that I hate him
    but I will complain: he is unfaithful.
When my complaint has been said, I love him more.
    Venus spare me, let me be his wife;
Brother, Love, change the hard heart of your brother
    that he will do service in your camp.[2]
If this cannot be, I who was first to love –
    I say this without the slightest shame –
can supply the love that will kindle the fuel
    for loving that he has within him.
But this is all delusions and lies, the dream
    that hovers before me is not true;
his mother's heart does not beat in Aeneas.
    You were conceived by rocks and mountains,
born of oaks on the high cliffs, of the savage
    beasts, or of raging seas, such a sea
of hostile tides as now you can observe, tossed
    by the winds, on which you will soon sail.
Where do you flee? The rising storm will stop you,
    indeed, it will be my gift to you.
Look now, how the wind tosses the rolling waves.
    What I had wanted to owe to you
I will owe to the winds of the storm because
    winds and waves are more than just your soul.
My worth is not great enough for you to die
    in fleeing from me on the high seas –
why can I not place a wrong value on you –
    if you are able to risk dying
to be free of me, then you have paid too much
    for this hatred you are indulging.
The winds must soon cease, and over the smooth waves
    old Triton will drive his sky-born team.[3]
Oh that you too might be so easily changed;
    and so you shall be changed, unless you
are harder than the oak. Why does one who knows
    the sea like you so trust the waters
whose power you have felt? When you have cast off
    your mooring because the sea is good,

59

there will still remain much to fear from the sea.
    It is right that this should be, for it
was from the sea, near Cythera, it is said,
    that the naked mother of the Loves
came, and so one who has been unfaithful should
    not tempt the waves that flow in that place.[4]
I am doomed, but I fear that I will ruin
    him who ruined me, that I will harm
him who harmed me, I fear my foe will be wrecked
    at sea and be drowned. Aeneas live,
I pray it, for by living you will be hurt
    more than you could be hurt by dying.
You will be well-known as the cause of my fate.
    Imagine – may this be no omen –
that the storm has swept you up, what will you think?
    You will think of me and your false tongue;
you will think of Dido forced to die because
    one from Phrygia was unfaithful;
you will see the tears of your abandoned bride,
    her shoulders bent in grief, hair undone,
all stained with blood.[5] What is it that you gain now
    to pay you enough that you can say,
'This was I justly owed, the gods forgive me,'
    as the thunderbolts are hurled at you?
Wait a little, for your meanness and the seas
    to calm, for your safe voyage will be
your reward for waiting. Perhaps you
    can ignore such things, still you must let
young Iulus live. You alone will have enough
    if it is known that you caused my death.
What is Ascanius' guilt, or your Penates'
    that they be worthy of such a fate?[6]
Have they been saved from a burning city so
    that now they can be lost in the sea?
But you are false. All this talk of your father
    and the gods, all borne on your shoulders
to escape the flames, is still more of your lies.
    I was not first nor will I be last
to feel the heavy burden of your deceit.

Do they ask about your son's mother?
She was left dead and abandoned by her lord.[7]
    You told me that, and I should have known
that you were only giving me fair notice.
    Now, let me be burned as she was burned
for such a punishment is very much less
        than the pain my crime should win for me.
And I am certain that your gods are angry
    for this is now the seventh winter
that you have been tormented by the harsh winds.
    The sea washed you up on my shore and
I welcomed you to a safe refuge; hardly
        knowing your name, I gave you my throne.
I wish these gifts had been all, that everything
        else could be buried and forgotten.
That awful day, when a sudden storm came out
    of the blue sky and we took shelter
in a high-ceilinged cave, was my doom. I heard
    a voice, I thought it was a nymph's song
but it was the Eumenides shouting out
    a warning of the fate that was mine.[8] *Oresteia*
Virtue lost, you may exact the penalty
    which I owe to Sychaeus, I go
in shame and misery to seek forgiveness.
    His statue stands in a marble shrine
among green branches and ribbons of white wool.
    From that sacred place four times I heard
a voice that I remember quite well faintly
    calling out to me, 'Elissa, come.'
He calls me to his bed because I am his.
    I am late because I have confessed
my awful crime, I come in shame, forgive me.
    He who caused my fall was worthy and
he makes my sin less hateful. It was my hope
    that his divine mother and the weight
of his old father would make a faithful son
        become for me a faithful husband.
If I have failed, my fault has a worthy cause;
    if he be true, I have no regret.

Now, near the end of life, my fate is unchanged
    and it will follow me to the end.
My husband's blood washed the altars of his house,
    my brother reaped the fruits of that crime.
I was driven out of Tyre into exile
    leaving both his ashes and my land.
My enemy pursued me along hard paths;
    I reached this coast, having escaped both
my brother and the sea, and I bought these shores,
    the land that I gave you, faithless man.
I founded my city, I laid foundations
    on which huge walls would rise, exciting
the jealous fears of the neighbouring kingdoms.
    A stranger and a woman, I found
myself soon threatened by war. Quickly, I raised
    gates and prepared a hasty defence.
I have a thousand suitors, each one eyeing
    me with fondness and all complaining
because I prefer a foreigner. Tie me,
    give me to Iarbas of Gaetulia;
I would permit it.[9] My brother might sprinkle
    his profane hand with my blood as it
was sprinkled once with the blood of my husband.
    Set aside your gods and holy things,
your hand profanes them. An unholy right hand
    should never worship a deity.
If it was decreed that you worship
    these gods who escaped a city's flames,
it might well be that these same gods now regret
    the fate that let them escape those flames.
But perhaps it is Dido, swollen with child,
    whom you abandon with part of you.
To the mother's fate must be added the child's,
    you will cause your unborn child to die.
Iulus' brother will soon die with his mother,
    one fate will take us both together.
'But the god has ordered this!' It is my wish
    he had prevented your coming here,
that Trojan foot never had touched Punic soil.[10]

Could this be the same god who led you
to spend so many years on the harsh seas, tossed
    and tormented by the hostile winds?
Surely, you could more easily return straight
    to Pergamum, if it but remained
thriving as it did when Hector was alive.[11]
    But the Simois of your fathers
is not what you seek, it is the Tiber's stream.[12]
    You will land in that place a stranger
while the land you seek is so hidden from sight,
    so draws back from the keels of your ships,
that you will never be able to approach
    until you have become an old man.
Stop this wandering! Choose me and my dowry –
    the riches of Pygmalion and
the people I brought to this place. Move Ilion
    to this safer Tyrian city,
take pleasure in a king's estate and divine
    rights that belong to a king' sceptre.
If it is war for which you thirst, if Iulus
    must have battlefields to prove his strength
we shall find enemies for him to conquer.
    Nothing will be lacking because we
shall have here a place for both the laws of peace
    and a place for the display of arms.
I ask only this and by your mother pray,
    and by your brother's arrows and by
your divine companions, gods of Dardanus,
    may those Trojans you saved survive fate,
may that awful war be your last misfortune,
    may Ascanius find joy at last
and may the bones of old Anchises find rest
    here in a peaceful grave. Only spare
this house that has been given into your hands
    without condition. I ask no more.
You can accuse me of nothing more than love.
    I do not come from Phthia nor
am I a daughter of Mycenae; neither
    husband nor father ever fought you.[13]

If some scruple prevents your calling me wife,
    then let me be merely your hostess.
Whatever you require of Dido, she will
    gladly do so long as she is yours.
Believe me, Aeneas, I know how the waves
    can break against these African shores.
They will let you sail or keep you here in port
    according to the times they decide.
When the wind is right you will raise the white sails,
    but then the seaweed may keep you here.
Trust me to watch the skies and guess the weather;
    I will see that you get underway.
Even if it were your desire to stay, then
    I myself will not let you remain.
Your sailors need rest and your fleet needs repair:
    shattered by storms, it is not ready.[14]
By your former kindness to me, by that debt
    which I will owe you after marriage,
give me just a little time until the sea
    and my love for you have both grown calm,
while with time and courage I acquire the strength
    to bear up bravely in my sadness.
But if you will not listen to me, then with
    my own hands I will pour my life out.
You have been so cruel and are cruel to me now;
    Soon, I will be able to escape.
You should see my face while I write this letter:
    a Trojan knife nestles in my lap;
tears fall from my cheeks on its hammered steel blade
    and soon it will be stained with my blood.
How fitting that this knife was your gift to me,
    for death will not diminish my wealth.
My heart has already been torn by your love,
    another wound will hardly matter.
Anna, my sister; you, my sister, wretched
    with the knowledge of my shameful guilt:
too soon, you must give my ashes their last grace.
    When I have been consumed by the flames,
do not write, 'Elissa, wife of Sychaeus',

but in the marble of my tomb, carve:
'From Aeneas came a knife and the cause of death,
from Dido herself came the blow that left her dead.'

NOTES

1. This passage recalls the story of Cycnus, who was a musician as well as King of Liguria, that region of Italy on the north-western coast of the peninsula. Cycnus and Phaethon were friends, and when Phaethon was thrown from the heavens, Cycnus in his grief wandered in the grove of poplars which had once been the grieving sisters of Phaethon. Finally, Apollo took pity on Cycnus and turned him into a swan; then he carried him to the heavens where he became the constellation of stars, Cygnus. Ever since, so the myth goes, swans sing melancholy songs just before they die.

2. As the son of Venus (Aphrodite), Aeneas was also the half-brother of Eros (the Roman Amor or Cupid), a god of love.

3. Triton was one of the many gods of the sea. It was said of him that he could calm the waters by blowing on a conch shell. In the *Metamorphoses*, I.330–47, it was Triton who, after the world had been inundated by the flood, was summoned by Neptune, the principal Roman god of the sea, to blow his horn. As the sound reverberated across the earth, the waters returned to their rightful places, shorelines reappeared, oceans, lakes and rivers went back to their bounds, and the world was reborn.

4. Cythera was an island in the Aegean which was thought to be sacred to Venus because it was here that she was said to have been born. The story of the birth of Venus was told and re-told many times throughout the centuries and was the subject of numbers of pictorial representations, most notably the *Primavera* of Botticelli. In this passage, Ovid refers to Venus as the mother of the Loves, rather than of Love. The plural form of Eros – Erotes – is sometimes used, suggesting that Love is more than one.

5. Phrygia was a large area of Asia Minor which reached the shores of the Black Sea and the Aegean. It is likely that Dido is here referring to the ancestry of Anchises, father of Aeneas.

6. Iulus and Ascanius are both names for the son of Aeneas. Iulus (that is, Julian) was the name given to the imperial dynasty of which Julius Caesar and Augustus Caesar were the most prominent members.

7. Creusa was the mother of Ascanius. She was a daughter of Priam and Hecuba. Though captured by the Greeks in the Trojan War she was quickly released through the intervention of Aphrodite. When Troy fell

she disappeared as Aeneas was fleeing the burning city. The suggestion by Dido that Creusa was in fact abandoned, as she herself is abandoned by Aeneas, is her – and Ovid's – addition to the story.

8. The Eumenides, sometimes known as the Kindly Ones, were goddesses who ensured the productivity of the earth. Aeschylus in his play *Eumenides* identified them with the Erinyes or the Furies, and clearly this is Dido's understanding of their nature.

9. Gaetulia was roughly the area of north-west Africa. The term was also sometimes used broadly to refer to the interior of the African continent, with the connotation of the wild and untamed.

10. The word Punic, or Phoenician, refers to the city of Carthage and its inhabitants.

11. Pergamum is the name given to the central fortification of the city of Troy. Hector was one of the sons of Priam and a famous warrior. Because of his great love for his wife Andromache, his fidelity was cited as an exemplar. Dido here contrasts the faithfulness of Hector with the seeming infidelity of Aeneas.

12. The Simois was a tributary of the river Scamander in the vicinity of Troy. As the Simois is associated with Troy, so the Tiber is with Rome. It would appear that Dido by referring to the Tiber is actually uttering an anachronism; she would not be expected to know of the Tiber before Aeneas established his city.

13. Phthia was a city in Thessaly, and was said to be the birthplace of Achilles. Mycenae, a very ancient city in Argolis, was the capital of Agamemnon's kingdom. Like Phthia, it is used here to indicate a source for the troubles of Aeneas which caused him to leave his homeland and embark on this painful journey.

14. Dido is here being disingenuous. Aeneas and his men have lingered in Carthage for several years. If his crew now needs rest and his ships repair it can only be because they have been wasted while in port. When Dido writes her letter the ravages of the crossing from Troy to Carthage must have been repaired.

VIII: Hermione to Orestes

This letter has as its point of conflict the fact that the maternal grandfather of Hermione, Tyndareus, arranged her betrothal in the absence of her parents to Orestes, while Menelaus, some years later, was responsible for her betrothal to Pyrrhus, Achilles' son, to whom she is now married. In the usual order of things Hermione would not have the freedom to choose a husband except with the permission of a parent or perhaps a surrogate parent. For Tyndareus the marriage of Hermione and Orestes would greatly consolidate his own dynasty. While Tyndareus was King of Sparta his daughters Helen and Clytemnestra were the wives of the Atreidae, so that the children of Clytemnestra and Agamemnon would inherit Mycenae. Towards the end of his life the male heirs of Tyndareus were killed and he transferred the throne of Sparta to his son-in-law, Menelaus. With that Helen became the wife of the King of Sparta. While Menelaus probably favoured a marriage of Hermione and Orestes, when faced with disaster before the walls of Troy such concerns became secondary to the overriding need for a quick victory.

If it were possible to have Hermione and Orestes joined in marriage then the two kingdoms would be effectively united, to the prosperity of both. This betrothal, which Hermione persistently regards as a marriage, occurred between two children after the abduction of Helen and after the departure of Menelaus and the other Greeks for Troy. At this juncture Tyndareus can certainly be regarded as the head of his daughters' families since there seems to be no one to act in this capacity.

While Hermione asserts that it is love which determines the viability of a marriage contract the reader must be aware of the fact that it is only by accident that she and Orestes have fallen in love after their betrothal. The facts of the matter are painfully simple: the wishes and desires of Hermione and Orestes are quite immaterial before, first, the overriding dynastic considerations in effecting a union of the two kingdoms, and second, the need of the Greeks to pacify Achilles. That such extrinsic considerations were so important only emphasizes the passivity required of the two principals. For Hermione and Orestes the expediencies dictated by transcendent affairs of state necessarily reduced their wishes in the matter to triviality.

It is interesting to observe the ways in which Hermione is able to imagine and address the concerns that might motivate Orestes. As she writes this letter Orestes has already murdered his mother, Clytemnestra, and her lover, Aegisthus, in the same house where they had earlier killed Agamemnon, his father. In the midst of his torment at this double murder – if we are to believe Aeschylus – Hermione calls on him to visit the same revenge on Pyrrhus. While the courage of Orestes may not be sufficient to accomplish one more murder, the strength of his claim to Hermione should prevail.

As in most of these letters the characters and the events of their lives are set within a historical context that sweeps them along. Hermione contrasts her present situation as a young woman with her position as a child heartlessly abandoned by her mother. Later on, when her mother has returned to Sparta, Helen fails to recognize Hermione and Hermione realizes that indeed her childhood is over and her helpless, childlike passivity has been transferred to her adult life.

Hermione's existence is characterized throughout by betrayal and loss. In childhood she loves and loses her mother – though one can well wonder whether there was much to be lost – and soon after she loses her father. Her childhood companion and cousin becomes her betrothed and as quickly is set aside in favour of a man for whom she has no love. Hermione protests at her fate but her complaint echoes the hopelessness of her situation. Her life is determined by an unwilling passivity which, at least in this letter, she seems unable to escape.

Pyrrhus – a man as strong-willed as his father,
    Achilles – holds me here a captive.[1]
All laws of heaven and earth are on my side.[2]
    I have done all that I can, I have

never been willing to be kept here by him;
    more than that a woman cannot do.
'Son of Aeacus, what have you done?' I cried.[3]
    'I have one to avenge me, I am
a woman, Pyrrhus, with a master.' Deaf as
    the sea to my cries of 'Orestes!',
he dragged me with hair undone to his palace.
    Could my fate have been worse if Sparta
had been conquered and I with all the other
    daughters of Greece had been made captive
by barbarian hordes? Andromache herself
    was less abused at the hands of her
captors when the victorious Achaean troops
    and their fires consumed the goods of Troy.[4]
Orestes, if you have any care for me,
    do not be bashful about your rights:
if a thief opened your gate and stole your herds,
    would you arm yourself? Your wife is gone;
can you delay a minute to catch the thief?
    Let my father Menelaus be
your model: when his wife was taken from him,
    he demanded her return; the theft
of this woman became a just cause for war.
    Had he lacked ambition, had he been
content to doze in his empty house, Paris
    and my mother would be wedded still.
Do not prepare a thousand ships with bulging
    sails loaded with Greek soldiers ready
to fight for me. Only you, alone, should come.
    Yet I could have been won in battle,
it is never improper for a husband
    to fight battles for his marriage-bed.
Do not forget that Atreus, Pelops' son,
    is grandfather to us and if we
were not husband and wife we would be cousins.[5]
    My husband, be a help to your wife;
my cousin, come to your cousin's aid. Both ties
    must be for you the call of duty.
Wise Tyndareus, a man of sober life

and many long years gave me to you,
this grandfather determined the grandchild's fate.[6]
    Still it might be claimed that my father
not knowing this, gave me to Aeacus' son.
    But my grandfather prevailed in this.
When we married, we brought harm to no one, but
    if I wed Pyrrhus, you must be hurt.[7]
Menelaus my father will forgive us:
    he too has been struck by love's arrows,
a love he enjoyed he must grant to the man
    his daughter chooses; and my mother
whom he loved will aid us also in her way.
    You are to me as he is to her
and the role once played by a stranger from Troy
    is the role that Pyrrhus plays today.[8]
Let him brag about his father's mighty deeds,
    your sire, too, is worthy of your boasts.
Tantalus' son ruled all, even Achilles.
    The one man was only a soldier
while the other man was commander of all.
    And there are your ancestors – Pelops
and his father. If you counted every one
    you would be the fifth of Jove's offspring.[9]
And your mighty deeds – your weapons were awful,
    you had no choice, your father gave them.
Your deeds should have required more courage from
  you,
    though the cause was not for you to choose.
But you heard and then obeyed the call; the pierced
    throat of Aegisthus gave up his blood
in the house your father's blood had stained before.[10]
    Aeacus' son attacks your name, turning praise
to blame, and is not shamed to stand in my sight.
    Anger breaks out of me, my face swells
with fury, my breast burns with a pain that is
    wrath caged up within my pounding heart.
Has any mean thing been said of Orestes
    within hearing of Hermione
and I have neither strength nor sharp sword at hand?

But I can weep; I can pour out rage
so that tears like a stream cover my bosom.
    Only these do I have, and freely
do I let them go; my cheeks are always wet
    and ugly from their unending flow.
Has some fate come to us, pursuing our house
    down the years even to my time so
that we, mothers of the line of Tantalus,
    are easy prey for any rapist?[11]
I'll not recite the false words of the swan nor
    complain about the feathers of Jove.[12]
Where an isthmus splits the sea Hippodamia
    was taken away by a stranger;
the woman born in Taenarus was carried
    across the seas by one from the slopes
of Mount Ida, a man welcomed as a guest,
    for whom the Argive men took up arms.[13]
I hardly remember, but I remember.
    There was only sorrow, everywhere
fear. My grandfather wept, as did my mother's
    sister, Phoebe, and the twins as well.[14]
Leda prayed to her Jove and the gods above.
    Though my hair was not yet long, I pulled
at it as I cried out, 'Mother, do you go
    away and leave me here, behind you?'
Do not think that I am not Pelops' daughter;
    for I am Neoptolemus' prey.
If only the bow of Apollo had missed
    the son of Peleus; a father
would damn his own son for such a reckless deed.
    In the old days Achilles never
rejoiced nor would he now to watch a widowed
    husband mourning for a stolen wife.[15]
Why does heaven itself oppose me, what stars
    have ranked themselves against my poor self?
My childhood knew neither father nor mother;
    one was away, the other at war.
Oh my mother, you did not hear your daughter's
    childish words, you neither felt her arms

around your neck nor felt her weight on your lap:
      it was not your hand that cared for me;
when I was married no one prepared the bed.[16]
      When you returned I went to meet you –
I tell the truth – but I did not know your face.
      You were the most beautiful woman
I had ever seen, you had to be Helen,
      but you asked which one was your daughter.
Fortune has given me only one kindness:
      Orestes to be my husband. But
he too will be lost to me if he does not
      fight for what is his. Pyrrhus keeps me
though my father has returned victorious.[17]
      It is this that I have from Troy's fall.
When Titan drives his resplendent team my soul,
      heavy with grief, finds some little joy;
but when night falls and consigns me to my bed
      with cries and wailing for my sad fate
I lie, stretched out, and tears, not sleep, are the gift
      that my eyes give to me and I shrink
back from my partner as I would from a foe.[18]
      My grief quite often leaves me insane:
I forget where I am, the fate that is mine,
      with unknowing hand I touch that man
from Scyros.[19] But then I wake, shocked by the deed,
      I draw back my poor hand now defiled.
Often I murmur in my sleep, 'Orestes,'
      rather than 'Neoptolemus,' and
your cherished name I take as a good omen.
      I swear, by our most unhappy tribe,
and by that parent of us both who disturbs
      the seas, the land, his heavenly realms,
and by your father's sacred bones, he who was
      my uncle, bones which require of you
a courageous revenge so that they can lie
      at peace within their burial mound:
I shall die in youth or I, Tantalus' daughter,
shall be the wife of a man born of Tantalus.[20]

NOTES

1. Pyrrhus was the son of Achilles by Deidamia.

2. While it is certainly true that Menelaus should not have broken the word of Tyndareus which gave Hermione to Orestes, it is difficult for Hermione to argue that the law is on her side. Her position is confirmed only to the extent that Orestes has the right to have the original contract come to fruition. While Hermione might insist that she has rights, only those of Orestes are directly at issue. By refusing to give her consent, Hermione – as she herself says several lines later – has done all that a woman can do in such a matter.

3. Pyrrhus was the great-grandson of Aeacus, the first King of Aegina. The lineage runs from Aeacus (by Endeis), to Peleus (by Thetis), to Achilles (by Deidamia), and so to Pyrrhus. It is significant that Aeacus during his lifetime became renowned for his piety towards the gods and his great respect for justice. That Hermione should here invoke the great-grandfather of Pyrrhus suggests strongly that she is contrasting the injustice of her situation with the justice and probity of Pyrrhus' ancestor.

4. Early in the Trojan War, as the Greek forces were conquering the cities of the outlying allies of Troy, Achilles sacked the city of Thebes which was ruled by Eetion, the father of Andromache. By that time she was married to Hector, the son of Priam. After the death of Hector, when Troy fell to the invading Greek forces, Andromache was taken into slavery and given to Pyrrhus as part of his booty.

5. Atreus had two sons, Agamemnon and Menelaus. Agamemnon was the father of Orestes and Menelaus the father of Hermione. These two – Agamemnon and Menelaus – were known to the ancient world as the Atreidae, the sons of Atreus. Because their fathers were brothers, Hermione and Orestes were cousins.

6. Tyndareus was King of Sparta, renowned in his lifetime for his great wisdom. It is probable that Tyndareus was instrumental in returning Agamemnon and Menelaus to the Mycenaean throne of their father. It should be noted, however, that while Helen was born to Leda during the time of Leda's marriage to Tyndareus, it is consistently maintained by various authors that Helen and her brother Polydeuces were the result of the union of Zeus and Leda, while Castor and Clytemnestra were the offspring of Tyndareus and Leda.

7. It is probable that Ovid is not asserting that Orestes and Hermione had actually been married prior to her being given to Pyrrhus; rather it seems reasonable to understand the term 'married' as 'betrothed'. Hermione has every incentive to argue for the strictest possible understanding of a marriage

contract. Though the facts do not quite support her assertion, she is insistent that she and Orestes are already married.

8. Again, Hermione insists that a marriage contract negotiated and entered into by her father and presumably consummated by her and Pyrrhus can be abrogated simply by the fact that her desires have not been met. In this, she denies every dynastic and political reason that might have made her marriage to Pyrrhus desirable. She does not hesitate to see Pyrrhus and Paris as fulfilling similar roles. She does, however, close her eyes to significant facts which make such a comparison dubious at best.

9. Showerman (op. cit., page 102) points out that Orestes is really sixth in the line of descent from Jove, his lineage being through Jove, Tantalus, Pelops, Atreus and Agamemnon. The text, however, would seem to indicate that Hermione (and Ovid) is counting only the actual descendants of Jove, of whom Orestes is clearly the fifth.

10. Aegisthus was taken by Clytemnestra as her lover and was her accomplice in the murder of Agamemnon. Later, Orestes killed both Aegisthus and Clytemnestra to avenge the death of his father.

11. Tantalus was a Lydian king, the father of Pelops. His well-known punishment in Hades was the result of a feast which he gave to entertain the gods. At the feast he attempted to test their perspicacity by serving up to them a stew made from the body of his son, Pelops. When they discovered the horror, the gods restored Pelops to life but consigned Tantalus to the Underworld. Another story tells us that Tantalus was punished because, after being invited to dine with the gods on Olympus, he stole nectar and ambrosia from their table and furthermore told their secrets to mortals.

12. Jove, in the disguise of a swan, ravished Leda.

13. Hippodamia was the mother of Atreus, Thyestes and Pittheus. All her potential husbands were killed in a test devised by her father, Oenomaus. Each suitor was required to take Hippodamia in his chariot and drive to the neighbouring Corinthian isthmus. Oenomaus in full armour followed with his horses. If he overtook the suitor's chariot he was free to kill the young man. Pelops managed to evade Oenomaus and finally to kill him, and took Hippodamia as his wife. The stranger, then, that Hermione refers to here was Pelops. It seems that Ovid (and Hermione) is here suggesting that Hippodamia went unwillingly with Pelops after the death of her father, just as Hermione went unwillingly to be the wife of Pyrrhus. This, however, is not generally the nature of the story.

Helen was born in Taenarus and Paris grew to manhood on the slopes of Mount Ida.

14. Phoebe and her sister Hilaeira were daughters of Leucippus. They were kidnapped by the twin brothers of Helen, the Dioscuri, whose wives

they became. Phoebe, then, is sister-in-law to Helen and aunt to Hermione.

15. Achilles was the son of Peleus and was killed by Paris who, standing on the walls of Troy, shot him with a poisoned arrow. The arrow was guided to its mark by Apollo, who took care that it struck Achilles in the only vulnerable part of his body, the heel, which alone had not been dipped in the waters of the Styx. Hermione is suggesting, in this rather convoluted allusion to the myth, that just as Achilles mourned when the slave girl Briseis was abruptly taken from him, so would he sympathize with the grief of Orestes now mourning the loss of the woman given to him.

16. That is, no one prepared the wedding-bed when she was so hastily married to Pyrrhus.

17. Menelaus gave Hermione to Pyrrhus, Achilles' son, in an attempt to spur Achilles and Pyrrhus to greater efforts in the battle against the Trojans. Now that victory has been won, Hermione suggests that Menelaus can no longer have a reason to give her to Pyrrhus.

18. 'Titan' refers to Helios, god of the sun. In fact Helios was sometimes confused with his father, Hyperion, who was also a god of the sun. Titan, or Helios, was commonly described as driving in a resplendent chariot drawn by a team of four horses across the sky during the hours of daylight. By night he returned to the point of the dawn by riding in a great golden cup on the current of the river Oceanus. Because he could see everything on the face of the earth, Titan was called upon to witness oaths.

19. Scyros, an island in the Aegean, was where Pyrrhus was fathered by Achilles.

20. Jove was the common ancestor of both Hermione and Orestes. By referring to Tantalus in the concluding lines of her letter, Hermione seems to suggest that while Tantalus may have sinned against his own child, she and Orestes will wrest a kind of salvation from the terrible situation in which they find themselves, a situation brought about by the unfortunate deeds of their forebears. There is also the suggestion here that whereas Tantalus was condemned always to have gratification and relief either just out of reach or whisked away as he was about to seize them, she and Orestes will be able to avoid this cruel fate.

IX: Deianira to Hercules

Deianira opens this letter by writing as an injured wife deprived by her lawful husband of what has been hers in law – Hercules and his estate, his possessions both tangible and intangible. As she enumerates in confusing detail his many escapades she also notes how he has conferred the fruits of his heroism on different women. The tone of her address, it would seem, is not so much one of jealousy as one of grief at her loss.

Given this emotional state, it is not difficult to imagine the reason why she depicts Hercules as enslaved by feminine charm and held captive by the attractions of other places. In simple terms Hercules by his marriage vows must be hers. For him to give either himself or his possessions to anyone else is to deprive her of something that has properly become hers. In a way Deianira invokes a paradox that runs throughout much of imaginative literature – the dichotomy that can exist between one's deeds and one's reputation. For Deianira, the conquest of Hercules by Iole and Omphale is especially bitter because it is the result of his own complicity in his downfall.

It does not seem far off the mark to argue that Deianira is a woman whose life and accomplishments have been entirely given over to those of her husband. Her only glory is his, her only life is the life he has given her. Without Hercules – and this possibility is quite real – she is reduced to the status of one who is nothing and has nothing. Deianira is most careful to recognize this link between her own sense of herself, her pride, and the presence of Hercules.

It is a curious aspect of this letter that Deianira is not so much cognizant of an injury to love as she is of an injury to her wifely status. The real threat for her is the possibility that Iole might become Hercules' wife. She seems to have little concern for the bond of love; rather she is concerned that the marital bond may not only be compromised but even broken. Deianira's concern for Hercules is familial and dynastic, but scarcely amorous and erotic.

Deianira scarcely mentions the injury being done to her. The emphasis which she develops so strongly is that Hercules is injuring himself. That he is making himself a ridiculous figure hurts her because he has already been hurt by it. Deianira reminds Hercules that only equals should marry. He is a hero of wide renown and she is a simple girl, and this is only balanced when his fame and property become, at least in part, hers in marriage. For him to marry another and remove these goods would be a violation of a contract rather than a violation of the claims of love.

You conquered Oechalia honourably
    and I give thanks, but I also grieve
because your victory has turned to defeat:
    rumour has suddenly spread itself
through the cities of Pelasgus, a rumour
    unfitting to one whose deeds belie
such words, that he who could never be crushed by
    Juno's unending labours is yoked
by Iole.[1] Eurystheus would be pleased,
    the Thunderer's sister would be pleased,
stepmother that she is; she would cheerfully
    know of this blemish on your virtue.[2]
But Jupiter himself, for whom just one night
    of love was not enough to father
your might, if one is to believe what is said,
    would be sad to learn of these events.[3]
Venus, more than Juno, has been your downfall;
    the one, crushing you, has raised you up,
but the other has your neck under her foot.[4]
    Look, wherever the blue waters of
Nereus pass a shoreline, there is the peace
    that was won by your guardian strength.[5]
You alone guarantee safety on the seas,
    your great deeds fill the sun's two houses,
heaven where you will live was once your burden.
    When Atlas was keeper of the stars
mighty Hercules bent his back to carry

their load.[6] What have you gained now except
the spread of your miserable shame if you
        cap your former deeds with this poor sin?
Can you be the infant, now grown, who strangled
        two poisonous snakes in his cradle?
Worthy of Jove, your beginning was better
        by far than your end, man and boy are
not the same, your most recent deeds are such that
        their fame is less than those of your youth.
The arrows of love finally have conquered
        that one who survived a thousand wild
beasts and Juno's hatred and the enmity
        of the firstborn son of Sthenelus.[7]
But men say that because I am your wife and
        your father is Jupiter, lord of
all the thunder, then I must have married well.
        An ox, yoked to one not his equal,
suffers like the wife who is less than her lord.
        Happiness in marriage demands that
only equals marry, anything less is
        without honour, it only seems just.
I so rarely see my lord that he is more
        a guest in our house than my husband;
he is always away, pursuing wild beasts
        and horrible monsters. I busy
myself, widowed and chaste, with praying at home,
        tortured by my relentless fear that
some vicious foe will bring him down; my mind's eye
        is filled with snakes and boars and lions,
with three-throated hounds pursuing their quarry.
        I am terrified by entrails left
on the altar, by an idle dream, and by
        omens sought in the confusing night.
In misery, I strain to catch the muttered
        talk of simple men; fear vanishes
in weakened hope, my hope vanishes in fear.
        Your mother is away, lamenting
that she ever pleased an all too mighty god.
        Neither your father, Amphitryon,

nor Hyllus, your son, are here; Eurystheus,
    who rules through the tricks of cruel Juno,
and the unending anger of the goddess,
    these I am left here alone to bear.
Is this not enough for me? You also add
    to my pain with loves that are more odd;
whoever wants becomes a mother by you.
    I will not mention Auge, betrayed
by you in the glades of Parthenius or
    your sorrow, daughter of Ormenus,
nor hold you responsible for the daughters
    of Teuthras' son, that crowd of girls
of which not even one was spared.[8] There is one
    new love, a new offence, that makes me
the stepmother to Lamus of Lydia.

    Meander, which flows back and forth through
the same lands, turning back his wearied current
    on himself sees jewelled chains hanging
from the muscled neck of Hercules, the same
    neck that bore the heavens easily.
Were you not shamed when your arms were bound with
  gold
    and gems were set on your bulging strength?[9]
Indeed, these arms crushed life out of the Nemean
    nuisance, a horrid beast whose pelt drapes
the left side of your body, but you do not
    hesitate to wrap your long unkempt
hair in ribbons cut for a woman.[10] The white
    poplar is more proper to your curls;
you have shamed yourself by tying up your waist
    with Lydian belts like some reckless girl.
Have you not recalled Diomedes feeding
    men's flesh to his mares?[11] If Busiris
were to see you now, he whom you defeated
    would blush for having fallen beneath
a conqueror such as you have now become;
    and Antaeus would tear the ribbons
from you for the shame of his bitter defeat.[12]
    They say you are changed, that your mistress

often frightens you with her threats; that the same
    hands that performed a thousand labours
carry baskets of wool for Ionian girls.
    Alcides, when you touch the basket
of wool does not your mighty hand cringe?[13] Can you
    draw out with your thumb the fibres and
give back to your shameless mistress the proper
    portion that she measured out for you?
How often have your hands crushed the spindle while
    your fingers twisted the wool to thread?
You have lain at her feet and told deeds of which
    you should say nothing: of serpents coiled
about your infant hand while you crushed their life;
    of the great Tegaean boar that prowls
in the cypress groves of Mount Erymanthus,
    shaking the earth with his body's weight.[14]
You could not omit telling of skulls hung up
    on Thracian walls, nor those mares fattened
on the flesh of men, nor the threefold marvel,
    Geryon, rich with Iberian cattle,
who was one in three bodies, nor Cerberus
    growing three hounds from one body, his
hair caught in a tangling snake, nor the fecund
    serpent rising from a fruitful wound,
enriched by her pain, nor that one whose weight hung
    on your left side, between your arm and
your body as you clasped his throat, nor the troop
    of beings, both horse and man, destroyed
by you in the mountains of Thessaly when
    they put their trust in their twofold form.[15]
Can you recite these deeds while wearing a gown
    cut in the Sidonian fashion?
Such garments should tie your foolish tongue in knots.
    The nymph-daughter of Iardanus has
even decked herself with your arms and triumphed
    over her vanquished hero.[16] Puff up
your courage, recite each one of your brave deeds,
    it is she who is the better man.
You, mightiest of men, have become much less

than she; conquering you, she has won
a victory greater by far than you won
    by conquering all your enemies.
Everything that you won by your mighty deeds
    has now been given to her; give up
as well whatever you own, for your mistress
    inherits now even your great fame.
It is shameful that the lion's pelt adorns
    her dainty body. You are wrong but
you do not know it. She has won that prize not
    from the beast but from you. You conquered
the lion but it is she who conquers you.
    A girl grasps the darts that drip the black
venom of Lerna, a girl not strong enough
    to carry a spindle of new wool;
she hefts the great club that conquered many beasts
    and at her mirror wears my husband's arms.[17]
But all this I had only heard; I could doubt
    the words of men, the pain struck gently.
But now my eyes can see the rival and I
    cannot deny the truth that I see.
You will not let me turn away: a captive,
    she is led through our city and I
can no longer deny the pain that I feel.
    But she is like no other captive
With ragged hair and downcast face, instead she
    walks on, a pretty sight, hung with gold,
dressed as you were dressed when you lived in Phrygia.
    She looks at the crowd, her head held high,
as if it were she who conquered Hercules.
    One could think that Oechalia still stood
and her father continued to live. Perhaps
    Aetolian Deianira will
be driven off so that this one can give up
    being mistress and become your wife.
Iole, the daughter of Eurytus and
    Aonian Alcides will be joined
by you in low shame with the bonds of Hymen.
    My mind cannot consider such things;

81

my body is swept with chill and my hand lies,
    unable to feel, in my poor lap.
Like her, you have had me among your many
    loves, but I come to you without shame.
Do not regret it now because you have twice
    fought to keep my love secure for you.
Weeping, Achelous gathered his shattered horns
    on the marshy banks of his river
and bathed his wounded face in its murky stream;
    Nessus, the half-man, sank down into
the Euenus with its blooming lotus and
    reddened it with the flow of his blood.[18]
But why should I go on about these deeds when
    rumour whispers that you are dying
of the poison in that cloak? What have I done?
    Alas, is this the madness my love
has driven me to embrace? Wicked woman,
    Deianira, why do you wait to die?[19]
Will your lord be torn apart on Oeta and
    shall you then, the cause of his dying,
still live? If I have done anything to win
    the title, wife of Hercules, let
my death then pledge our union. Meleager,
    you too will find in me a sister
worthy to be counted among your sisters.[20]
    Deianira, why do you wait to die?
Alas for my faithful house. Agrius sits
    on the high throne, Oeneus has lost
all and sterile old age weighs him down. Tydeus,
    my brother, lives in exile on some
foreign shore; another brother's life was hung
    over the flames of fate; our mother
pierced her heart with a steel blade.[21] Wicked woman,
    Deianira, why do you wait to die?
I ask forgiveness for just one thing only,
    and this I ask by the sacred bonds
of our marriage-bed, that I seem to have planned
    your death. Nessus, when the arrow lodged
in his lusting heart, said, 'This blood has power

over love.' I, not understanding,
sent his bloodied robe to you. Wicked woman,
Deianira, why do you wait to die?
Farewell old Father, farewell to you, Gorge,
my sister, and to you my native
land, to you my brother and to you, this light
that is the last light strike my eyes.
To you my lord, farewell – how I hope it can be;
and at last to Hyllus, my son, I say farewell.

NOTES

1. At the time Hercules was conceived by Zeus, Juno (the Greek Hera), wife of Zeus, had professed an undying enmity for all the many illegitimate offspring of her philandering husband. Through no fault of his own Hercules spent his life attempting to free himself from her hatred. The labours to which Deianira refers were actually imposed by King Eurystheus as conditions to be met before he would purify Hercules of the guilt incurred when he murdered his own children. That murder was committed in a fit of madness sent by Juno. Therefore it could be said, as Deianira says here, that the famous tasks were 'Juno's unending labours'.

It seems fairly certain that Oechalia was a city in Greece, though it is not at all clear where it was located or what its modern name might be. It is interesting to note that Hercules when a boy was taught to use an archer's bow by Eurytus, King of Oechalia.

2. That is, Juno, who was not only the sister of Zeus but his wife as well; thus in a sense Juno could be said to be Hercules' stepmother.

3. There was a myth that the conception of Hercules was so momentous that even Zeus required more than one night to accomplish the task.

4. The many stories of Hercules quite often focus on what appears to have been an insatiable sexual appetite combined with a boundless sexual capability. In every way, Hercules was a man of heroic stature. The irony to which Deianira here refers is that Juno's hatred has actually caused him to flourish while the affection of Venus has destroyed him.

5. Nereus was an ancient god of the sea. He was known to have significant prophetic powers and he also had the curious ability to change his shape as he wished. Certain of the nymphs led Hercules to the lair of Nereus. Though Nereus confusingly adopted many different appearances, Hercules was finally able to bind him hand and foot and force the god to reveal the location of

the Garden of the Hesperides where the golden apples grew. To secure these apples and bring them to King Eurystheus was one of the labours exacted by the king. The suggestion in this passage is that by subduing Nereus, Hercules also managed to bring a degree of calm to the waters.

6. Deianira is here summarizing the beneficial impact that the heroic deeds of Hercules have had on the earth. The reference to the two houses of the sun – that is, the house from which the sun departs at dawn and the house to which he goes at sunset – is another way of saying that the heroism of Hercules is to be found wherever the sun's light is cast. The reference to heaven as a burden is to the account of Hercules coming, as he travelled in the western extremities of the world, to the spot where Atlas stood, carrying the weight of the sky on his shoulders. Because this place was near the Garden of the Hesperides, and because Atlas presumably knew its exact location, Hercules offered to hold up the sky for a little while if Atlas would go to the garden, pick the apples, and bring them back to him. Atlas hurried to oblige. However, when he had once transferred the weight to Hercules and after he had obtained the apples, he had no intention of returning to bear the weight of the sky but instead offered to deliver the apples himself to Eurystheus. Trapped beneath the great weight, Hercules was forced to rely on his wit rather than his strength. He pretended to agree to Atlas's request, but said he would need to raise the load so that he could place some kind of protection on his back. Atlas agreed, and as soon as the sky had been returned to him Hercules took the apples and hurried away to King Eurystheus.

7. Amphitryon, the husband of Alcmene at the time Zeus fathered Hercules by her, killed Alcmene's father Electryon. After the murder, Sthenelus, the brother of Electryon, sent Amphitryon into exile at the court of Creon, King of Thebes. When Alcmene was pregnant by Zeus and very near the time of her confinement, Zeus boasted to the gods on Olympus that on that very day a boy would be born of the line of Zeus who would rule the lands of his birth. Hera, pretending to be amazed at something so unlikely, asked Zeus to swear an oath that indeed the boy would be a great ruler. At once, Hera took steps to delay the delivery of Alcmene and hurried to cause a son to be born to the wife of Sthenelus. As a great-grandson of Zeus through Perseus, this boy, Eurystheus, became King of Tiryns and Mycenae and in due time imposed on Hercules the legendary labours.

8. Auge was a priestess of Athena and one of the many women seduced by Hercules in the course of his adventures. According to one account the child of this union, Telephus, was exposed on Mount Parthenius at the same time that Atalanta was also exposing her child by Meleager, Parthenopaeus. This story has the two infants raised together by shepherds until such time as Telephus sets off as a young man to find his parents.

84

Ormenus was the grandson of Aeolus, god of the winds, and father of Amyntor and the nymph Astydamia.

Thespius was the son of Teuthras. A savage lion had been taking animals from the flocks of both Amphitryon and Thespius. Thespius had heard of the great strength of the young Hercules and invited him to visit his kingdom. For fifty nights he entertained Hercules in regal splendour and because he wanted to enrich his line by having the sons of Hercules as his own grandsons, he sent in the course of those fifty nights each of his fifty daughters successively to the bed of Hercules. Another variation claims that on each of the fifty nights all fifty daughters were sent to Hercules. It is interesting to note that Deianira is telling the story with great sympathy for the daughters who, she implies, must have been ravaged by Hercules. The more traditional accounts, on the other hand, would suggest that it was Hercules who deserved sympathy. At all events, Ovid is reiterating the idea that Hercules is a man whose sexuality, like all his other characteristics, is indeed of heroic proportions.

9. After murdering Iphitus, the elder son of Eurytus and the brother of Iole, Hercules found himself afflicted by a terrible disease of the skin. Seeking to be cleansed, he sought the advice of the Oracle of Delphi. The advice, which was notably straightforward, was that if he sold himself into slavery for three years and gave the price of his servitude as recompense to the sons of Iphitus he would be cured. Accordingly he was sold to Omphale, Queen of Lydia, the daughter of Iardanes and the mother of Lamus. Deianira suggests that Hercules has gone willingly to Omphale; the myth, however, quite explicitly emphasizes that Hercules can only be cleansed of his terrible affliction if he will give up his freedom and embrace slavery. For Deianira, this is a significant misunderstanding of the facts. Or perhaps we can argue with some cynicism that she has correctly understood the situation.

10. After enjoying the hospitality of Thespius, Hercules seems not to have gone on to pursue the horrid beast that was ravaging the area. Deianira here refers to the first of the labours of Hercules: that he slay the Nemean lion. This beast was very much more than an ordinary lion. It was of a great size and its hide was such that it could easily repel any weapon, whether of stone, bronze or iron. Hercules confronted the beast in its mountain lair. At first, he attempted to shoot it with an arrow but the arrow simply fell away from the animal. Hercules then took more heroic measures. He blocked up one of the entrances to the den, and entered the other carrying no weapons. He met the animal and promptly killed it with his bare hands. He left the cave wearing the lion's pelt over his shoulders like a cape. For the rest of his life he wore this pelt as a sign of his strength.

11. The eighth labour prescribed for Hercules was to seize and bring back to King Eurystheus the mares of Diomedes. Diomedes was a barbarous and

warlike king in Thrace who had four mares of great ferocity who were fed on human flesh. Hercules went to Thrace where he stole the mares from their grooms. But as he prepared to drive them to the sea, he found himself attacked by the Bistones, the followers of Diomedes. To protect himself he gave the horses into the care of his young manservant, Abderus. After routing the attackers he returned to find that the horses had killed Abderus and had eaten most of his body. Another source says that Hercules calmed the mares by feeding their former master to them. He then took the four animals to Eurystheus who set them free.

12. Busiris was an Egyptian who attempted to end a drought by offering to Zeus a sacrifice of foreigners who were living in Egypt. To avenge this outrage, Hercules brought Busiris to justice by killing him in combat. In this episode, Hercules served his father Zeus as an avenging arm, because Zeus was the patron of all travellers and enforced the law of hospitality.

Antaeus was a giant, the son of Poseidon and Ge, the earth goddess. Any visitor to Antaeus' homeland of Libya would be invited to wrestle with the giant. The giant, however, found his great strength in his mother, the earth. Even if the foreigner began to win the contest, he would find as he pressed Antaeus to the ground that the giant would immediately be renewed by contact with his mother. As a result, Antaeus always won the bout and the foreigner invariably lost his head. Hercules in his travels came to Libya and observed the paradox that Antaeus seemed to find victory in defeat. Accordingly Hercules, in wrestling with Antaeus, lifted the giant over his head and, when the giant's body was no longer in contact with the earth, crushed and killed him.

13. At birth Hercules was given the name of his grandfather, Alcaeus. This name was later changed to Hercules. The use of 'Alcides' here refers to the fact that Hercules was a descendant of Alcaeus, who should have an interest in the current turn of events. Once again Deianira is using Hercules' past as a reproach for his present actions.

14. Deianira here refers to the two serpents which Hercules strangled in his crib to prove his divine parentage. The capture of the Tagaean or Erymanthean boar was one of the labours prescribed by Eurystheus. The fact of the boat hunt is much less interesting than the events leading up to it in which Hercules, to reach Mount Erymanthus, passes through the land of the centaurs, a place to which they had been exiled after their disruption of the nuptial feast of Pirithous and Hippodamia.

15. In this passage Deianira catalogues a number of the more notable of Hercules' accomplishments.

The skulls hung on Thracian walls is a reference to Antaeus, who hung each of the severed heads of his victims on his wall, or as one source says, on his roof.

The fattened mares are the mares of Diomedes.

Geryon was a man with three heads (or as some say – as does Deianira – a one-headed man with three bodies) who owned a herd of quite splendid cattle. Hercules killed Geryon's herdsman, stole the cattle and killed Geryon when he followed in pursuit.

Cerberus was the watchdog at the gates of Hades. When Hercules went to the Underworld, he brought Cerberus back to Eurystheus. Cerberus had the body of a dog and three heads.

The fecund serpent probably refers to a strange creature found in a cave, who had the body of a snake from her waist down. She admitted to having stolen the horses of Hercules but refused to surrender them until Hercules had begotten three sons with her. He acceded to her request and when his horses had been restored he eventually continued his travels.

The reference to one whose weight hung on the body of Hercules could be to any of several incidents in his exploits. Usually he killed his victims by strangulation.

The centaurs, beings that were both man and horse, were driven to a new homeland by Hercules.

16. The nymph-daughter of Iardanus was Iole.

17. The weaponry of Hercules contained arrows whose tips had been touched with the venom of the Hydra which he found at Lerna. After dipping his arrows, Hercules extracted the venom from the Hydra's body. As time passed, this venom would be the cause of death for many until, finally, Hercules himself was poisoned by it.

18. Achelous was a river god who wrestled with Hercules, the winner to have Deianira for his wife. Though the god used every evasion possible, including a frequent change of shape, he could not win the contest. Finally Achelous became a bull, in which guise he was finally defeated by Hercules who shattered its horns.

Nessus was one of the centaurs who were driven out of Arcadia by Hercules. He became a ferryman and on one occasion carried Deianira across a river while Hercules swam across alone. Taking advantage of the situation, Nessus attempted to rape Deianira, but Hercules shot him. As the centaur was dying, he advised Deianira to make a love potion composed of his blood and semen, all the while knowing for a certainty that his blood was poisoned by the Hydra's venom on the arrow. Later it was this potion, tainted with the Hydra's venom, which caused Hercules' death.

19. At the end of his life, Hercules decided to avenge himself on Eurytus for refusing to give him Iole after he had rightfully won the girl. He raised an army, defeated Oechalia, killed Eurytus and captured Iole. Because he wished to make a proper and appropriate sacrifice to his father Zeus, Hercules sent messengers to Deianira asking her to send him a ceremonial garment for the event. Fearing that Hercules would become enamoured of

Iole, Deianira wished to take steps to ensure that he would love only her. To do this, she applied the love potion given her by the dying Nessus to the lining of Hercules' cloak. This deed would cause the death of Hercules and at the same time guarantee that he would, finally, love only Deianira. In Ovid's account the cloak is the one Nessus had worn at his death, rather than a fine cloak that Deianira had surreptitiously spread with the potion given her by Nessus.

20. The reference to Meleager, Deianira's brother, at this juncture is somewhat tenuous. Meleager was mourned by his sisters who were still living in their mother's household. Deianira, on the other hand, had gone away with Hercules and so could not have known of their grief at the time of Meleager's death. While she might well have grieved for the death of her brother, her grief would have been tempered by the fact that he was not the entirety of her love since she was married to Hercules. Now, however, if Hercules is indeed dying – and the reader must know that by the time Deianira has learned of his terrible suffering he has in fact already died – then she has lost her husband in addition to her brother and has no choice but to join belatedly in the terrible grief of the other sisters of Meleager. It is noteworthy that in one account of the death of Meleager the maiden sisters and their attendant women mourn with such extravagance that Artemis is infuriated and causes all of them to be changed to guinea-hens, which were known in antiquity as meleagrides.

21. Agrius, brother of Oeneus and uncle of Meleager, became King of Calydon after Meleager's death left Oeneus unable to retain the throne. Tydeus was the brother of Meleager and Deianira, and after the death of Meleager he was driven into exile by his uncle, Agrius.

X: Ariadne to Theseus

Ariadne's letter to Theseus is interesting as much for what it does not say as for what it says. Like so many of her companion heroines Ariadne has given up everything so that she might have the partner she desires, but she has also lost the love she expected to have. As the letter opens, Ariadne has in a painfully short time lost the privileges she enjoyed as the daughter of Minos, one of the richest and most powerful of men, and finds herself deserted on a barren island with nothing to sustain her. Theseus had come to Crete in captivity, prepared to give his life in tribute to the pre-eminence of Minos and the Cretan hegemony. But he destroyed the Minotaur and broke the claims that Crete had on Athens so that he returned home with a splendid victory won by stealth and deception at the expense of Ariadne.

It is difficult to find in this letter anything of love. Ariadne complains more of her loss of safety and social position. While Theseus is undoubtedly attractive and a worthy object of her passion, the primary consideration in this letter is that Ariadne has been seduced and then abandoned, bereft of her virtue, dignity and possessions.

Ovid's readers must surely have known that in other accounts the story ends well, for eventually Ariadne is found by Dionysus and becomes his wife in a vast celebration. But here, at the time of the letter, no such good news has come to pass. Without a happy ending, without any reward for her kindness to Theseus, Ariadne is little more than a pitiful if not despicable victim of her own foolish infatuation. She succumbed to the conniving opportunism of a man who desired her only peripherally while he acquired everything she could give.

All wild beasts are gentler than you and not one
　　could have abused my trust more than you.
The words you are reading, Theseus, have been sent
　　from the shore where you deserted me,
the shore from which the sails carried off your ships.
　　On this island I was betrayed both
by you and by the sleep I could not resist;
　　in my sleep you plotted my ruin.
It was autumn, not long before the first frost,
　　when hidden birds would sing their complaint
from the trees. At the moment of waking, I,
　　still drowsy, turned on my side and reached
to touch my Theseus but I could not find him.
　　I withdrew my hands, and reached out a
second time, moving my arms across the couch.
　　But he was gone. Fear cut through my sleep.
Terrified, I rose from the abandoned bed,
　　my hands beat my breasts and tore my hair,
dishevelled as it was from my night of sleep.
　　I strained my eyes to see by moonlight,
there was nothing to see but the ocean's shore.
　　Running back and forth without a plan,
the loose sand slowed my young feet and all that while
　　I screamed 'Theseus' along the shore
and only the rocks returned my cry. Each time
　　I called to you, the place itself felt
my great grief and tried to ease my misery.
　　A mountain rises out of that shore
with shrubs growing from its peak and a steep cliff
　　that is carved out by the ocean's waves.
I ascend – strengthened by my spirit – to where
　　I can see for a very long way.
The winds were also cruel: your sails blowing
　　out were stretched tight in a southern gale.
I had never thought I would see such a sight;
　　suddenly I was cold and quite faint,
life nearly left my body. But anguish roused
　　me, and made me cry with all my strength:
'Where did you go? Wicked Theseus, come back.

Turn your ship, one of your crew remains.'
Those were my words. When my voice became weak I
    beat my breast and mixed my words with blows.
In the event that you saw but could not hear,
    I hung my veil in a tree and waved,
and hoped that those forgetting would remember.
    Then you were gone beyond my sight and
only then did I free my tears. Until that
    moment my eyes had been dulled by pain.
What more could those eyes do than weep for me when
    your sails had disappeared from my sight?
Alone, with my hair unbound, I wandered like
    a Bacchant roused by the Ogygian
god, or I sat on a rock to watch the surf,
    cold, a rock like that on which I sat.[1]
Often I go to the couch where we once slept,
    a couch that would not see us again,
and I touch the hollow left by your body –
    it is all that remains – and the cloths
that once were warmed around your flesh. I lie down
    on the bed wet with my tears, and cry,
'We were two lying together, give back two;
    let us leave together as we came.
Unfaithful bed, where is he gone, the greater
    part of me, where is he gone to now?'
What will I do? Where can I go? The island
    is not ploughed, I am left here alone.
I see neither man nor woman, no cattle.
    The sea binds the land on all sides; there
is no sailor, no ship to make way. Suppose
    I found companions, wind and ship, where
could I go? My father's lands are closed to me.
    If my luck were good and Aeolus'
winds were gentle for me and my ship's keel sailed
    peacefully, I am still an exile.[2]
Crete, island of a hundred cities, I can
    never again look at you, a land
known to the boy Jove, a land ruled by my sire –
    how dear to me, but betrayed by me.

You would have died in the twisting halls without
    the string that I gave to be your guide.
You said to me, 'I swear by these perils that
    as long as we live, you will be mine.'
We are alive, Theseus, but I am not yours;
    though buried by your deceit, I live.
You should have killed me when you killed my brother;
    my death would have freed you from your oath.
Now I see not only what I must suffer,
    what anyone abandoned sees, but
my thoughts churn with a thousand kinds of dying:
    I fear death less than I fear delay.
Always, whether here or there, I expect wolves
    to attack and tear my flesh apart.
Could it be that this shore nurtures the lion
    and shelters the fierce tiger as well?
I have heard it said that the powerful seal
    is sometimes cast up on this shoreline;
and who is there remaining who might protect
    me from a sword that pierces my side?
But what do I care so long as I am free
    and not held captive in harsh bondage,
spinning out some task with hands bound by slavery?
    I, the daughter of Minos; I, whose
mother is descended from Phoebus; I – there
    is no memory more dear to me –
who was betrothed to you, promised to be yours.[3]
    When I have surveyed the sea, the land,
and the wide-ranging shore, I know great dangers
    threaten me on both water and land.
The sky is out of my reach but even there
    the gods would come to me in visions.
I am helpless, subject to ravenous beasts,
    and if men live here I fear them too.
I can no longer trust men I do not know;
    you have made me fearful of strangers.
I wish my brother, Androgeos, still lived;
    I wish that the land of Cecrops had
not been punished for its impiety with

the death of its children, and I wish
that your raised arm, oh Theseus, had not killed
    that being, man and bull, with your club,
and I wish that I had never given you
    the thread that guided your safe return –
thread caught up and passed through the hands it led
on.[4]
    It is no wonder that you conquered
the beast that struck the earth of Crete with his bulk.
    Even his great horns could not have pierced
your iron heart. Without a shield, your breast was safe.
    Your flesh displayed the hardness of flint
and the toughness of fine steel, there you displayed
    a Theseus harder than anything.
Miserable sleep, why did you keep me here?
    It would have been far better for me
had I been crushed beneath unending darkness.
    You, winds, were cruel and far too eager
as were you, breezes, quick to begin my tears.
    And how cruel that right hand that has brought
my brother and me to our death; and cruel
    that pledge – empty words – you gave to me.[5]
My own sleep, the wind and your treacherous oath:
    one innocent girl, three times betrayed.
Dying, must I die without my mother's tears
    and will no one's fingers close my eyes?
Must my sad soul travel the alien airs?
    Will no friendly hands arrange my limbs
anointing them with spices and fragrant herbs?
    Are my bones to lie unburied, prey
to the birds that are waiting here by the shore?
    Is this the tomb my kindness deserves?
You will return to the safety of Cecrops
    to be received with pride in your home
and you will stand before the crowds reciting
    the glorious death of the man-bull in
those great winding passages cut from the rock.
    Be sure, then, that you also include
me, abandoned on a desolate island

93

for I belong among your honours.
Aegeus cannot be your father; Aethra,
    daughter of Pittheus, cannot be
your mother for I am sure that you were born
    from a union of rocks and the sea.
I could pray that you had seen me from the stern,
    that my sad figure had moved your heart.
Yet try to see me now, not with your eyes but
    with your mind, as I cling to this rock
that is drenched again and again by the waves.
    See my hair, loose like one in mourning;
look at my garments that are soaked with these tears
    falling on them like rain from the sky.
My body shudders like grain in a north wind;
    the words I write are frail as my hand.
I do not ask for what is due to me for
    you have denied me that, let nothing
be owed to me for what I have given you.
    But do not leave me here to suffer.
If I had not saved you from danger it would
    still be wrong for you to injure me.
These hands are weary of beating my sad breast
    but I stretch them out to you across
the vast sea; what is left of my hair, in grief,
    I display and beg that you notice.
By these tears, tears produced by what you have done,
    turn your ship, take another tack, sail
back swiftly. And if I die before you return,
it will be you who carries my bones from this place.

NOTES

1. The Bacchants, or maenads, were female worshippers of Bacchus (the Greek Dionysus). As used here, 'Ogygian god' is an epithet for Bacchus. 'Ogygian' was also used to refer to the city and the surrounding countryside of Thebes. According to one of the myths, Dionysus was the son of Semele after her seduction by Zeus. When Hera discovered that Semele was pregnant she appeared to her in disguise as the girl's old and trusted nurse. She

convinced the girl that it would be well for her to demand that her secretive lover reveal himself in the full glory of his deity, as though Semele were his legitimate wife. The girl lost no time in tricking Zeus into granting her anything she might wish. When Zeus magnanimously acceded to her request, she made the demand suggested by Hera. Realizing the inevitable outcome, Zeus agreed with the greatest reluctance. At his manifestation, said to be either in the form of a thunderbolt or enthroned in a chariot and surrounded by thunder and lightning, Semele was struck dead. At once, Zeus took from her body the unborn child and stitched it into his own thigh where it grew until the time came for it to be born. This 'second birth' of Dionysus is the origin of the common name for him 'Twice-born'.

2. Aeolus was keeper and guardian of the winds.

3. Pasiphaë, the mother of Ariadne, was one of the daughters of Helios, god of the sun. The name Phoebus was sometimes given to Apollo as an indication that Apollo was often identified with the sun. Here, however, the distinction between Helios the sun and Phoebus Apollo is blurred by emphasizing a common characteristic.

4. Androgeos was a son of Minos and Pasiphaë substantially older than Ariadne. The boy seems to have been raised to manhood at Athens, where he became an outstanding athlete, and died as he was attempting to kill a wild bull which had ravaged the countryside around the city. Minos, however, suspected that Aegeus, the Athenian king and father of Theseus, had somehow arranged for the death of Androgeos – the 'impiety' to which Ariadne refers. It was after Minos had waged war against the Athenians that Athens successfully sued for peace by agreeing to provide as tribute seven young men and seven young women in every ninth year.

Cecrops was one of the legendary kings of ancient Athens. Both the city of Athens and its surrounding area, Attica, are sometimes called by this name.

5. One of Ariadne's brothers – either Taurus or Asterius – died while trying to prevent the escape of Theseus and Ariadne from Crete.

XI: Canace to Macareus

This letter of Canace to Macareus is one of the most interesting characterizations in the *Heroides*. Canace has been gravely hurt but she does not accuse her brother, who is also her lover; it is her father against whom she complains. While another author might well have cast Macareus as the villain and Canace as the victim of his aggression, Canace herself only alludes to the fact of incest in the blandest of terms while she deplores the horrible violence of their father Aeolus' punitive and retributive anger. Perhaps Canace is too ingenuous, too innocent to be credible. Or perhaps the compelling presence of love may have swept away every inhibition, leaving her nothing but still intact virtue about to be destroyed by her father's appeal to justice rather than love.

Such a pattern of guiltless fault creates a curious and unique tension within the poem. As Canace presents the case for their love they are innocents caught up in a most private action that has, finally, a catastrophic and public conclusion. The initial infatuation, the all-too-willing seduction, has conferred little or no guilt. The pain, the fear of discovery, derives almost entirely from the fact that Canace is pregnant. Yet even the foetus which resists every attempt at abortion and becomes finally her child is presented as an object of pity because it too is helpless before the overpowering anger of Aeolus. The cries of the new-born child contrast with the cries of Aeolus. The child that resisted death before its birth is mourned because it will have survived the hazards peculiar to its gestation and delivery only to die horribly when its dependence is passed from its mother to Aeolus. The naive innocence of Canace contrasts sharply with the worldly practicality of the nurse. Where Canace regards her conception and pregnancy with wonder, it is the nurse who reacts immediately and with neither shame nor modesty.

Though Canace and Macareus are guilty of incest it is the insane rage of Aeolus that becomes opprobrious. And it is a clever stroke on

96

Ovid's part that the reaction of Aeolus to this discovery is so much in keeping with his turbulent temperament. The reader could well imagine that had the father of Canace and Macareus been of a different personality the outcome of their love might well have been different. That Aeolus, like the winds, is unable to control his own rage is the single most important fact for Canace.

This letter invites comparison with the letter of Phaedra (IV). Both women are writing in the context of an incestuous passion and both address the danger of discovery. But the differences between the two are starkly drawn. Most significantly Phaedra is an older woman attempting to seduce her reluctant stepson, at the same time, perhaps, as intending his ultimate destruction. While the character of Phaedra is filled with every kind of deceit and deception that of Canace is almost a model of virtue. Where Phaedra is so calculating as to be the personification of evil and disordered desire, Canace is loving and kind and finally pitiful.

At the beginning of her downfall Canace could not resist the force of passion and finally she cannot resist her father's impetuous rage. In both instances she and Macareus are victimized by the irrational rush of love and its concomitant, death. The inevitability with which these children are swept to their doom is prefigured by the inevitability and foolishness with which they first loved one another.

If these words are blotted out, you should know that
    my blood will have stained this little roll.
The pages lie here flattened, my right hand holds
    a pen and my left hand holds a sword.
The scene I describe for you is Aeolus'
    daughter addressing a letter to
her brother. In this way, I suppose, I may
    win the approval of my father.
I can only wish that he were here to see
    my end; that his command will be done
in the presence of him who gave the order.
    Though he is fierce, harsher even than
his east winds, he would watch me without a tear.

Can anything good come from a life
this is lived among the winds? Like his subjects,
    his temper is stormy. He governs
Notus and Zephyr and Thracian Aquilo,
    as well as your quills, reckless Eurus.[1]
These four mighty winds he rules but he cannot
    stop the blast of his inflated wrath.
Compared to his faults, his kingdom is tiny.
    I am descended from Jove himself:
my ancestors' names are written in heaven;
    but that distinction is worthless now.
Is this steel – my funeral gift – less deadly
    because it is in a woman's hand?
Macareus, how I do wish that the hour
    that made us one had come after death!
Brother, you loved me more than a brother should;
    why was I more to you than sister?
Burning with love I felt that god in my heart
    and knew him to be what I had heard.
I could not eat, my cheeks were pale, I grew thin;
    my sleep was uneasy, time had stopped,
I groaned without pain, I could not give reasons
    for this strange behaviour: I could not
know what it was to be in love, but surely
    I had found myself caught up in love.
The first to notice my distress was my nurse,
    in the way an old wife sees such things:
'Daughter of Aeolus, you must be in love.'
    I was a maiden and blushed; shame forced
my eyes down and I confessed without a word.
    Quite soon, the burden of my erring
body grew; my weakness felt its secret weight.
    Every herb and every remedy
my nurse brought, applying each one shamelessly
    to evict from my flesh – the only
secret we kept from you – the burden growing
    there. It was too much alive, it stood
firm against her attacking skills and remained
    safe never knowing its enemy.

Nine times the most splendid sister of Phoebus
    had risen and now another moon
was beginning to rouse her horses.[2]
    I did not know the cause of such pain –
I had not known the pain of labour before –
    I was a recruit new to combat.
I could not hide my groans. 'Why reveal your sin?'
    said my nurse, as she covered my mouth.
What am I to do, unhappy as I am?
    Pain forces me to groan but my fear,
my nurse and my shame together silence me.
    I choke my cries, I try to capture
the words that have slipped away from me, I force
    myself to drink the tears I have shed.
Death stood in my sight, and Lucina denied
    me aid.[3] If I died, death would leave guilt.
But bending down over me, you pulled aside
    my robe and my hair, you warmed my flesh
back to life by pressing your breast against mine
    and you said, 'Live, my dearest sister;
live so that yours is not the cause of two deaths.
    May good hope be your strength. You shall be
your brother's bride; he who made you a mother
    will also make you his cherished wife.'
Though I was dead, believe me, your words gave life
    so that I gave birth to my womb's shame.
Do not rejoice. Aeolus sits in the hall
    of the palace,the sign of my sin
must be hidden from his eyes. My old nurse goes
    to prepare a basket of fruits and
olive branches and in among them she hides
    the child, wrapped in light cloths. She pretends
that she will go to the place of sacrifice,
    she mutters some prayer, the people step
back and my father himself opens a way.
    Nearly at the door, my father hears
the new-born's cry and the child is lost, betrayed.
    Aeolus seizes the child and shows
the mock sacrifice to all. The house echoes

again and again with his mad cries.
As the ocean trembles at the passage of
    a little breeze, as the ash tree shakes
in a warm breeze from the south, you might have seen
    my whitening flesh shiver: I shook
so that my bed itself was shaken. He rushed
    in shrieking my shame for all to hear;
he scarcely could keep his hand from my poor face.
    I was utterly confused, helpless;
I could do nothing but let tears pour out,
    my tongue was dumb with cold, icy fear.
Then he ordered that his grandchild should be left
    for the dogs and the birds. The baby
began to scream – did he understand his fate? –
    as though he were pleading for his life.
What were my feelings, my brother? – look at yours –
    my enemy rushed the child away from me
to the dark forests, that the fruit of my flesh
    be consumed by wolves. He left my room.
I could beat at my breasts and score my poor cheeks
    with my sharp nails. Then, one of his men
wearing a grieving face came to me and said
    these shameful words: 'To you, Aeolus
sends a sword and wishes you to know its use
    from your deed.' I know and I shall use
it bravely. I shall bury my father's gift
    in my breast. Father, is this the gift
you have chosen to give me for my marriage?
    Is this the dowry that you will give
to make me rich? Hymen, remove your torches,
    flee this wicked place.[4] Black Erinyes,
come with your torches and brighten with your blaze
    the pyre on which my body is laid.[5]
My sisters, you are wed happily under
    a better fate, remember me, lost.
With so few hours of life, what was his crime?
    How could he, just born, bring injury?
If in some way he deserved to die, poor child,
    it is my sin that causes him pain.

My son, your mother's grief, prey of hungry wolves,
    torn apart on the day you were born;
my son, pitiful pledge of unholy love,
    this day is both your first and your last.
I was not allowed to let my tears – the tears
    that are owed to you – fall upon you;
I was not allowed to clip a lock of hair
    that I might carry it to your tomb;
I was not allowed to bend over your flesh
    and take a last kiss from your cold lips.
Now, vicious beasts are tearing into pieces
    the child's body that my flesh produced.[6]
I too will follow the shade of this infant,
    I will give myself the blade so that
not for long will I be known to all the world
    as both grief-stricken and a mother.
And you, you for whom your poor sister always
    hoped, gather up, I beg you, the bits
and pieces of your son and bring them to me
    their mother, that we may share one tomb,
that one small urn may contain the two of us.
    Live on, do not forget me, pour out
your tears over my fresh wound, and do not leave
    her whom you did love and who loved you.
I beg you, obey the sister you loved too well;
    for myself, I will obey our father's command.

NOTES

1. Notus was the south wind, Zephyr the west, Aquilo the north and Eurus the east. Though Ovid here seems to personify the four winds, most authors only characterized Zephyr and Aquilo (also known as Boreas). In all probability this distinction was made because these two were the prevailing winds in the area and were the most indicative of the weather and its changes.

2. The epithet Phoebus, or 'shining', was often given to Apollo, who was the brother of Artemis (the Roman Diana). Artemis was often associated with the moon, either directly or by the name of Selene (the Roman Luna),

and Phoebus Apollo with the sun or with the sun god, Helios. In this passage Canace says that the moon has passed through nine cycles, or nine months, and the tenth month is about to start.

3. For the Romans, Lucina was the goddess who was called to attend a woman in childbirth.

4. Hymen was the god of marriage; there are no myths specifically associated with him.

5. The Erinyes were spirits whose mission was to punish those who had committed offences against their own relatives, particularly children who had grievously injured their parents. The Erinyes were known to the Romans as the Furies.

6. Canace laments that she cannot mourn over her dead child as would have been the case had he died of natural causes. After the infant has been killed as Aeolus commanded, it will not be possible for her to perform this maternal service because the body will have been destroyed by its ignominious death.

XII: Medea to Jason

The story of Medea was widely known and often told. Ovid was clearly aware of this rich literary tradition because Medea figures prominently in the *Metamorphoses* as well as in the *Heroides*. Among the lost works of Ovid there was a tragedy devoted to her story.

The major accounts of Medea which survive – the *Argonautica* of Apollonius of Rhodes, the *Metamorphoses* and *Heroides* of Ovid, and the *Medea* of Euripides are unanimous in their portrayal of Medea as a person of astounding and unparalleled evil. But there is a larger view and this is worth examining. Medea is a barbarian. She lacks all the graces that follow upon civilization. While it might seem that this civilization is of the nature of etiquette and custom, there is here something more basic, more fundamental, which every Greek valued: that is, a formed ethical or moral sense in which the measure of every act was the standard of moderation. When set beside this the character of Medea necessarily fails. Once the reader catches sight of this consideration, it becomes quite obvious why Medea is so easily supplanted by Creusa in Jason's affections.

While it would appear that Jason has every reason to abandon Medea because of the new wealth and power that Creusa can give, it also must be noted that in the *Heroides*, as in other texts, Medea's barbarous beginnings have become if not an embarrassment certainly a liability. As a priestess of Hecate, Medea has skills which frighten those around her. In the past as well as in the present she has been willing to use these to achieve her desired ends, which alienates her from those who might be a source of safety and assurance.

Medea is a woman of deep and abiding emotions, but as swiftly as they are felt they are as swiftly out of control. Such a person living always on the edge of madness cannot be tolerated in a society which prizes the rule of law, in both the state and its individual citizens. Like all the heroines of the *Heroides* Medea has been hurt. She has given everything to win the love of a man and when she has lost all she herself has been cast aside in favour of another. But none of the heroines seeks a revenge quite so horrible as Medea's.

Another aspect of the personality of Medea is developed in the *Heroides* and is almost entirely the invention of Ovid. A character totally driven by a particular virtue or vice, or even one who is entirely virtuous or vicious, quickly becomes flat and uninteresting because the character is static. Ovid provides a variation on the traditional characterization of Medea and this is accomplished largely by the epistolary style.

Medea makes no attempt to deny or even to mitigate the horrors she has committed and will soon commit. She does not deny the deeds which are the identification given her by the world. Rather she uses her letter to argue that she is a woman of great feeling who has been gravely injured. As she outlines the intensity of her love for Jason and the grief for her family betrayed, we see a woman of somewhat greater depth than the monster we find in more traditional accounts. That the Medea of the *Heroides* is quite different from the Medea of the *Metamorphoses* is significant.

The narrator of the *Metamorphoses*, though apparently all-knowing, quite often misses the subjective states of a character while the objective facts of a character's actions are recited with apparent accuracy. This simple distinction of narrative styles is important because it is the means by which Ovid is able to create a work significantly different from one that tradition would seem to warrant, though the differences are not so much variants as enrichments of the material at hand. Yet for all the humanizing elements introduced by Ovid, it would be hazardous in the extreme to read this as an attempt by him to portray Medea more favourably. Whatever extenuations are offered by Medea in her own defence, her criminality is never denied. Rather, Medea grieves that while she cannot resist the temptation to revenge she will in all probability regret her act even as she regrets the loss of her family to gain the love of Jason.

But Medea's recognition of her own guilt is at best defective and not of such a degree as to rehabilitate her in the eyes of the reader. While we cannot ignore the crimes of Medea, her preoccupation with her folly, her naivety, her gullibility, her hasty willingness to be deceived by Jason, are less than admirable. Medea writes out of a sharp sense of events and her guilt in them, while revealing a degree of self-deception that is without parallel in the *Heroides*. Ultimately it is this self-deception, this ability to act out of a seriously compromised moral sense, that makes Medea such a perfect model of depravity.

While Ovid permits Medea to reveal another side to her character, the reader finally realizes that even as she pleads mitigating circumstances her argument is so flawed that finally she cannot be pitied. Whenever we are likely to be persuaded of her girlish innocence we are confronted with a woman who betrays and murders. While she attempts some sort of explanation or justification for her awful deeds, we must finally conclude that if there had ever been an innocent Medea that person is so irretrievably fixed in the past as to be inaccessible.

In the course of this letter Medea's fortunes are turned full circle. When Jason comes to her she holds all power and is able to dispense the estate of her father to the needy Argonauts. At the end she has nothing but her rage and her magic, agents only of destruction. At the beginning her family must be abandoned so that she can gain Jason; in the end Jason and Creusa must be lost so that she can take her revenge. At the beginning Medea, safe in her power, can scold Jason for his infidelity; in the end the infidelity has reached a conclusion that leaves her only her injured pride. She passes from bitter invective to revenge. The transition is momentous.

It is worth noting that this letter begins almost in mid-sentence, as though some conversation or correspondence had been interrupted and is now being resumed. But it is also possible – and I think this the more probable explanation – that the dialogue which seems to begin so abruptly has in fact been going on in Medea's disordered imagination. At all events, from the outset we are shown a greatly distraught character. The ending of the letter further elucidates the distraction of Medea because, as the text becomes disjointed and fragmentary, she makes reference to the anger seething within her, at one point even giving way to threats of horrible retribution which will in fact come to pass. By the time the last few lines are written Medea is a person who is almost totally overcome with rage, so much so that though there is still a struggle between a womanly concern for Jason and her sons and the overwhelming desire to destroy those who are destroying her, there is now little possibility that she will restrain her great powers for evil.

And I remember that I, Queen of Colchis,
    found time when you came begging for help.
Indeed, those sisters who spin the threads of life
    should have unwound at last my spindle.[1]
Then Medea would have ended well. But now
    the life I live is a life of pain.
Why was a ship made from Pelion's wood rowed
    so quickly over the seas by young
arms searching for the ram of Phrixus? Why did
    we of Colchis see the *Argo*? Why
did your Greek crew stoop to drink from the Phasis?[2]
    And why did I take too much pleasure
in your golden hair, your fine ways and the lies
    that fell so gracefully from your tongue?
Yet I did delight too much. If I had not
    your odd hull would have beached itself and
unloaded your brave men and the unwitting
    son of Aeson without any fear
and without an anointing of precious oils
    to save his life would have confronted
the flames exhaled by those awful bulls, he would
    have sown the seeds; the sower himself
would have fallen in the battle his sowing
    had begotten. What great treachery,
wretched man, would then have died with you and what
    awful grief would have been turned from me.
I find that I can take some little pleasure
    in accusing you with the favours
I did for you. I will enjoy that pleasure,
    the only pleasure I'll have from you.
Directed to turn your ship towards Colchis,
    you set your feet on my native land.
In that place I was as your new bride is here,
    as rich as her father, so was mine.[3]
Her father rules Ephyre, between two seas,
    my father rules everything along
the shore of the Pontus, to the Scythian snows.
    Aeëtes welcomes the young Greek men
to his house and these Pelasgian heroes

rest their bodies on the couches draped
with embroidered cloth. It was then that I saw
    you, then that I began to know you,
then that came the first step of my soul's downfall.
    I was helpless and the sight of you
enflamed me not with the usual flames but
    like a knot of pine kindled before
some powerful god. While you were wonderful
    to see, fate was rushing me to doom.
The splendour of your eyes robbed mine of vision.
    You saw it, unfaithful one, for who
can very well hide the signs of love? It shines
    brightly and is its own betrayal.
You were given the task of yoking the strong
    necks of those fierce bulls to a plough. They
were the property of Mars, they menaced all
    with more than horns, for they exhaled flames;
with hooves of solid bronze and snouts of wrought
    bronze,
    their muzzles were blackened by their breath.
And more, you must scatter over the broad field
    with docile hand seeds that will beget
a horde of men to attack you with weapons
    that grew like their bearers from the soil.
This is a harvest that will be nothing but
    pain and suffering to the farmer.
For your final task you must somehow deceive
    the unsleeping eyes of the watchman.
Aeëtes finished his speech. You and your men
    rose, sobered, the table was taken
from the benches. Creusa and the kingdom
    that is her dowry, Creon's daughter
and Creon, father of your bride, must have been
    far from your minds. You leave dejected,
my tearful eyes follow you, and I whisper
    so faintly, 'May you have good fortune!'
I go to my neatly arranged chamber and
    lie on my couch, deeply hurt. Weeping
I pass the night. I could see so clearly all

that happened – the bulls, the horrible
crop, as well as the serpent that never sleeps.
        Love and fear competed within me
and fear sharpened in me the pangs of loving.
        At dawn my sister entered and found
me, with tangled hair, lying face down weeping
        so that everything was wet with tears.[4]
She prays that the Minyae be aided, one prays
        for them, but another implores, and
it is the son of Aeson who is given
        the answer to her demanding prayers.[5]
There is a deeply shaded grove of pine trees
        and the limbs of the holly oak where
the piercing light of the sun seldom reaches.
        In it stands – or once stood – Diana's
shrine, with her gold statue wrought by barbarian
        hands. Do you know it, or have places
left you as I have slipped away from your mind?
        You and I came to that place, you spoke
with your unfaithful lips: 'Fortune has given
        you the means of my salvation. Whether I
live or whether I die, my future is placed
        in your hands. To destroy me, if one
took pleasure only in power, is one thing
        but saving me is greater glory.
I pray, by our misery, which you can lift;
        by your race and by the deity
of your all-knowing grandfather, the bright sun;
        by the mysteries and by the three
faces of Diana, by my family's gods –
        if it is gods that we have – by these
take pity on me, take pity on my men.[6]
        With kindness you will have me always.
If you do not scorn a Pelasgian suitor –
        can the gods easily grant my wish? –
I swear that my soul shall cease to be before
        one other than you becomes my bride.[7]
As pledge, I call Juno, in whose shrine we stand,
        the guardian of all marriage contracts.'

Such words – and I write but a few of them – moved
   my simple heart as your hand held mine.
Then you wept – your tears aided the deception –
   and I, a maiden, was quickly caught.
Swiftly you yoke the bulls that are shod with bronze
   and your flesh is not harmed by their flames;
you turn the dense turf with the plough as ordered,
   you cast the teeth around you like seed
and there comes from the earth a band of warriors
   fully armed with shield and sword ready.
I sat by that field, pale with fear and wonder,
   I, the provider of that potion,
watching these men so suddenly born and armed
   until the brothers, sons of the earth –
what a marvellous deed – drew arms and approached,
   the struggle of each with each other.
Then there appeared the unsleeping guardian
   rattling his scales, hissing as he swept
the ground with his coiling body. What about
   the rich dowry now? Where is that royal
companion, what about that finger of land
   dividing the currents of two seas?[8]
I, the lass who is become a barbarian
   to you, the lass who is become poor,
the lass who is now a source of injury:
   with my drug, I brought sleep to those eyes
shutting their flaming gaze in harmless slumber
   and I gave the fleece into your hands.
By this act I betrayed my father, gave up
   my throne and the country of my birth,
and my reward for all of this is exile.
   My girlish innocence belongs now
to a brigand who came from foreign places;
   my dear mother and sisters are gone.
But my brother, him I did not leave behind.
   My pen scratches, it cannot write on.
What my hand did willingly, it cannot write.
   I too should have been torn apart.[9] Yet
I had no fear – what was left to strike terror? –

I, a woman covered with guilt, sailed
away from that place. Is there no more justice?
    Are there no more gods? Let the sentence
we deserve catch us at sea, you for deceit
    and me for my eagerness to trust.[10]
Now I wish the Symplegades had found us
    and crushed our bones together or that
Scylla had drawn us into her chambers where
    we might be consumed by her fierce dogs.[11]
That would have been proper, for Scylla brings grief
    to ungrateful men. She who vomits
out so often the torrents and swallows them
    back, should have brought us beneath the wave
that washes the shores of Trinacria.[12] But
    without harm and victorious, you
return to the cities of Haemonia
    and the fleece is set before your gods.[13]
I'll not repeat the story of Pelias'
    daughters who for love of their father
were led to evil and their hands to butcher
    their father's corpse.[14] Others will blame me
but you for whom I have been compelled to act
    can have no choice, now you must praise me.
But you – words fail my fitting anger – have said,
    'Depart from this, the house of Aeson.'
As you ordered, I have left your palace and
    I take with me now our two children
and what will remain with me, my love for you.
    All at once my ears heard Hymen's songs
and my eyes saw the reckless blaze of torches.[15]
    The pipes blared a wedding march for you,
for me they cried in muted funeral tones.
    Caught up in fear I could not believe
such guilt might live in anyone, still my heart
    within my body grew cold and chill.[16]
The crowd of revellers hurried on shouting
    loudly, 'Hymen, O Hymenaeus.'
As they came nearer to me the more awful
    their wild songs and shouts became for me.

My servants turned away from me, weeping but
    trying to hide their sadness from me –
could anyone ever bring news of such things?
    Much better then if I had not known,
but my heart was sad, as though I truly knew,
    when the younger of our sons perhaps
by accident, perhaps anxious to see, stood
    by the outer door and said, 'Mother,
come here by me, a parade is coming and
    Jason, my father, is at its head.
Dressed in bright gold, he drives a team of horses.'
    Then I knew. I tore my cloak and beat
my breasts; I cried out and my nails tore my cheeks.
    My heart drove me into that mob and
I tore the blossoms out of my new-combed hair.
    With my hair down over my body,
I could not contain my shrieking, I wanted
    to cry out, 'He is mine,' and hold you.
Wounded father, be happy. You Colchians,
    abandoned by me, be happy now.
My brother's ghost, accept from this my downfall
    the sacrifice I have owed to you.
Now I am alone, deprived of all, my throne,
    my country, my home, and my husband,
who was more than all that I ever wanted.
    I have subdued serpents and raging
bulls, but a single man I could not control;
    I have turned back the raging fire with
cunning potions, but I cannot turn aside
    the consuming flames of my desire.
My spells, my herbs and all my skill have left me;
    my goddess has forsaken me, and
Hecate ignores the sacrifice I make.[17]
    My days are unpleasant, and my nights
are vigils of bitterness; sleep deserts me.
    My magic made the dragon's eyes close
but nothing I can do will bring sleep to me.
    I benefit others more than me.
That slut is caressing the body I saved;

my art and my work serve her pleasure.
Perhaps you will entertain her stupid ears
    with slanders against my foreign ways.
Let her laugh now and be merry at my faults
    while she reclines on Tyrian purple,
soon enough she will weep as she is consumed
    in a blaze that is hotter than mine.
So long as I have poison, fire and weapons,
    Medea's foes will all be punished.
If by chance my petitions touch your iron heart,
    listen well to these my humble words.
I am as much a beggar now as you were
    then: I throw myself down at your feet.
If this cheapens me in your eyes, ignore me
    and consider only our children:
no stepmother would treat them with kindness; they
    came from my body looking like you.
I cannot see their faces without weeping
    because they are more your sons each day.
By all the gods, by the brightness of the light
    my grandfather shines forth, by my gifts
to you and by our two sons who are the pledge
    that we made once each to each other
return me to the bed for which I rashly
    let so much escape my hands. Be true
to your word; give me your help as I helped you.
    I do not ask your aid against bulls
and men; nor must you calm a serpent for me.
    I want only you for it is you
I deserve. By you I became a mother
    and by me you became a father.
You might ask about my dowry. I counted
    it on the field which you turned over
before you took the golden fleece. My dowry,
    which if I demanded it you would
refuse, is that well-known ram. My dowry is
    yourself, safe. My dowry is your crew
of young Greek men. Miserable man, compare
    all this to the goods of Sisyphus.[18]

That you still have life, that you can take as wife
    one who comes with regal rank, that you
can be ungrateful to me, you owe to me.
    Listen well – but why should I tell your
future? My wrath labours to bear all my threats.
    I will not hesitate to follow
wherever this anger leads, you can be sure.
    I will loathe the revenge I take but
now I hate myself because I was concerned
    for the good of a faithless husband.
Let that be in the care of the god who prods me;
    I do not know for certain what is in my soul.

NOTES

1. This is a reference to the Fates who determine the succession of events in every human life. The Fates were, in a sense, merely personifications of destiny. However, while the Fates in this passage are seen as important to the end of life, they were also often present at birth. The idea that they spin out the destinies of men has its greatest development in Homer. They are often shown pictorially not only as spinning but also measuring and finally cutting the thread of life.

2. The *Argo* was constructed of the finest timber from the slopes of Mount Pelion, on the peninsula of Magnesia, where Jason was raised to manhood by Chiron.

The ram of Phrixus was the ram with a fleece of gold.

Medea, in saying that the Argonauts drank from the Phasis, means that they made landfall and refreshed themselves along the principal waterway of Colchis.

3. Medea, as she writes this letter, is in Corinth, where she had been taken some years before by Jason. They had lived together in that city until he set out to divorce her and take Creusa as his wife. In Corinth, Creusa as the king's daughter would have a place of great prominence, while Medea would only occupy the position of Jason's wife.

4. This sister is usually identified as Chalciope.

5. The Argonauts were frequently called Minyae or Minyans because it was thought that most if not all of them were descended from Minyas, a legendary hero in Boeotia. It would seem, however, from an examination of the list of the men who followed Jason aboard the *Argo*, that only Jason and

possibly one other could have come from this line. The sense of this passage is that Chalciope prays the Argonauts will receive some form of divine assistance, but Medea prays with an even greater urgency. Chalciope sought aid for them because her sons had befriended the Argonauts and thus incurred the wrath of Aeëtes. Medea here emphasizes that while Chalciope feared for the loss of her sons, she, Medea, feared even more that she would lose Jason. But Jason is favoured with safety and the prayers of both women are answered.

6. Jason refers to Helios (the sun), father of Aeëtes and grandfather of Medea, who from his vantage-point in the sky sees everything that happens on the face of the earth.

In many of her manifestations, Diana (the Greek Artemis) appeared to both gods and men in a multitude of disguises. This could also be a reference to the fact that in various accounts the attributes of Diana and other goddesses are often confused.

7. It is quite clear that Jason and Medea were descended from very different racial and cultural stock. For Jason and the Argonauts, to be Pelasgian was to be pre-eminent in all things. Note here the irony that when Jason proposes to marry Creusa he is abandoning Medea because she is of barbarian ancestry and hardly worthy to be married to one of Jason's stature. In other words Medea has no more to give Jason, and it is at this point that her barbarian origins come into prominence.

8. This is a reference to Ephyre, the kingdom ruled by Creon, Creusa's father. Medea is also contrasting the riches brought to Jason by Creusa with the riches that she herself has given him and presumably will continue to give. In Medea's view, such a comparison will find Creusa gravely wanting.

9. As Jason and Medea fled Colchis they killed her brother Absyrtus, dismembered his body, and threw the pieces from their departing ship to delay the pursuing Colchian fleet.

10. After rehearsing her many deeds, deeds which the reader must regard as criminal, the only crime Medea acknowledges is that of having trusted unwisely.

11. The Symplegades or the Clashing Rocks were two rocks on opposite sides of the channel at the northern entrance to the Bosporus. It was said that in a very high wind they clashed together with a terrifying and exceptionally dangerous force. After the Argonauts had passed through, assisted by Athena, the rocks became fixed in place and ceased to be a hazard.

Scylla was a monster who captured and ate seamen as they made passage through the Strait of Messina, a narrow channel separating the island of Sicily from the Italian mainland. Her lair was on a high place overlooking the whirlpool, Charybdis. Scylla was usually depicted as having the head of a woman and a body composed of the bodies of six dogs to give her mobility. The Argonauts sailed through the strait safely because they had divine protection.

12. Trinacria, or Thrinacria, was an ancient name for Sicily. It was the place where Helios kept his flocks. In the *Odyssey* it was also the place where Polyphemus and the Cyclops lived.

13. Haemonia was another name for Thessaly.

14. The daughters of Pelias, at the instigation of Medea, killed their father in the hope of being able to restore him to youthful vitality.

15. Hymen was the god of marriage.

16. That is, Medea professes herself unable to believe that such guilt for having abandoned her could live in the heart of Jason.

17. Medea suggests that even her goddess, evil as she is, has forsaken her. Coming from Medea, these words can only heighten the irony.

18. Sisyphus was a king of Corinth and presumably it was his wealth, inherited by Creon, that was being delivered to Jason as at least a part of Creusa's dowry.

XIII: Laodamia to Protesilaus

Laodamia's letter is unusual in the *Heroides* because she and Protesilaus are married and deeply in love, and separated only by the Trojan War. This is significant; in other letters written by women to their husbands – Penelope, Oenone and Deianira (letters I, V and IX) – there is a very clear suggestion that the husband is absent for some iniquitous reason. However, Protesilaus has merely been caught up in the war and then loses his life through an impetuous though probably heroic act – that of being the first Greek to set foot on the Trojan shore.

The letter concerns itself with a nearly ideal love between a man and his wife. While others of the heroines argue that love must and certainly can be clandestine, here there is nothing to hide. They are married, they hold regal power and the dynasty which engendered them has every expectation of continuity in their lives. There are no issues of rightful place, property, or the exercise of authority. The issues drawn are very simple: a married woman misses the presence of her husband and worries about his safe return to their house.

But while such emotions are quite ordinary in the *Heroides*, here they are unique because they are not mingled with either guilt or injury. There are no rivals, for there is no jealousy. Laodamia seeks no revenge. There is only one fact before her: her life is profoundly enmeshed with that of Protesilaus. To her mind they have quite literally become two in one flesh. The dynamics of the situation are very instructive because I believe that Ovid presents in this letter, not a love without pain, but a love devoid of pain gratuitously and even frivolously inflicted. The reader knows that her deepest fear will be justified – Protesilaus must die – and that according to the various sources Laodamia will also meet her death. As she warns Protesilaus about Hector, who is the very paragon of Trojan courage and military prowess, wc know that it is Hector who will kill Protesilaus.

The relationship of Hector and his wife Andromache, which is so splendidly developed in the *Iliad* (VI.390–502 and XXIV.723–45), is suggested in this letter when Laodamia imagines a nameless Trojan warrior leaving his wife at the beginning of the day's battle and returning to her welcoming arms at the day's end. But like all the other heroines, Laodamia finds that the desires of love are not entirely met by life. What she most wants, the continued union with her beloved in life, will be denied. Her hopes will all be shattered. Having tasted the sweetness of love fulfilled, she must now experience the bitterness of love denied. But the denial is through no fault of any of the participants; Laodamia's love is snatched away by blind fate aided only slightly by the over-eagerness of Protesilaus to engage the enemy. And perhaps, if Protesilaus were allowed to speak here, he might argue that he was first to leave the ships because he was overcome by the desire to see the war fought to its conclusion so that he might return quickly to his beloved Laodamia. But because he seems not to know the prophecy his action is finally careless rather than careful.

The great affairs of state, of competing kingdoms pillaged for the sake of a sexual insult, of commercial ventures that require trust and honesty – all these are secondary to the fact that Laodamia and Protesilaus are deeply in love. Laodamia certainly sees the great riches that are part and parcel of the war, but this is all of very little consequence in comparison with her overwhelming hope that her desire to love and be loved can continue to be fulfilled.

Laodamia sends greetings and best wishes
    from Haemonia to Haemonia's lord
and it is the wish of her loving heart that
    this letter will go as it is sent.[1]
I am told the winds detain you at Aulis;
    where were these winds when you sailed from me?
Then the tides should have risen against your oars;
    then was the time for a raging surf.
I could have kissed my lord and given him more
    requests, I wanted to say so much.
But you were hurried away by a wind your

crew loved; it was not a lover's wind.
I forced my arms to free you, Protesilaus,
    the words I would have said went unsaid;
my very tongue was stopped in my mouth so that
    there was hardly time for one 'Farewell'.
Boreas flew from the skies to stretch and fill your
    sails; soon my Protesilaus was gone.[2]
I took delight in watching you as long as
    I could, I followed your eyes, and when
I could see you no more, I followed your sails
    a long while. When I could no longer
see either you or your sails my eyes fell down
    to the sea as the light went with you.
Darkness rose up around me, my blood faltered
    within me; they tell me my knees failed
me and I sank to the ground. Not your father,
    Iphiclus, nor mine, Acastus, nor
my mother, who was crushed with sorrow, could cause
    cold water to bring me back to life.
They went about their well-meant chore but it did
    nothing. I am shamed – I did not die.
When I awakened, my pain returned to me.
    A wife's love tears at my faithful heart.
I have no desire to dress my hair, garments
    of finest gold give me no pleasure.
I am like those who are touched by the two-horned
    god with his rod, I run back and forth
driven along by madness.[3] The ladies of
    Phylace come around me and shout,
'Laodamia, put on your regal robes.'
    Is it fitting, then, that I go out wearing
robes dipped in costly purple while you, my lord,
    are in battle by the walls of Troy?
Should I arrange my hair while a great helmet
    weighs down his head? Should I put on new
garments while he is burdened with heavy arms?
    Let them say I imitate your life
dressed coarsely; it is fitting for me to spend
    this time of war forsaking all joy.

Doom-filled Paris, whose beauty thrives in the fall
    of his family, be as weak in strife
as you were faithless in another man's house.
    I could wish that you found no pleasure
in the face of that Taenarian wife or that
    your face had given her no pleasure.[4]
Menelaus, you grieve too much for one stolen;
    how many must grieve for your revenge?
O you gods, I pray, keep evil far from us
    let my lord one day offer his arms
to Jove in thanksgiving for a safe return.
    But when the war comes to mind it comes
with terror and my tears flow like snow that melts
    in the sun. Ilion and Tenedos,
Simois, Xanthus and Ida are fearful
    names that frighten by their very sound.[5]
That stranger would not have dared to steal unless
    he knew the extent of his own strength.
It is said that he set foot on the Greek shore
    dressed in rich gold, bearing on his back
a sign of the all-powerful Phrygian wealth,
    the men and the ships that are needed
to wage a winning war – how much of his strength
    do you think was brought along with him?
Daughter of Leda, the sister to the Twins,
    by such as these you were overcome
and it is by such as these that the Danaans
    now are suffering such misery.[6]
Beware the man they call 'Hector', whoever
    he might be, if you have care for me.[7]
Keep his name in your heart. As you avoid him
    avoid every Trojan. Imagine
many Hectors. As you put on arms, whisper,
    'Laodamia bids caution for her.'
If Troy must fall to the Argolic forces,
    let its fall find you still unwounded.[8]
Let Menelaus hurry to meet his foe,
    let the husband seek his captured wife.
But it is not the same for you. Fight to live,

to return to your wife's loyal embrace.
Sons of Dardanus, spare just this one; the blood
    that is mine must not flow from his flesh.[9]
This man should not enter battle with bare steel,
    giving his body to enemies.
His strength is greater by far in making love
    than making war on a battlefield.
Let other men march forward into battle;
    let Protesilaus enjoy love.
Now I admit freely, I would have called you
    back, but my tongue was still in my mouth
because I feared an evil portent. But when
    you crossed the doorstep of your father's
house, you stumbled, and I saw a sign.
    I groaned, and said to myself, 'Let this
be a sign that my lord will return to me.'
    I did not tell you this until now,
but now I tell it to you with the hope that
    you will not rush recklessly into
combat. It is for you now to be sure that
    my fears can vanish as the winds go.
I have heard of a prophecy that foretells
    an unjust death for the Danaan
whose foot is the first to touch the soil of Troy.
    Unhappy the woman who is first
to weep for a husband slain. May the gods keep
    you from being too eager. Of all
the thousand ships may yours be the last to cleave
    the weary surf. Also, let yourself
be the last to leave the ship; the shore you touch
    is not your father's. When you return,
hurry your ship with oars and sails together;
    do not rest until you reach this place.
When you are here, do not wait. If Phoebus hides
    behind the earth or rises above,
rush to me by day, hurry to me by night.
    All the better if you come at night
for we women are happier if an arm
    embraces our necks in night's darkness.

For now, I find comfort only in my dreams –
    when true joy fails, false joys must delight.
But why does your pale face appear in my dreams?
    Why do reproaches fall from your lips?
I wake and I pray to the phantoms of night.
    Every altar in Thessaly is smoking;
I pour out incense and wet it with my tears,
    the flame flares up as though quenched with wine.
How long until I hold you, safely returned;
    how long until I am lost in joy?
How long before we are joined together, here
    on my couch, and you tell me your deeds?
While you talk, though your speech is delightful, you
    will take kisses and give many back.
Favourite stories well told are often halted;
    the tongue is freshened by sweet delay.
But when Troy comes to my mind, I think also
    of wind and the sea; good hope is sunk
by nervous fear and soon fails. I have also
    noticed that while the winds keep your ships
you still prepare to sail in spite of the winds.
    Would anyone be so foolish as
to return to his home port in a bad wind?
    Yet you have set sail to leave your home
though the sea and all the elements resist.
    Why should Neptune open the sea lanes
when it is his city that you would attack?[10]
    Where will your mindless hurry take you?
All of you, go back to your homes. Danaans,
    Where will your mindless hurry take you?
Alter your plans to suit the opposing winds.
    This delay is no accident for
the all-powerful gods have sent it to you.
    What do you seek but a common slut?
There is still time for you to turn back your sails,
    ships of Inachus.[11] What have I said?
Do I call you back? Rather, may gentle winds
    and peaceful seas bring you back to me.
Though they see the dismal luck of those they love,

121

I am jealous of the Trojan wives.
With the enemy so near, the new bride sets
    a helmet on her husband's head and
puts in his hands the Dardanian weapons.
    Buckling armour to his body, she
will kiss and be kissed by him in turn; it will
    be pleasant duty for both. She will
lead him from their house and command his return
    saying, 'Bring back these weapons to Jove.'
With her reminder fresh in his mind, he will
    fight with care that he return safely.
When he is back again with her, she will take
    his shield from his body, his helmet
from his head and then at last she will welcome
    his weary flesh to her warm embrace.
But we can never know. Our persistent fear
    compels us to imagine the worst
that could be as already having happened.
    While you are away, a soldier in arms there,
I keep a wax figure of you here that brings
    to my sight the dear lines of your face.
It hears the cherishing phrase, it hears the words
    of love that are rightfully yours and
it receives my longing embrace. Believe me
    when I say, this figure is more than
it might seem. Add only a voice to the wax,
    and it will be Protesilaus.
I gaze at it, I hold it to my bosom
    in the place of my true lord and I
reproach it for your long absence as if it
    might somehow make a reply to me.
I swear, by your return and by yourself, you
    who are my god, and by the torches
that burned both for our love and our marriage day;
    from wherever you call I will come
to you whether what I fear shall come to be
    or whether you can go on living.
Let one brief request be the close of my letter:
if you have any care for me, care for yourself.

NOTES

1. Haemonia (the land of Haemon) was another name for Thessaly. Haemon, the lover of Antigone, was the son of Creon, King of Thebes.

2. Boreas was the god of the north wind.

3. Bacchus (the Greek Dionysus) was often depicted with two horns growing from his brow.

4. Helen was born in Sparta, which was often called Taenarus by the poets. Properly speaking, Taenarus (now Tainaron) is a point in Laconia which is the most southerly extension of the Peloponnese. The area was said to contain a cave which was the entrance to the Underworld.

5. These are all geographical features of the area around Troy. Ilion is the name by which the country was known; Tenedos is an island off the coast; Simois is a river of Troy, as is the Xanthus, also known as the Scamander; and Ida is a range of mountains that lies south and east of the site of Troy, whose principal peak is Mount Ida.

6. This is another reference to Helen, whose mother was Leda and whose brothers were the Dioscuri.

The Greeks were often called Danaans after Danaus, a very early king of Argos. See HYPERMESTRA in Appendix 1: Principal Characters.

7. Hector, foremost of Priam's many sons, was the greatest of the Trojan warriors.

8. Argolis is the name given to that area around the Gulf of Argolis in the Peloponnese. Its principal city was Argos, and the area included Epidaurus, Midea, Mycenae, Nauplia, Nemea and Tiryns. Because Argolis encompassed much of Greece – though not its entirety – Laodamia here uses the term to include the whole.

9. The Trojans were often known as the sons of Dardanus who was said to be the common ancestor of the people of Troy.

10. The city of Troy was especially sacred to the sea-god, Neptune.

11. The Inachus is the principal river of Argos. In this context the term applies to all things Greek. Inachus was also said to have been the first of the Argive kings.

XIV: Hypermestra to Lynceus

While it might seem that Hypermestra saved Lynceus because she loved him, that is actually not quite the case. Throughout her letter Hypermestra refers again and again to her horror at the massive slaughter in which he was spared, but her dismay is not because these men – or Lynceus – might have been objects of amorous desire but because they are human beings who should not die before their appointed time.

The present relationship between Hypermestra and Lynceus is one of piety, or *pietas*, not of love in the sense of *amor* or passion. This distinction is very important both for what it says about the character of Hypermestra and the nature of her love for Lynceus, his brothers, and presumably for all human beings. The heroism of Hypermestra is the heroism attendant upon a higher good. She does not lament the loss of a beloved man, nor does she complain at his treatment of her. In this account Lynceus bears no guilt, yet his only endearing characteristic is that before he could demand his marital rights he fell into a drunken sleep.

Hypermestra's act of magnanimity is driven not by infatuation but by a single-minded act of total piety, an unswerving devotion to a principle that unstintingly works for Lynceus' good. Lynceus, then, is not so much the object of Hypermestra's generosity as the catalyst which makes it possible. Though his identity is interesting, his importance to the letter is simply that he was allowed to survive. In his survival we find summarized the totality of her self.

Hypermestra is depicted finally as under sentence because she has not only refrained from evil, she has in fact performed a good action. In this way the letter becomes an essay on virtue, but virtue without its proper reward. The dismal ending which Hypermestra unflinchingly expects is in fact frustrated. But within the constricted frame of this letter there is no cause for hope and Hypermestra has no reason to believe that she will be granted the freedom and the life which she so generously granted to Lynceus. The heroism of Hypermestra resides precisely in the fact that she has disobeyed her father because a higher good must be preserved. The virtue which she preserves intact is not her virginity but a sharply drawn sense of moral obligation which she refuses to violate.

While Hypermestra maintains throughout the letter a tone formed by a lofty moral imperative, in the concluding distich of the letter we suddenly find an extremely realistic admission of weakness and frailty. The woman who had the strength to raise a sword, though unwillingly, is here weighed down by her chains; the woman in whom fear and piety existed as complementary virtues finds piety gone and fear sapping her strength. These lines do not compromise the moral integrity of Hypermestra and her truly heroic deed; they reveal her as a person in whom heroism and humanity are uneasily mingled.

Hypermestra admits that her courage has lapses, that virtue is oppressive and that before the magnitude of her deed she is frightened for her own safety. Though she has maintained a moral principle she has also made herself vulnerable to the weaker side of her own nature.

Hypermestra sends this off to the living
    brother of so many who are dead,
killed by the crime of their brides. Because I was
    faithful I am confined in this house,
bound tightly with heavy chains. My hand could not
    thrust a steel blade into a throat so
I am charged with a crime; if I had done it,
    I would be praised as a heroine.
But better a criminal than to have pleased
    my father; these did not shed blood,
I have no regrets. Let me burn with the flames
    I would not violate, he can thrust
the bright torches from my wedding in my face,
    or he can hold to my throat the sword
he so deceitfully gave me and then I,
    the wife, can die the death my husband

escaped – but he will never force me to say,
    'I regret my deed, forgive my crime.'[1]
To regret my loyalty denies my faith.
    Danaus and my wicked sisters,
rather, should repent for repentance is right
    to follow when evil has been done.
My heart shudders with fear when I remember
    that bloody night, my right hand shakes and
its very bones are bound by sudden trembling.
    The woman you think might have killed her
husband cannot write of crimes by other hands!
    But I shall try to write. Earth enters
twilight, day is ending, night has just begun.
    We, the daughters of Inachus, are
led into the richly appointed house of
    Pelasgus.[2] There, our husbands' father
welcomes the armed women who will wed his sons.
    Everywhere lamps trimmed with gold are lit,
incense that has not been made holy is poured
    on unwilling sacrificial fires.
The rude mob screams, 'Hymen, O Hymenaeus.'
    But the god ignores all this, Jove's spouse
has left the city that she had once chosen.[3]
    Addled with wine, they come in a rush
as their friends cheer them on; with fresh flowers hung
    in their sweaty hair, they joyfully
burst in the bridal chambers – bridal chambers
    which will become their tombs – and they press
their bodies into the couches that will soon
    serve them better as funeral beds.
Now, brought down by the weight of food and wine,
  they
    slept and a carefree quiet settled
over Argos. Then from all around I thought
    I could hear the moans of men dying;
indeed, I heard, and my fears were true. My blood
    grew still, my body and soul were chilled
and I lay cold on my new-made wedding-bed.
    As Zephyr's gentle breeze makes the thin

stalk of grain quiver, as the blasts of winter
    stir the poplar's leaves, so did I – and
even more – tremble.[4] But you were still,
    gripped by wine and the deep sleep it brings.
Then I remembered my father's edict and
    fear went away. I rise, my trembling
hands grasp the steel. I will not lie now: three times
    my hand wickedly raised the sharp blade;
three times it fell back. I put it to your throat –
    I admit the awful truth – I put
to your throat the blade my father gave. But dread
    and piety stayed the brutal stroke;
my pure right hand refused the deed commanded.
    Tearing my purple robes and tearing
my hair I spoke in a whisper words like these:
    'Hypermestra, your father is cruel;
obey his order, send your husband to be
    with his brothers! I am a woman
gentle in her years and gentle by nature.
    Fierce weapons do not suit my young hands.
But come now, while he lies there helpless, follow
    the example of your brave sisters –
it must be that they all have killed their husbands.
    Yet if my hand had strength to murder,
it would be red with the death of its mistress.
    These men all deserved this fate because
they seized their uncle's kingdom, while we, helpless,
    wander with our old, helpless father.
But what if our husbands did deserve to die,
    what then have we done? What is my crime,
that I must be burdened with guilt? What have I
    to do with swords; what have the weapons
of war to do with a girl? My hands were meant
    to work with new wool and a distaff.'
These were the words I muttered to myself and
    while I spoke, my tears followed my words
and from my eyes fell down upon your body.
    As you fumble for my embrace you
throw your arms about, clumsy with sleep, so that

your hand is almost pierced by my blade.
Fear of my father, his servants and the dawn
    filled me and I woke you with these words:
'Wake up and flee, child of Belus, the living
    brother of so many who are dead;
unless you hurry this night will be for you
    unending night.' In terror you wake
and see the mighty sword in my fearful hand.
    You ask the reason: 'Night permitting,
flee,' I answer. While the last darkness of night
    permits, you escape while I remain.
At dawn, Danaus counted his sons-in-law
    that lay there dead. Only you are missed;
he grieves at the loss of your death and rages
    that not enough blood has yet been shed.
By my hair they drag me from him to a cell
    repaying me for my piety.
It is well-known that Juno's wrath persisted
    from the time that young woman became
a heifer to the time she was a goddess.
    That anger made her a lowing beast
who could not keep the love of Jove. By the stream
    of her father, the new heifer stood
looking at her image in the water; horns
    that had never been hers, a mouth that
could utter no lament but only lowing;
    she was frightened by her shape and voice.
Why be angry, miserable one? Why seek
    your image in the river's shadows?
Why do you count the feet your new form requires?
    You are the lover of Jove and you
are the dread rival of his sister. Still you
    satisfy your hunger now with grass
and leaves torn from trees, you drink from bubbling
  springs
    wondering at your image in the pool,
and you are fearful that your hooves might wound you.
    You once were rich, rich enough, you thought,
to be worthy of Jove; now you lie naked

on the naked earth. You range over
land and sea and related streams, oceans part
for you, your way is the land and streams.
But why do you flee? Why wander the great seas?
You cannot escape your own features.
Child of Inachus, to what place do you flee?
You both follow and flee, all the same;
You are at one time guide to your companion
as you are companion to your guide.
The Nile, which flows to the sea through seven mouths,
strips away the features of the mad
heifer and restores the woman that Jove loves.[5]
Why should I bother with such stories,
tales told me by the old? My own life gives me
ample cause to lament. My father
and my uncle are at war; we are forced from
our kingdom and driven from our home;
we are thrown off to the most remote places.
Of that great horde of brothers only
the least part remains. For those killed, and for those
who did the killing, I weep. I lost
many brothers; I lost as many sisters.
Let these two contingents have my tears.
But because you have survived, I will be kept
to suffer the pain of punishment. But what,
I ask you, happens to guilt when I am charged,
a felon, for deeds that should be praised?
What happens when I fall in misery, once
the hundredth member of a family
of whom only one brother remains alive?
Lynceus, if you have any care
for me, your sister, and if you are worthy
of my gift, come and help me. But if
not, you shall give me over to death and when
this poor body is done with living
stealthily place it upon the pyre. Entomb
my bones when you have wet them with tears
and let these few words be carved above that place:
'Hypermestra, in exile, suffered

the sad death she saved her brother from dying,
    an unjust reward for piety.'
I would write more to you, but the weight of these
    chains
and an awful fear has left my hands without strength.

NOTES

1. That is, she would rather burn with the flames of unrequited love than violate the ceremonial of the wedding torches.

2. The Inachus was the principal river of Argos and it was often referred to as a god. Inachus was also the father of Io, from whom Hypermestra and her sisters claimed descent. For the story of Io, see note 5 below.

3. Jove's spouse was Juno (the Greek Hera). The worship of Hera had been established in Argos by Inachus and the city was sacred to that goddess.

4. Zephyr was the west wind.

5. Hera seems to have spent much of her time and energy harrassing the many paramours of her husband Zeus (Jupiter). Hera at one time was served in Argos by a priestess, Io, who was the daughter of Inachus. Io caught the attention of Zeus, who came to her many times by night and in her dreams invited her to join him in the meadows along the river Lerna, where the flocks of Inachus were kept. As a punishment for her dalliance with Zeus, Io was turned into a cow, either by Hera to frustrate Zeus or by Zeus himself who was embarrassed to find Hera observing his transgressions. Zeus then swore to Hera that he was innocent of any transgression with Io. Forever after the gods were lenient of lovers' deceptions. Io, in bovine form, was forced to wander across the earth. Finally, on the shores of the Nile near the Egyptian city of Memphis, Zeus found her and caused her to become pregnant. Io, with her humanity eventually restored, gave birth to Epaphus. In Euripides' play *The Suppliant Women*, the Danaides – daughters of Danaus – assert that despite their Egyptian birth they are really Argives because they are descended from Io. Earlier in this letter, Hypermestra refers to herself and her sisters as the daughters of Inachus; she would therefore seem to claim the ancestry that is reported by Euripides.

XV: Sappho to Phaon

This letter is unusual for a variety of reasons. First of all, Sappho was an historical figure rather than a character of myth. She was a lyric poet who spent most of her life on Lesbos, but little more is known about her. Phaon, on the other hand, exists largely through this letter and very probably is a fiction. Neither Sappho nor Phaon is assigned any regal or even aristocratic position. Though Sappho writes the letter after she has become a renowned poet, she makes no claim to a lofty birth or even a distinguished genealogy, and Phaon is nothing more elevated in life than a boatman. The aristocracy which Sappho invokes is that of beauty for Phaon, and talent for herself.

Yet at the time Ovid wrote the *Heroides* the story of Sappho and her young lover was widely known and there were probably versions of the story which are now no longer extant. The January–May love affair is a perennial favourite, though in such accounts it is usually the man who is aged and the woman who is young and beautiful. But the point of this letter is that Phaon has abandoned Sappho quite without ceremony. It is a strong possibility that having once had the freedom of Sappho's charms, the young man has fled in some degree of chagrin to find other, more appropriate sexual alliances in a place far from Lesbos.

Sappho's complaint against Phaon is interesting. She has been loved and left, seduced and abandoned; her complaint, however, is that this brief affair has effectively turned her eyes away from the beauty of many young women to that of one young man. But this is not all. While she is no longer attracted to these young women, she finds herself now unable to sing of their beauty. Not only has Phaon summarily departed, he has taken with him the source of her poetry, her reputation and her success. Sappho describes the affair with Phaon in terms that suggest a strong and sensual passion. All this is gone because she is no longer excited by feminine loveliness and the only masculine beauty she has ever desired has fled.

Lurking in the background of this letter is the great potential for comic, if not ludicrous, episode. Though Sappho argues that love affairs can and do cross the boundaries of race and ethos, she is hard-pressed to argue that the boundary of age can be crossed so easily. This problem also arises in the letter of Phaedra to her stepson, Hippolytus (IV). There, however, the age difference is obscured by the fact of incest. But Phaedra in her disappointment remains a woman of resources who can and does manage to destroy Hippolytus; Sappho is more than old and rejected, – she is also powerless to effect a change in Phaon's determination and to alter her own situation. The cure that she seems finally to seek will be not some magical remedy for the pangs of love, rather it will be the finality of death which cures both pain and joy.

Sappho is very careful to outline the nature of her genius. She compares herself with certain of her contemporaries and finds that her accomplishment is equal, if not superior, to theirs. Not content with this she reminds Phaon that her sexual skills were most pleasing to him. Though she never suggests that she brought Phaon her virginity, she clearly asserts that she could hardly have failed his expectations. And the suggestion is never far from Sappho's words that such pleasure was his because he was the beneficiary of her great experience, an experience that could only be the product of her years.

For Sappho Phaon is more than a beautiful young man. In his absence he has become – much to her surprise – an obsession. Phaon permeates her imagination so thoroughly that her dreams become intensely erotic and in waking she is disappointed that they have come to an end. Because of Phaon, Sappho's inner tranquillity – derived from her former life and its satisfactions – is utterly destroyed.

The story of Sappho and Phaon fills a curious niche in ancient literature. While homosexual love was openly acknowledged among persons of aristocratic and divine nature, it always carried with it a social stigma. It is probable that the stigma derived from the fact that if practised exclusively by an individual it would effectively prevent the begetting of new generations and consequently prevent the transmission of both culture and property. By all accounts Sappho seemed to enjoy a very close, if not intimate, relationship with the young women of her circle. The fact that she married and bore a child is seldom mentioned. There is a long-standing tradition – supported by Ovid in this letter – that Sappho was an unattractive woman, but it is also possible that one could read this to mean that in becoming old Sappho has lost her youthful beauty.

Phaon represents heterosexual passion outside marriage. This is important. Sappho first caught sight of the young man when she was no longer young. Phaon seemed to have responded to her attentions but then he disappears from her life, though not from her imagination. Sappho tells the classic story of the older person surprised by a passion for a much younger lover who is unable to maintain or perhaps even recognize the kind of stability demanded by the older. Perhaps the relationship was totally impossible for all concerned; perhaps Phaon, having enjoyed the passion of Sappho, had no more interest in her. Perhaps he merely went on to be welcomed by so many other women that he did not so much reject Sappho as simply forgot about her. It is important, however, that in this letter Sappho asserts that Phaon is responsible for turning her eyes from 'the hundred others I have loved in shame' – a clear suggestion that having enjoyed heterosexual passion she is no longer able to enjoy homosexual relationships.

When you saw these letters from my eager hand
    could your eye recognize the sender
or did you fail to recognize their author
    until you could read my name, 'Sappho'?
Since I am famous for the lyric do you
    wonder why my lines vary in length?
But I weep and tears fit well the elegy –
    a lyre cannot bear the weight of tears.[1]
I am on fire and wasted like a burning
    field with its grain turning to ashes
in the east wind's blast. The fields where you are now,
    on the slopes of Typhoeus' Aetna,
Phaon, are far away but no less subject
    than I to the flames that come by storm.[2]

I do not make songs now for a well-tuned string,
    for songs are the work of carefree minds.
No Pyrrhan girls please me now, nor do those from
    Methymna, nor any from Lesbos.[3]
Anactoria is nothing to me now,
    nor is that dazzling beauty, Cydro.
Atthis no longer brings joy to my eyes as
    she did once. Nor do I find pleasure
in the hundred others I have loved in shame.[4]
    Yours is now the love these maids once had.
Your face, the beauty that astonished my eyes,
    your years are ready for life's pleasures.
Take up a lyre and a quiver of arrows,
    you will seem to us like Apollo;
or let horns burst from your brow and be Bacchus.
    Phoebus loved Daphne and Bacchus loved
the maiden from Cnossos.[5] But neither of them
    knew the lyric mode. Still the daughters
of Pegasus come to me with sweetest songs;
    my name is known all over the earth.[6]
Alcaeus himself has no richer fame: he
    who shares not only my gift for song
but also my homeland, though he sings a song
    of more dignity than my lyrics.[7]
If nature denies me the gift of beauty,
    let my name's measure be my stature.
If this my beauty does not dazzle your eyes,
    then recall that dark Andromeda
was beautiful to Perseus though she was
    dark with the hue of her native land.[8]
What is more, white pigeons often mate with birds
    of a darker colour and the black
turtledove is loved by birds of green plumage.
    If no woman can be yours unless
her beauty is thought to be great enough, then
    there is no woman who will be yours.
But my beauty seemed sufficient when you heard
    me read my songs; you insisted then
that those words made me forever beautiful.

I would sing – I remember, for all
lovers remember all – and while I sang you
    were busy stealing kisses from me.
You even praised my kisses. I must have pleased
    you in all things but especially when
we toiled at the task of love. Then, I recall,
    my playful abandon delighted
you more than you had known before: a quick joke,
    a sudden embrace to spice our game;
and when our joys were at last one joy, the deep
    weariness that filled our spent bodies.
But you seek new quarry – Sicilian maids.
    What does Lesbos mean to me? I wish
that I were a girl on Sicily. Send him
    back to me, you Nisaean mothers
and Nisaean daughters.[9] Do not be tricked by
    the lies that fall so easily from
his charming tongue. What he says to you he said
    to me. You, Erycina, who roams
the mountains of Sicania – I am yours;
    lady, you must protect your singer.[10]
Must my sad fortune go on as it began,
    always bitter in its swift passage?
Only six birthdays had come and gone for me
    when I swept up my father's bones, dead
too soon, and let them drink my young tears. Caught up
    with a whore, untrained in loving ways,
my innocent brother bore the foulest shame
    and suffered the greatest loss. Beggared,
he roams the blue oceans with a quick oar while
    the riches he wasted in evil
pleasure he seeks now to win by evil means.
    Because I scolded him often and
faithfully, I have now only his hatred;
    truthfulness and duty brought me this.
And, though I have much to give me endless care,
    a young daughter completes my worry.
But the last thing of which I complain is you.
    My boat is not propelled by friendly

breezes; look, my hair tangles about my neck,
    my hands display no glittering gems,
I wear a rough shift, no gold is sprinkled in
    my hair, my curls have no foreign scents.
For whose pleasure should I dress and for whom should
    I adorn my body? You are gone,
you, the only right cause for my adornment.
    My tender heart is easily hurt
by the slight shaft; I always have good reason
    to be in love. But then, what happened?
Can it be that when I was born the Sisters
    set this as a law for my nature
but did not spin out for me a living thread
    tough enough to bear this fateful weight?[11]
Or is it that desires become character
    and my mistress, Thalia, softens me?[12]
Can it be any wonder that I am swept
    away at the sight of your manhood
as it shows itself at the start of those years
    when men's love reveals its first stirring?
It seems now that I must be afraid that you,
    Aurora, would steal him away and
put him in the place of Cephalus, and so
    you would, but your first choice holds your eye.[13]
Phoebe should see him, she who sees all things, and
    it will be Phaon that she preserves
in sleep; Venus might well have taken him off
    to the skies in her ivory chariot
but she knows all too well that he might have caught
    the eye of her Mars himself![14] Neither
just a man nor still a boy, age joins with charm.
    Splendour and great glory of your age,
come here to me; sail back, O beautiful man,
    to the warmth and strength of my embrace.
My plea is not that you should love but rather
    that you let yourself be loved by me.
As I write my eyes let the welling tears flow
    like dewdrops; only observe the blots
that blur the lines I have written. If you wished

so strongly to leave, you could have gone
away from me with a greater dignity;
    at the very least, you might have said,
'Farewell, woman of Lesbos.' You did not take
    my tears, you took no kisses of mine.
I felt no fear for the pain I would suffer.
    You left nothing, nothing but my hurt;
and you took nothing, nothing to bring to mind
    your abandoned lover. I gave you
no commands, though I would have given you none,
    but the hope you would remember me.
By our love, may it never be far away;
    by the holy nine, my goddesses:
I swear that when I heard, 'Your joy is fleeing
    away,' I could neither weep nor speak.[15]
Eyes could not form tears and tongue could not form
    words,
    my heart was frozen with a cold frost.
When I recovered grief, I beat my breast and
    tore my hair and without shame I shrieked
like that loving mother who lifts to the high
    funeral pyre her son's empty body.
The heart of my brother, Charaxus, rushes
    with joy at my misery; he comes
before my eyes, and fades from my sight. Hoping
    to make my woe improper, he says:
'Her daughter is still alive, she need not grieve.'
    Love and decency are not the same.[16]
No one could avoid seeing me; still I tore
    open my robes and exposed my breast.
It is you, Phaon, who are my concern, you
    it is that comes to me in my dreams –
dreams that come brighter than the beauty of day.
    There, in my dreams, I find you, though you
are far away; the joys of sleep are too short.
    So often, it seems, I press the weight
of my neck against your arms and so often
    do I place my arms beneath your neck.
I know the kisses, the tongue's caresses which

once you enjoyed giving and getting.
It seems I fondle you while uttering words
   that are near the truth of wakefulness
and my sensation is guarded by my lips.
   I blush to say more, all comes to pass:
Throughout every part of my body a great
   pleasure rushes and I discover
that now I can no longer control myself:
   I am no longer joyless and dry.
Then when Titan appears and lights the earth, I
   am sad that sleep has left me so soon.[17]
I go to the woods and the rocky hollows –
   if only such places could help me.
There I run in a frenzy as though maddened
   by the touch of Enyo.[18] My hair loose
in the wind, it flies about my neck. I see
   the coarse rocks that hang above the paths;
places that once were like Mygdonian marble.
   I find the forest which so often
was a bower in which we lay, shading us
   with heavy leaves. But I do not find
him who was lord of both that forest and me.
   Now it is cheap and has no value,
he was the gift that enriched that remote place.
   I see the crushed grasses in the turf,
the sod that took on the impress of our weight.
   I have reclined and touched the place where
you rested, the grass that once was welcoming
   to me has been watered with my tears.
Even the branches have given up their leaves
   and no birds are singing their sweet songs.
Only the bird of Daulis, that grief-stricken
   mother who brought an awful revenge
to her lord, cries for Itys of Ismarus.
   The pitiable bird sings of Itys,
while Sappho sings her song of love abandoned.[19]
   There is no more but night-time silence.
I found the sacred spring of water more pure
   than the finest crystal – many think

a spirit dwells in its depths – above it spreads
    a water lotus, itself a grove.
Here the grass grows green and tender. I laid down
    my tired body and let the tears flow
when suddenly before me stood a Naïad.[20]
    Standing there she said, 'Because you burn
with flames that are unsatisfied, you must find
    the land that is called Ambracia.[21]
In that place, Phoebus surveys from the heavens
    the great stretch of sea that touches both
Actium and Leucadia.[22] In this place
    Deucalion, consumed with love
for Pyrrha, threw himself down, striking the sea
    without harming his body. The man's
passion left the heart that was beneath the waves
    and Deucalion was free of love's pain.
This is the law of that distant place.[23] Go now;
    search out the high cliff of Leucadia
and do not let yourself be afraid to leap.'
    The advice was given, her words stopped
and she vanished from my sight. I rose, frightened,
    and the tears would not stop their flowing.
Nymph, I am off to seek the cliff you described.
    Fear, begone; my passion evicts it.
Whatever shall come to pass will be better
    by far than my present misery.
You breezes, hurry to me; raise up my flesh,
    it is not a thing of much substance.
Sweet Love, bear me up on your wings, lest my death
    be the fault of Leucadia's waves.
Then I will dedicate to Phoebus the shell
    that has always been our common good.
Beneath it let there be engraved in the stone
    one verse followed by another verse:
'Phoebus, the grateful poetess, Sappho, brings
    a lyre, a gift proper to us both.'[24]
But why is it that you force me to Actium's
    coast, despondent as I am, when you
could so easily turn your steps back to me?

You would be better by far for me
    than Leucadia's surf; you can be Phoebus
to me in beauty and in kindness.
But if I die, you who are more dangerous
    than cliffs or waves, can you bear the shame?
Better it would be to press my breast to yours
    than to fling it from the rocky cliff.
This, Phaon, is the woman's bosom you praised,
    the woman who seemed to have genius.
I wish that eloquence were mine now, but grief
    kills my art and woe stops my genius.
The gift of song I enjoyed will not answer
    my call; lyre and plectrum are silent.
Daughters of Lesbos who will marry or who
    are married, daughters of Lesbos whose
names one time were sung to my Aeolian lyre,
    daughters of Lesbos whom I loved and
for whose love I am ashamed, stop there,
    do not come to hear my shell's music.
Phaon has destroyed what you once held so dear –
    poor me, I nearly said, 'My Phaon' –
bring him back, you will find your singer restored:
    he was my genius, it left with him.
Are my prayers good for nothing, has his low-born
    heart been moved or does it remain cold
and unfeeling while Zephyr carries away
    these words that fall with such idleness?[25]
I wish that the breezes which scatter my words
    would bring your sails back to this island.
If your heart had any care then such a deed
    would be proper for one so delayed.
If it remains your plan to return to me,
    but you are still delayed by the need
to fashion a gift to mount on the ship's stern,
    why do you destroy me with delay?
Leave your anchorage. Venus was born out of
    the sea and opens passages for
the lover. The winds will hurry you along
    if you but leave your mooring. Cupid

will be your pilot as he sits in the stern,
  with his delicate hands he himself
will open then fold the sails. But if you wish
  to flee from Sappho of Pelasgos –
though you can find no reason for such a flight –
  at least you must permit a letter
cruel though it must surely be to tell me this woe
and I will find my fate in Leucadia's waves.[26]

NOTES

1. In this letter Ovid's fictional character, Sappho, is writing in elegiacs, a form which is in every way quite foreign to Sappho the lyric poet.

2. Typhoeus was a dangerous monster imprisoned by Zeus beneath the island of Sicily. The volcanic activity of Mount Aetna was explained by the presence of Typhoeus.

3. Pyrrha and Methymna were cities of Lesbos. Sappho reproaches Phaon for successfully turning her attentions from all the young women of her circle.

4. The beauty of Anactoria is celebrated in the first book of Sappho's poems. Anactoria came from Miletus, which was the name of two different cities, one located in the Ionian colonies of Asia Minor and the other on Crete. Anactoria eventually married a Greek soldier and went with him to Sardis. Nothing is known of Cydro, except that she must have been a friend or companion of Sappho. Her name is not mentioned in the extant poems of Sappho. Neither is anything known of Atthis, except that she too must have been a friend of Sappho. Unlike Cydro, Atthis is mentioned in several of Sappho's lyrics.

5. Apollo was the Greek god who was patron of musicians, prophets and seers, archers, practitioners of the healing arts, and young people. Apollo and Artemis were the illegitimate children of Zeus and Leto. Because of the enmity of Hera, the wife of Zeus, Apollo was often occupied with various hazards and challenges. Apollo enjoyed two affairs with young men: Hyacinth and Cyparissus; both of these loves ended in tragedy for the youths.

Bacchus, or Dionysus, was the Greek god of wine. Because he was the illegitimate son of Zeus and Persephone, he too earned the enmity of Hera. In his infancy, to shield him from Hera, he was reared by foster parents who disguised him as a girl. In his youth Dionysus sought passage from Icaria, an Aegean island, to Naxos in the Cyclades. According to some accounts, during the voyage the sailors were so taken with his great beauty that he was either seduced or attacked and raped by them. Dionysus was followed by a crowd of devotees of both sexes. The cult of Dionysus was characterized by orgiastic rites that seem to have involved very much sexual licence.

Apollo was also known by the name Phoebus, which means 'shining'. This indicates the identification of Apollo with the sun.

Daphne was a nymph who refused to have any dealings with men. Leucippus fell in love with her, but she rejected his advances. He determined, then, that the best way to attract her attention would be to come to her in the guise of a young girl. He did this, pretending to be the maiden, Oeno. In this disguise he requested permission to join the hunt with Daphne and her companions, and this was readily granted. After the hunt, Daphne and her companions wished to bathe in a river, but giving some excuse, Leucippus declined to join them. Daphne and her companions, however, playfully stripped off his clothing. When they discovered his masculinity, they killed him with their spears. It is possible that this happened because Apollo wanted to have Daphne for himself. Another version of the story omits the episode with Leucippus, but Daphne is still made to suffer greatly because she has avoided men. In this account Apollo pursues Daphne through the forest until, in desperation, she prays for divine help and is turned into a laurel tree. Frustrated, Apollo can do nothing except fashion a branch into a wreath to wear on his head. From that time on, the laurel was sacred to Apollo. At some point in his travels Dionysus came to the island of Naxos, where he found the daughter of King Minos of Crete, Ariadne, who had been abandoned there by Theseus.

6. Pegasus was a winged horse who, with Chrysaor, was born from the neck of Medusa when Perseus severed her head. Their father was Poseidon. Pegasus was a great favourite of the Muses, patrons of the arts. Most authorities agree that the Muses lived on Mount Helicon, where Pegasus is said to have started the spring called Hippocrene by stamping his hoof.

7. Alcaeus, a lyric poet whose life is approximately contemporaneous with that of Sappho, lived in the city of Mytilene on Lesbos. Though Alcaeus seems to have written some love poems, he also wrote verse which was political in nature, as well as some drinking songs. However, even the topical poems frequently have a strong meditative and reflective quality.

8. Andromeda was an Ethiopian princess who was chained to a rock by her father, King Cepheus, in order that he might appease a terrible monster that had come from the sea. Perseus, however, rescued her and carried her back to his home in Argos where she became his wife and bore him many children. For the Greek geographers and historians, Ethiopia was a quite well-defined place situated at the headwaters of the Nile, to the south of Egypt. Ethiopia would therefore have had no access to the Mediterranean,

since its closest body of water would have been the Red Sea. Homer, on the other hand, locates Ethiopia on the shores of Oceanus, and at times it seems to be a land either in the far east or the far west. Certainly, it is safe to say that any reference to Ethiopia must carry with it the notion of the fabulous and the unbelievable.

9. Nisus was a legendary king of Megara, a city on the Corinthian isthmus in an area known as Megaris. After being betrayed by his daughter Scylla, Nisus was turned into an eagle.

10. Erycina was the area surrounding Mount Eryx in the extreme north-western corner of Sicily. It is interesting to note that Venus was sometimes addressed as Erycina, since there was a well-known temple to Venus on the summit of Mount Eryx. Eryx was also the name given to a son of Venus who was defeated by Hercules. The Sicani were a tribe which came from either the Iberian or the Italian peninsula to settle in this part of Sicily. The name, as used here, refers to the whole of Sicily.

11. A reference to the Fates, those goddesses whose duty it was to determine the course of every human life. Generally the Fates are depicted as spinning the thread of a life, measuring it, and then cutting the length of the thread to measure.

12. Thalia, one of the Muses, was commonly said to be the patron of comedy or light verse.

13. Aurora (the Greek Eos) was the Roman goddess of the dawn. Cephalus was the son of Herse and Hermes, and as a young man was of such unique beauty that he was kidnapped by Aurora. Shortly after, Aurora gave birth to Phaethon, the son of Cephalus.

14. This is a rather oblique reference to the myth of Endymion. Phoebe, or Selene, was originally a Titaness who after a period of time came to be associated with Diana, goddess of the moon and sister of Apollo. Endymion, the King of Elis, caught the eye of Phoebe, who fell in love with him and over many years bore him fifty daughters. Zeus granted the king the rare privilege of being able to determine his own fate. It was Endymion's choice that he should sleep for ever and never grow old. This wish was granted, and it is said that in each passage of the moon, Selene – or Phoebe – takes new pleasure in his physical beauty.

The reference to Venus and Mars seems to be not so much to some specific event as to the fact that Venus was notoriously generous in helping lovers achieve their desired union with the beloved. The reference to Mars, how-ever, suggests the possibility that the beauty of Phaon is such that he might engender homosexual as well as heterosexual attention. Throughout my-thology, the gods certainly had many male lovers, both human and divine.

15. The 'holy nine' refers to the Muses.

16. Charaxus suggests that the only justifiable cause of Sappho's grief would be the death or loss of her daughter. Since this has not happened, then she has no legitimate reason to grieve.

17. That is, at dawn. Helios, the sun-god, was sometimes known simply as Titan.

18. Enyo was a goddess who frequently accompanied Ares, the Greek god of war, into battle. Ares corresponds to the Roman god Mars.

19. This is a reference to the story of Tereus, Procne, Philomela and Itys. Tereus was a king who ruled in the Phocian city of Daulis. He married Procne, and she bore him a son, Itys. After a few years, Procne told Tereus that she wished to have a visit from her younger sister, Philomela. Tereus hurried to the kingdom of Pandion, and when he saw Philomela he immediately fell in love with her. Without hesitation, he began to plan for seduction. Pandion, however, was unwilling to let Philomela go until she begged him for his permission. At last Pandion reluctantly consented and Tereus immediately set sail with her. Landing in his own territory he took Philomela to a hut in the forest where he raped her. In her anger, Philomela threatened to tell the world of his crime. To silence her, Tereus tore out her tongue. He left Philomela in the cottage and returned to his palace and his wife, where he told with much grief and many tears a tale of the death of Philomela. Procne believed Tereus and mourned the death of her sister. Meanwhile, a year passed and Philomela was finally able to make a garment into which she wove an account of what had happened. She caused one of her guards to carry the finished cloak to the queen. Procne deciphered the message and, in silence, went to the hut where she freed Philomela and dressed her as a Bacchante, since it was the time of the biennial festival of Bacchus. The two returned to the palace where Procne plotted an appropriate revenge. Setting eyes on Itys, she noticed the boy's resemblance to his father. With no compunction, Procne killed her son, cut the body into pieces, placing some in a pot of boiling water and others on a spit to be roasted over the open fire. Then she herself served the cooked flesh to Tereus, who willingly ate his own son. When the meal was ended he asked her to send Itys to him, and she replied that Itys was already there. As he realized what had happened, Tereus cursed the sisters. He pursued the two through the palace but as they fled from him they were transformed into birds, becoming a nightingale and a swallow. In this passage, Ovid associates Itys with Ismarus, a city ruled by Tereus.

20. The naiads were water nymphs, goddesses of the water.

21. Ambracia was an area of southern Epeirus, north-west of Argos.

22. Phoebus was another name for Apollo.
Actium is a point due west of Argos on the northerly side of Acarnania.

Leucadia, also known as Leucas, is one of the Ionian Islands. It is west by south-west of Argos.

23. This episode in the history of Deucalion and Pyrrha is not well documented in other sources. There is a suggestion in the *Metamorphoses* (I.318–415) that if Pyrrha had been lost at sea Deucalion would have followed soon after. But this particular story is not told in conjunction with the account of Deucalion and the flood. It is probable that Sappho's version was invented by Ovid for this passage. It should be noted that the high place at Actium which overlooks the sea is a great distance from Lesbos and would require a difficult voyage from there through the Greek islands. Alternatively, Sappho could travel from Lesbos to the mainland, and then cross Greece to reach Leucadia. However, this latter route would also be extremely difficult and hazardous.

24. That is, she will dedicate to Phoebus, god of music, the musical instrument she has used to accompany her lyric poems. The earliest lyres were made of the shell of a turtle; consequently Sappho refers to her lyre as a shell.

25. Zephyr was the west wind.

26. Pelasgus was the mythical founder of all the Greek tribes. His name was given to the whole of Greece and its inhabitants were known as Pelasgians.

XVI: Paris to Helen

The reputation of Paris in the ancient world and in the myths of the period was never good. Paris is usually depicted as something of a dilettante, a ladies' man whose proper activity is best conducted indoors and within the bedchamber. In this letter Paris is careful to present the strength and courage which he displayed first when his flocks were attacked by robbers and then when he participated anonymously in the funeral games. Still, in matters of love Paris is his own law and recognizes no bounds beyond his own desires. That he is consumed by passion becomes in his mind sufficient reason for its indulgence. This profound self-deception is only complicated by his failure to understand the prophecies surrounding his birth.

In this letter Paris refers to Menelaus as the unworthy husband of Helen. It is quite clear that the promise of Venus – a promise to which Paris is sole beneficiary and, significantly, sole witness – cuts through any legal and social niceties which might have stood in the way of his desire to have Helen. Paris portrays Menelaus as unworthy of Helen's affections by virtue of his ancestry and his background. But more to the point, Paris has been given a mandate by Venus which not only expedites his journey from Troy to Sparta but also frees him from the observance of any laws which might prevent him from taking Helen as his wife. The disregard of Paris for Helen's marital circumstances is mirrored by the fact that he has also abandoned his own wife, Oenone (see letter V).

It is useful to read this letter in the light of what we know about the Mediterranean world. In all the literary accounts the house of Atreus and the house of Priam clearly possessed great riches and power. Paris carefully denies that he has come as a merchant. However, it would appear from this statement, privately delivered to Helen, that Paris and his many ships had been welcomed on the assumption that they were engaged in some kind of commercial venture. For the purpose of Paris' real intentions such a deception must be maintained until the very last minute.

Paris argues that the love which he feels for Helen – the love of a Phrygian for an Achaian – is an appropriate love. There is here the suggestion that Paris is of such a different racial and ethnic background that his love for Helen might be viewed in Sparta as improper. While a Greek might well enter into commerce with a kingdom from outside the Grecian hegemony, that same Greek might very well and with every justification refuse to allow the amorous or marital involvement of one of his women. The lines drawn in antiquity between Greek and barbarian were no less compelling than those drawn by the Romans in their day. Yet we know that in traditional love stories two lovers often surmount, or attempt to surmount, such barriers. Whether the love is appropriate or even wise, the point of the story is that love will at least attempt to conquer any obstacle.

While the *Heroides* is a work in which much of the action is anticipated by significant and substantial ironies, the ironies surrounding the life of Paris and the prophecies associated with him are particularly rich. It is common, and indeed trite, for various characters in the *Heroides* to refer to love as a flame or an arrow. This particular choice of symbol is certainly not unique to Ovid. However, both the imagery of the flame and that of the arrow become especially notable in the myths surrounding Paris and the Trojan War because they are so central to the action of the story.

Though possessed of the gift of prophecy, Cassandra was also cursed by the fact that her prophecies were not to be believed. Yet the problem here is even greater because the prophecy surrounding the birth of Paris, which is so graphic and so particular, is also ignored. While Paris does believe her prophecy – an apparent contradiction of Apollo's curse – in fact he disastrously misunderstands its import. He attributes it to his own state of mind rather than the consequences of the action which that state of mind will bring about.

The reader could almost conclude that there is here a conspiracy among Priam and his family to avoid any information which might suggest future events that are in opposition to their pursuit of immediate gratification.

I, son of Priam, send to you, the daughter
of Leda, prayers for my well-being:
something that will come to me only from you.
Should I speak or is my flame of love
so visible to all that I need not speak
and my love is all too apparent?
I would prefer that it be hidden until
the time came for me when joy and fear
might be distinct. Could a man conceal
flames when their light can be seen by all?
However, I will enhance the fact with words:
I am consumed by the fires of love!
Now, you have the words that bear my heart's message.
I beg you, forgive my confession;
do not read what follows with a hardened face
but with a face that shows your beauty.
For a long time now I have been cheered because
you welcomed my letter and perhaps
in time you might extend that welcome to me.
I hope that what the mother of Love
has decreed should come from this journey, will be,
just as she herself caused the journey.
I hope that her promise, that you would be mine,
has not been made foolishly because
I have set sail for your shores at her command.
You should not sin without knowing this:
I sail from my port, and no minor goddess
has favoured me with her protection.
The prize for which I am in contest is great,
but I want nothing that is not mine.
She who came from Cythera has already
promised you for my wedding chamber.
With her as my pilot, I left the beaches
of Sigeum behind me; riding
in a stern built by Phereclus, I have sailed
the doubtful ways of the ocean's flood.[1]
She it is who favours me with gentle winds
and a kindly breeze – without a doubt
she rules the sea because she came from the sea.

May it be that she still favour me:
may she still quiet the surges of my heart
    as she calms the tumult of the wave;
may it be granted to me that with her help
    my pledges will find their safe harbour.
I carried with me the flames of my desire,
    this blaze was not kindled in this place.
Neither a harsh storm nor a lost way brought me;
    it was the cause of such a voyage,
from the beginning my ships were on a course
    that only took them to Taenarus[2]
And do not think that I come as a merchant,
    plying the sea-lanes with a hull filled
with goods – what I have, may the gods keep.
    Nor have I travelled to see the sights
in your Greek towns – the kingdom from which I sail
    has cities that are richer by far.
It is for you that I have come, it is you
    whom bright Venus promised for my bed,
you alone were the one desire of my heart
    even before you were known to me.
You were in my mind before I saw you with
    my eyes; rumour first brought hurt to me.
But let it not seem odd that I am in love
    from so far off. With a bow so strong
the arrows of love were able to find me.
    So said the Fates.[3] You must not refuse
to heed their decree; hear the words I tell you,
    words that are true and faithful to them.
Late in my mother's womb, slow to be born, I
    made her body heavy with my weight.
In a dream, she seemed to see a vision that
    she gave birth to a great blazing torch.
Terrified, she awoke and told the fearsome
    vision from deep night to old Priam
who quickly told the dream to his prophets. One
    of these sang that Ilion would be burned
by the flame of Paris.[4] That was my heart's torch
    and I tell you, it has come to be.

My beauty and my wit, though I seemed to all
    low-born, were signs of my noble birth.
In the wooded valleys of Mount Ida, far
    from footpaths and shaded by pines and
the holm oak, is a place where slow-moving sheep
    have never grazed, nor the nanny goat
that clambers on the cliff, nor the ponderous
    cattle.[5] There I was, resting against
a tree, gazing down on the walls and high roofs
    of the city of Dardanus and
the sea when much to my great surprise I felt
    the earth shake as though many feet walked
on it – my words are true, though hard to believe –
    and there appeared, carried on swift wings,
the grandchild of great Atlas and Pleione –
    I could see this, now I may tell it –
the god carried a rod made of gold and then
    three goddesses, Venus, Pallas and
Juno, set their delicate feet on the turf.[6]
    My hair stood on end, I trembled and
lost speech. 'Do not fear,' said the winged messenger.
    'You are the final judge of beauty,
end the contentions of these three goddesses;
    decide which of them has such beauty
that will conquer the other two.' He called on
    the name of great Jove, that I might know
there was no escape and then he returned through
    the ethereal paths to the stars.
My frightened heart took comfort, I became bold
    enough to study each one of them.
All were worthy; I sighed because only one
    could win. Still one of them pleased me more;
you must have guessed: it was she who causes love.
    Every one of them wanted to win,
they tried to sway my judgement with splendid gifts.
    Loudly, Jove's wife offered royal thrones;
his daughter pledged victory in war.
    How could I choose between power and
a courageous heart? But Venus smiled sweetly,

'Paris, do not be convinced by these,
because both will bring to you worry and fear.
   My gift for you is the gift of love
and the daughter of Leda, more beautiful
   than her mother, come into your arms.'
So she spoke. With both gift and beauty approved
   she, the victor, returned to heaven.
While this was happening, perhaps because fate
   wished to see my prosperity, I
was found by all the right signs to be a child
   of the royal house. After a long time
the son returned to his right home and the house
   rejoiced as Troy made the day a feast.
As I desire you, women have desired me;
   you can have what others have prayed for.
Not only the daughters of princes and lords,
   even nymphs have felt the pangs of love.
Which beauty is greater than Oenone's?
   After you, there is none more proper
than she to be the bride of great Priam's son.
   Tyndaris, I tell you, they weary
me since I have had the hope of winning you.[7]
   You fill my vision by day and it is you
my soul sees by night when my eyes are asleep.
   What can it be when I see your face,
you who have conquered without my seeing you?
   I was blazing with love, though the flame
was far away. I could no longer deny
   myself of what I hoped to have so
I set course on the dark blue path that I might
   find at last the substance of my prayers.
Groves of Trojan pine were put to the axes
   of Phrygia that ships might sail the seas;
the towering woods were stripped away from the broad
   reaches of Gargara so that soon
Ida's broad slopes produced beams without number.[8]
   The oak is bent into a frame for
my swift ships, the curved keels are woven into
   the ribs. Yards rise into place and sails

are hung from the mast. The raked sterns are painted
    with bright figures of gods. My ship has
the goddess who promotes our union and with
    her is painted a tiny Cupid.
After the last hand has finished its work and
    all is done, I am anxious to sail
the breadth of the Aegean, but I am stopped
    by the prayers of father and mother
who have managed to delay my departure
    with solicitous words. Cassandra,
my sister, with her hair undone, as my ships
    were ready to set sail, cried: 'Where will
your impetuous course take you? You will bring
    back to Troy an all-consuming flame.
You cannot know how great are the flames you seek
    beyond these waters.' She spoke the truth.
I know the flames of which she spoke for there burn
    now in my heart flames of harshest love.[9]
I sail from that harbour and with kindly winds
    I make landfall on your shoreline, nymph
offspring of Oebalus.[10] Your master receives
    me as a guest in his house – even
this followed the plan of the gods. He showed me
    everything of beauty and value
in Lacedaemon, but I wanted to see
    your famous charm, nothing else mattered.[11]
When I saw your beauty, I was without speech,
    astonished; new worries swelled in me.
Such features, I was certain, I had seen when
    Cytherea submitted to judgement.
But if you had joined her that day, Venus' prize
    would have been doubtful. Fame has told all,
your beauty is made known to every nation.
    No woman of beauty is like you,
not Phrygian nor anywhere under the sun.
    Only believe me when I tell you –
your reputation is less than the truth and
    has all but denied your charms. I find
more now than I was promised by the goddess

and you exceed by far that promise.
It was only right that Theseus should feel
        the flames of love for he knew your charms
and it was right that you became his spoil when –
        as your family so often does – you
competed in the games of the palaestra,
        a naked maiden with naked men.[12]
I revere his act, I can only wonder
        why he ever let you be returned.
Booty so grand should have been kept securely.
        I would sooner have let my head leave
my blood-spattered shoulders than would I have seen
        you taken from my marriage chamber.
For one like you, could these hands of mine ever
        have willingly given a release?
For one like you, could I, if I still had life,
        let you leave the closure of my arms?
If it must have been, I would have sought your pledge
        that my love would not have been in vain.
I might have picked your virgin's bloom or stolen
        perhaps something else instead that could
have been taken without bringing any harm
        to the state of your virginity.
Give yourself to me and know the loyalty
        of Paris; only the blazing pyre
can extinguish my love for you. I rank you
        first before the kingdoms which Juno,
Jove's cherished sister and bride, once offered me;
        that I might fold your neck in my arms,
I spurned the strength that Pallas would have given.
        I have no regret, nor will I think
my choice silly. My heart's desire is unchanged.
        I have one prayer, you who are worthy
to be pursued with such great labours, that you
        will not let fall my fond hope to earth.
I am not of low birth trying to marry
        one of nobler birth, nor should you find
yourself disgraced, I tell you, to be my wife.
        If you care to search out such things, you

will find a Pleiad and a Jove in our line,
    to say nothing of our race since then.[13]
My father rules Asia – no place is richer;
    a land so huge, one does not cross it.
Houses of gold in cities without number
    I will show to you and temples that
you will think are properly built for their gods.
    You will see Ilion and its great walls
strengthened with lofty towers that rose up to
    the wonderful tunes of Phoebus' lyre.[14]
Should I tell you of its crowds of men? The land
    hardly nourishes those who live there.
Troy's women will throng to meet you and the halls
    of our great palace will barely hold
the daughters of Phrygia. Often you will say,
    'Achaia is so poor.'[15] Any house,
any household that you might choose, will reveal
    to your gaze the wealth of a city.
Do not look back to your Sparta with disgust,
    to me, the land of your birth is rich.
But Sparta is a sparse place and you deserve
    to be maintained in riches. A place
like that is hardly appropriate for one
    with beauty so surpassing as yours.
Beauty that is like your beauty should always
    be enhanced with endless adornments;
beauty that is like your beauty should always
    revel in delights endlessly new.
When you have seen the garments worn by Trojan
    men, how, would you think, are the daughters
of Dardanus clothed? Be patient a little
    bit more, do not reject a Phrygian
for husband, you who were born in Therapnae.[16]
    It was a Phrygian, one of our race,
who is now among the gods, mingling water
    and nectar for their drink.[17] A Phrygian
became Aurora's spouse and was carried off
    by that goddess, she who determines
the limits of night's advance.[18] It is also

Anchises, the Phrygian, with whom
the mother of the Loves delights to be joined
    on the topmost ridges of Ida.[19]
And I cannot believe that Menelaus,
    when compared to our beauty and years,
will be more esteemed by you than I. Be sure,
    I will not bring a father-in-law
who scatters the sun's light and turns from a feast
    the sun's terrified team of horses.
Priam also has no father stained with blood
    from the slaughter of his wife's father,
nor has he a father who left in the wild
    Myrtoan surf a sign of his crime.
No ancestor of mine lunges for the fruit
    of the Stygian stream, nor does one
of mine bend over seeking to find water
    in the very middle of water.[20]
What good is this if one of theirs has you and
    Jove is father-in-law in this house?
Outrageous! For the length of the night that
    man unworthily keeps you and he
enjoys the closeness of your embrace, while I,
    I see you when the tables are spread
and even then I am hurt by many things.
    I can only wish that enemies
might enjoy such banquets as I have endured
    when the wine cups are put before us.
That I am a guest in his house pains me when
    that country fellow touches your neck.
And I swell up with envy – I will tell all –
    when he warms your shoulders in his cloak.
But when you kiss him before the company,
    I lift my cup in front of my eyes,
when he presses your body to his I drop
    my eyes and food I have not tasted
sticks in my mouth because I cannot swallow.
    How often I have groaned and then you –
I know how playful you can be – I noticed
    you could not stop laughing when I groaned.

How often I would have drowned my flame in wine,
　　but the blaze increased and wine became
fire added to fire. I try to avoid pain
　　by lying on the couch with my head
turned from you, but I find that I cannot keep
　　my eyes from looking at you again.
I do not know what I will do: seeing this
　　brings grief, but I grieve more when your face
is absent from my sight. However I can,
　　and with what strength I have, I struggle
to hide such madness. But my love reappears.
　　This is no deception, you know well
the hurts that are mine, indeed, you know too well.
　　I do wish that only you knew them.
How many times I have turned my face aside
　　when tears came so that man would not see
and ask the reason for my tears? How often,
　　after drinking, have I told of some
affair hoping you would see me in that tale
　　that you might learn something of my love?
Believe me, if you have not known before, I
　　was that lover. Indeed, I will be
still more honest and I will tell you more truth:
　　that I was drunk was only pretence.
Once, I remember, your robes fell open and
　　your breasts were revealed to my eyes – breasts
so much whiter than snow or milk or whiter
　　than Jove as he embraced your mother.
While I sat there enraptured by such beauty,
　　the wrought cup I held fell from my hand.
If you kissed your daughter, Hermione, I
　　hurried to kiss her young lips finding
there the kisses you had left.[21] And I would sing
　　of past affairs, reclined carelessly
on my back. And I would nod to you with signs
　　that should have remained hidden from all.
Most recently, I have tried to flatter your
　　friends, Clymene and Aethra. They said
only that they were frightened by all of this

and left me, my pleading unfinished.
    The gods should make you a prize in some contest,
        letting you become the victor's couch
as Hippomenes received his runner's prize,
        the daughter of Schoeneus, and
as Hippodamia was given over to
        a Phrygian's arms, as Hercules broke
the two curved horns of Achelous in the hope
        of winning your embrace, Deianira.[22]
My courage could have made its way boldly through
        challenges like these. You would have known
what it is to be the goal of my labour.
        As it is now, I have no choice but
to beg you, most beautiful one, and embrace
        your feet, if only you permit it.
Esteemed one, the glory of the twin brothers,
        worthy indeed to be wed to Jove,
if he were not already your ancestor,
        either I return to the harbour
of Sigeum with you my bride or I die
        exiled, covered with Taenarus' soil.
I have not been merely scratched by the arrow's
        deadly point, the wound goes to my bones.
I remember, it was this that my sister,
        always truthful, spoke in prophecy:
I would be impaled on a heavenly shaft.[23]
        Helen, I beg you, do not reject
a love established by fate; obey the gods
        so that they may listen to your prayer.
Though I can think of many more things to write,
        only welcome me into your bed
in the silence of the night and we can speak
        together, lying there face to face.
Perhaps you are ashamed and afraid to break
        the bonds of married love and be false
to a bed's purity that is yours by law.
        But that is too simple, even crude;
Helen, can you still think that beauty like yours
        can ever remain in chastity?

You must change, either your beauty or your firm
    resolution; beauty and virtue
are in contention. Jove and Venus both have
    found their delight in the sins of stealth,
and such a secret sin made Jove your father.
    If character is conveyed by seed,
the child of Jove and Leda could not be chaste.
    But you can be chaste, though not until
you have safely come within my Trojan walls;
    let your sin, I pray, be mine alone.
We will sin together now, but sin will be
    undone in the hour of our marriage.
My only prayer now is that the promise
    Venus once made to me will be true.
Your husband himself forces you to this by
    his actions, though hardly by his words:
that the guest may steal, he has removed himself.
    This was the only time he could find
to visit his kingdom on Crete. Surely he
    is a husband wonderfully shrewd.
'In my place, I commend to your care all of
    my affairs and our guest from Ida,'
he said, preparing to leave.[24] I swear to you,
    if you neglect the stated wishes
of your master, you do not care for your guest.
    Do you hope, Tyndaris, that a man
so dense will know the riches of your beauty?
    You are in error, he does not know.
If he valued what is his, he would not trust
    it to the hands of some foreigner.
Though you are moved by neither words nor passion,
    I am forced to seize the advantage
he gives. I would be foolish if I did not,
    more foolish even than your husband
if I were to let a time of such safety
    pass me by because of laziness.
Your lover has been brought to you almost by
    his guileless hands, seize now the moment.
Now alone, you spend the long nights on your bed

while I too am alone on my bed.
Be with me, enjoy with me our shared delights
    and that night will be brighter than day.
I will swear by any gods you choose and I
    will be bound by that oath to observe
the ceremonies which you prescribe and then
    I, unless I am false to our pledge,
I will myself plead with you to come with me
    as we together seek my kingdom.
If you are ashamed and afraid that it seems
    you have followed me, I will confront
this accusation without you for I will
    do as your brothers and Aegeus' son.
There is nothing closer to you than this for
    you were carried off by Theseus
and your brothers carried off the twin daughters
    of Leucippus.[25] All men will count me
as fourth to do such a thing. My Trojan ships
    are waiting, ready with arms and men;
in a moment they can be at sea driven
    on by beating oars and a fresh wind.
Through the towns of Dardanus you will travel
    in triumph like a great queen, and men
will think that earth has received a new goddess.
    As your party progresses, new flames
will be enriched with cinnamon; as it dies
    a victim will strike the bloody earth.
My father with my brothers and sisters and
    their mother, the daughters of Ilion,
and everyone in Troy will bring gifts to you.
    I can tell you only the smallest
part of what will come to pass; believe me, you
    will be given more than I can say.
And do not fear that if I steal you away
    terrible wars will pursue us as
Greece stirs up her mighty arms. Of all those who
    have been taken before, has any
one of them ever been followed by armies?
    I tell you now, your fears are foolish.

The Thracians seized the child of Erechtheus
    in Aquilo's name and Bistonia's
shores were safe from invasion; from the country
    of Phasis, Jason of Pagasa
carried off a maiden in his new-built ship
    and no men from Colchis journeyed then
to Thessaly for revenge. As he stole you,
    Theseus also stole Minos' daughter
but the men of Crete were never called to arms.[26]
    In matters of this kind, too often
the fear is so much greater than the danger,
    it is shameful to fear everything.
But suppose, if you wish, that a war breaks out:
    I too have power and deadly arms.
In no way is the wealth of Asia less than
    yours, we are rich in men and horses.
And Menelaus, the son of Atreus,
    will not have more energy than me
nor will he be thought superior to Paris
    in the business of combat. When I
was hardly grown to man's stature I regained
    our herds by killing an enemy.
For that I received the name I proudly bear.[27]
    While still a child I bested others
in the games, among these were Ilioneus
    and Deiphobus.[28] But if you think
I am feared only in the heat of conflict,
    my arrow can be placed where you choose.
Do you claim such deeds for his young manhood? Can
    Atreus' son lay claim to deeds like mine?
But if all fame were his, would he have Hector
    for a brother? Hector alone has
the strength and the courage of many soldiers.
    You cannot know my power and you
have never seen my warrior's skill in action.
    Though a bride, you do not know the man.
They will either demand that you be returned,
    but with no threat of war, or the Greek
troops will be forced to surrender to my skills.

For a bride like you I would quickly
take up arms for great rewards encourage strife.
If all the world were in contention
for one like you, you can be sure that your fame
will forever be known among men.
Now, be hopeful, put away your fear, leave this place;
take up this gift of the gods for they are with us.

NOTES

1. Venus (the Greek Aphrodite) was the goddess of love. Her son was Cupid (the Greek Eros) who was also known as Amor. Cythera, an island near the southern coast of the Peloponnese, was the centre of the principal cult of Aphrodite, and because of this she was sometimes called Cytherea. She was said to have been born from the waters of the sea. In citing Venus as the cause of his voyage to Sparta, Paris is also alluding to the promise made to him by Venus at the time he was called on to judge the beauty of the three goddesses, an event known as the Judgement of Paris.

Sigeum was a coastal town in the vicinity of Troy. While Sigeum was on the shore of the Aegean, Troy was set back from the sea.

Phereclus was the shipwright who built the ship on which Paris sailed from Troy.

2. Taenarus is a name sometimes used in a poetic context for Sparta.

3. The Fates were divinities who planned and set the pattern of events in every life. They were used to explain the fact that a man could not usually determine his own destiny.

4. At the time of Ovid, Ilion was simply another name for Troy.

5. Ida is a range of mountains in Dardania, near the site of Troy. The principal peak is called Mount Ida.

6. Dardanus was the son of Zeus and Electra and was born in the area in which the city of Troy was later built. He founded a city, Dardania, which seems later to have become part of Troy. Dardanus was revered by the Trojans as the founder of their city.

Mercury (the Greek Hermes), the messenger of the gods, was the grandson of Atlas and Pleione. His parents were Zeus and Maia, one of the Pleiades, who was the daughter of Atlas and Pleione.

Venus, Pallas and Juno are the three goddesses whose quarrel about which of them was the most beautiful was to be adjudicated by Paris. Venus was the goddess of love. Pallas, also known as Pallas Athena or simply Athena, was the virginal patron of war and art and the daughter of Juno and Jupiter. The Romans identified Athena with Minerva. Juno, the wife of Jupiter, was the Roman goddess of marriage and childbirth.

7. Tyndaris is a reference to Helen as a female descendant of Tyndareus, who was a Spartan king and the husband of Leda, Helen's mother. There is some irony in Paris' use of this name, since the commonly held myth was that the father of Helen was Zeus, who seduced Leda in the guise of a swan. It would seem that Paris here anticipates the way in which he will acquire Helen.

8. Phrygia was a vast area of Asia Minor which included much of Anatolia and had access to both the Aegean and the Black Sea. The Phrygians were allies of Priam's Troy. This close commercial and political relationship was reflected by the fact that Hecuba, Priam's wife, was of Phrygian ancestry.

Gargara was one of the peaks in the range of mountains called Ida. It was also the name of a town in the vicinity of Troy.

9. Cassandra was the sister of Paris, a younger daughter of Priam and Hecuba. As a young woman, she became a priestess of Apollo. In the course of performing her sacred duties, the god caught sight of her. Apollo, because he hoped to win her attention and ultimately seduce her, conferred on her the gift of prophecy. However, Cassandra rejected his attentions, causing him to curse her with the fate that though she would always prophesy truthfully, she would never be believed. In the course of her lifetime she was thought to be quite mad.

10. Oebalus was King of Sparta and the father of Tyndareus. Strictly speaking, Helen was not a nymph and the term is used here to refer to any young woman having nymph-like qualities. Perhaps Ovid is indulging his own sense of irony by describing as a nymph a married woman who has already borne at least one child. There was a pre-Homeric tradition that Helen was a goddess worshipped with her twin brothers, the Dioscuri, at Sparta. Helen as a literary figure originates with Homer for whom she is an entirely human character who, as the wife of Menelaus, was taken by Paris to Troy.

11. Lacedaemon was a son of Zeus and Taygete. He married Sparta and through her inherited the kingdom to which he gave his own name. He founded a city in that area and gave it the name of Sparta, after his wife.

12. As a very young woman, before her marriage to Menelaus, Helen was kidnapped by Theseus (see HELEN and THESEUS in Appendix I: Principal Characters) and Pirithous. She was rescued by her brothers, Castor and Polydeuces (or Pollux), the Dioscuri.

The palaestra was an arena set up for wrestling. It was surrounded, much like our boxing or wrestling rings, with an area for spectators as well as dressing rooms and baths. The games held in the palaestra were for men and the presence of a woman in such a place, especially a woman as beautiful as Helen, would have been most unusual. That she should have attracted the violent attentions of Theseus is not to be wondered at.

13. The Pleiad was Electra who, with Zeus as sire, bore Dardanus.

14. By making music on his lyre, Phoebus Apollo caused the walls of Troy to rise for Laomedon.

15. Achaia here refers to Greece. In antiquity, various areas of the Peloponnese were given this name, either in this or variant spellings. In the *Iliad* Homer refers to all men of Greek origin as Achaians.

16. Therapnae was a small town near Sparta which was said to have been the birthplace of Helen and the Dioscuri.

17. This refers to the myth of Ganymede who was an unusually attractive young man of the royal house of Troy. Though various accounts identify him as a son of nearly every Trojan king, it is most likely that he was the son of Laomedon. According to Homer (*Iliad*, XX.231–5), Zeus carried the young man to Olympus to serve as his cup-bearer. Many other accounts, however, add to this the observation that Ganymede was abducted to be the lover of Zeus.

18. Aurora (the Greek Eos) was goddess of the dawn. She was known for her amorous adventures with many men. One of her affairs was with Tithonus, one of the young sons of Laomedon. As a mark of special favour she won for him the gift of immortality, but she neglected to ask Zeus that he should also remain ageless.

19. Anchises was a Dardanian king. As a young man he was unusually handsome and thus attracted the attention of Aphrodite. Because Aphrodite had on many occasions ridiculed the gods and goddesses for their frequent infatuation with mortals, Zeus caused her to fall in love with Anchises. In disguise the goddess seduced Anchises and the child of that union was Aeneas.

20. These are references to the horrendous crimes which are to be found in the ancestries of both Helen and Menelaus. Paris is hinting, and not very subtly, that the father of Menelaus is the notorious Atreus. Because Aerope, Atreus' wife, was seduced by Thyestes, the brother of Atreus, Atreus slaughtered the unfortunate children of the union and served the cooked flesh to their unwitting father. At its discovery of this abomination the sun turned back in its course and Thyestes, learning of what had happened, cursed the entire house of Atreus. As Paris sees the situation, he could hardly be less desirable to Helen than Menelaus.

Paris also makes reference to the story of Pelops, who caused the death of King Oenomaus by bribing the king's charioteer, Myrtilus, to accomplish the murder. Later, Myrtilus reminded Pelops that Pelops had promised him half the kingdom and one night in the bed of Hippodamia in return for the death of Oenomaus. Pelops responded by throwing Myrtilus into the Myrtoan Sea, south of Attica. Each member of the house of Pelops: Atreus and Thyestes, Agamemnon and Menelaus, successively bore the curses that their ancestors had earned for their evil deeds. Finally, Paris refers to the torments of Tantalus, the father of Pelops, who was condemned because he murdered his son and served the boy's flesh at a banquet to which the gods were invited.

21. Hermione is the author of letter VIII. See HERMIONE in Appendix I: Principal Characters.

22. The story of Atalanta and Hippomenes is told in the *Metamorphoses*, X. Schoeneus was King of Boeotia. Atalanta, his daughter, was a renowned athlete who ran more swiftly than any other, man or woman. The oracle told her that she would be taken by a man and would lose all to him, never escaping his bondage. Therefore it was determined that any man who entered a race with her and lost would also lose his life, while the man who outran her would receive her hand in marriage. Many eligible young men entered the competition and lost both the race and their lives. Hippomenes entered the race, but as he ran dropped at various stages along the course three golden apples given to him by Venus. During the race, Atalanta stooped to retrieve each apple; thus Hippomenes won the race and her hand in marriage.

Hercules (the Greek Heracles) fought with Achelous, god of the river of the same name. The river god had two horns growing from his brow, which Hercules tore from the god's body. Both Achelous and Hercules came to the home of Oeneus, father of Deianira, to seek the hand of Deianira in marriage. The two exchanged insults and a fight broke out. Hercules won both the fight and Deianira.

23. In point of fact Paris will die in the Trojan War after being shot by an arrow from the bow of Philoctetes. That he persistently misses the import of various prophecies is a major flaw in his character.

24. Menelaus went to Crete because he wished to attend the funeral of Catreus, his maternal grandfather – the absence of Menelaus was not simply a foolish act on his part. That Paris should refer in so cavalier a manner to the sacrosanct law of hospitality is simply another example of his disordered conscience.

25. The Dioscuri abducted Phoebe and Hilaeira, the daughters of their uncle, Leucippus.

26. Erechtheus was King of Athens and his favourite daughter, Orithyia, was abducted by Boreas, the north wind, who was also known as Aquilo.

Boreas, who was convinced that the ways of gentle persuasion would have no impact on Erechtheus, let his stormy and harsh nature prevail and seized Orithyia, taking her to the land of the Cicones, in southern Thrace. Bistonia was a region of Thrace. Paris is saying that while the story was that Orithyia had been abducted by Boreas, in fact it was the Bistonians who had abducted and detained her. The tale is told in the *Metamorphoses*, at the conclusion of Book VI.

In his reference to Jason, Paris also refers to Medea, whose homeland was the city of Colchis in Phasis. See JASON and MEDEA in Appendix 1: Principal Characters.

Theseus abducted Ariadne. See THESEUS and ARIADNE in Appendix 1: Principal Characters.

27. Paris here refers to an attack on his flocks, when he defended both the sheep and the other shepherds; for this he gained the name Alexander 'the defender'.

28. A reference to the games which Paris entered at the time he was recognized as the son of Priam.

XVII: Helen to Paris

Helen's letter is written in reply to that of Paris and addresses the points and arguments made by him. It is interesting to note that her letter displays great worldly sophistication. Paris, both in his own letter and as he is described in Helen's, is obviously a man who acts impetuously and with little or no foresight. Helen, on the other hand, coolly reveals the practical consequences of every aspect of his suggestions. As Helen offers some encouragement, but with only the barest hint that the absence of Menelaus might be advantageous, it is obvious that her interests are on the immediate goods of a handsome body and an accomplished lover. It does not seem that she acquiesces in Paris' long-term plans; rather her interest seems to lie in a brief affair lasting no longer than the time that Menelaus will be away.

Almost bluntly, Helen rejects the offers of Paris. While he emphasizes the wealth she will have as his wife, she sees with great clarity the precarious position that will be hers in Troy. And of course she is never able to free herself of the fear that Menelaus and his Greek comrades will pursue them with war and destruction. But in spite of such protestations of practicality Helen does not deny the possibility of a clandestine affair in the house of the absent Menelaus.

The reader's imagination must bridge the gap between the close of this letter and her journey to Troy. Did Paris manage to overcome her every objection? Or did he in fact abduct her and transport her under duress? No explanation is given here and the question remains open. Ovid gives a partial answer in the opening lines of Book XII of the *Metamorphoses*, where it is said that Paris first seduced and then stole Helen away from her husband. Perhaps it is more accurate for us to see the event as one of theft, regardless of Helen's complicity or lack of it. Helen was not likely to leave Menelaus of her own volition; whether she went with Paris against her will or quite willingly, Paris was guilty of taking her away from Menelaus.

For Helen to move from her position as a virtuous wife affronted
by the unwanted and unwelcome attentions of a guest to that of a
woman who is at least interested in his beauty, she must have taken
several fateful steps. But the interaction between his desire and her
coquetry is profound. It would seem that no compromise is possible
between the two. The reader cannot be surprised that the persuasion
of Paris, coupled with his physical attractiveness and certainly aided
by the fleet he had brought, should prevail.

Since my eyes have been outraged by your letter,
   there is now no glory in silence.
You, an alien, have broken the sacred law
   of hospitality so that you
might trifle with a lawful wife's faithfulness.
     Surely, our shores of Taenarus gave
safe landfall when you were battered by wind-torn
   tides and, though you came from another
race, the doors of our royal house were not shut
   against you.[1] After such a welcome
your actions have become a most grave offence.
   Did you come as guest or enemy?
I do not doubt that though my reproach is just,
   you have decided that it is crude.
Then let me be rustic, I will keep honour
   that my life can be lived without fault.
Though I do not let you see a gloomy face,
   nor sit with wrinkled brows, my good name
still remains and I live my life without guilt –
   no secret lover brags about me.
So I wonder why you have such confidence
   in your scheme; what gives you such reason
for hoping that you might one day share my bed?
   Because Neptune's hero captured me
with such violence, must I now conclude that since
   I have been stolen once it is right
that I be stolen a second time by you?
   Had I been enticed, I would not be

blameless: I refused him nothing except that
    I refused to give him my consent.
But he did not reap the crop he had desired,
    I returned untouched except by fear.
Though a man with no shame, he took little but
    the few kisses I could not prevent.
Beyond that, he got nothing of mine. But you
    in your depravity would not be
content with so little – may the gods help me –
    that man was not so evil as you.
I was returned untouched and his modesty
    reduced the guilt that should have been his,
the foolish young man willingly repented
    of his rash deed.[2] Did Theseus repent
that Paris might follow in his steps so that
    my name remains always on men's lips?
But I am not offended, would anyone
    become angry with a new lover?
I only hope the love you profess is real.
    You can be certain that I know my
beauty is quite good reason for confidence.
    But I must harbour my doubts because
a too hasty trust will injure a woman,
    and they say you cannot be trusted.
You argue that others yield and a woman
    of chastity is indeed quite rare.
Why should I join that crowd to benefit you?
    If my mother seems to you to be
an example and if you think that you might
    sway me by citing her, you are wrong.
Her downfall came by deception: her lover
    was hiding within a bird's plumage.[3]
If I fell, I could plead no ignorance; no,
    there would be no doubt to mask my crime.
In good faith she erred, she herself paid the price.
    For what Jove would I say, 'happy fault'?[4]
And you go on, bragging of your descent, your
    distant forebears, and your royal name;
but my house glories in its nobility.

I say nothing of Jove, my husband's
ancestor, or of Pelops' glory, son of
    Tantalus or of Tyndareus.
Tricked by the swan, the bird she took to her breast,
    Leda gave me Jove as my father.
Now, tell us the first beginnings of your race,
    of Phrygians, Priam's Laomedon.
I revere each one of them, but he who is
    your greatest glory and fifth from you
is first before me among my ancestors.[5]
    Although I do not doubt the power
of Troy's regalia, ours is no less mighty.
    For certain, if this my native land
on balance has less riches and men than yours,
    yours remains a barbarous country.
It is true, your letter proffers gifts so fine
    the goddesses themselves might be moved
but if I cross the boundaries of honour
    I will instead have done it for you.
Either I keep always my unstained name or
    I go with you rather than your gifts.
I do not reject them; gifts are welcome when
    their donor makes them precious. I prize
more your love, the love that has caused your labour,
    the hope that led you over the seas.[6]
I can observe your insolent behaviour
    each time our tables are laid. Though I
pretend not to see, you gaze boldly at me
    and attack with eyes I hardly meet.
You sigh and then lift the cup closest to me;
    you drink from the same rim where I drank.
How often I have noticed the little signs
    your fingers make and how often have
I seen your brow send – almost words – messages
    meant for me. And how often I feared
that my husband too could see so that I blushed
    at the signals you did not conceal.[7]
How often I have murmured, or not even
    speaking have I thought, 'He is shameless.'

And what I said then was never false. And I
    have seen, traced on the table's flat top,
my name spelled in spilled wine, and there beneath it,
    the two words, 'I love'. I doubted this
and let my face show puzzlement – I have learned
    too well the language of expression.
These are the winning ways, had I sought to sin,
    by which you might have turned my desire,
by these my heart might have been made your captive.
    I confess, the beauty of your face
is without compare and any woman might
    with eagerness permit your embrace.
Let others have joy without blame, rather than
    let my honour pass to a stranger.
Learn from me, and live without pretty faces,
    seek virtue by forsaking delight.
Have you ever once thought how many young men
    must want what you desire but are wise?
Perhaps, Paris, only you have eyes to see.
    But you see no more clearly than they,
your boldness is more rash than theirs; your spirit
    is not greater, it is more assured.
I wish now that your swift ship had come when my
    hand was sought by a thousand suitors;
you would have been first if I had seen you then.
    My husband will pardon what I say:
you are a latecomer now, tardy to joys
    already taken and possessed; with
hope delayed, you seek what another man has.
    Even if I were your bride in Troy,
never think that Menelaus holds me here
    a reluctant and unwilling bride.
Do not batter my weak heart with your sweet words,
    do not injure one you claim to love;
let me keep the place I am given, do not
    shame me now by seeking my honour.
You claim to act out the promise of Venus,
    that somewhere in the wilds of Ida
three goddesses appeared naked before you:

that the first offered a kingly throne,
the second material triumphs, and the third said,
    'Tyndareus' daughter will be your bride!'
It is quite hard to believe that heaven's own
    would submit their beauty to your eyes,
but if true, then for sure the rest of your tale
    is a made-up thing, when I am said
to be the reward given you for your choice.
    I do not consider my beauty
so great that I should ever be the finest
    gift a grateful goddess could bestow.
I am content with knowing that my beauty
    is well thought of in the eyes of men;
if my beauty were to be praised by Venus
    I fear it would occasion envy.
But I will make no denial, I am pleased
    to hear the compliments you convey.
Why should these words that I write to you deny
    what is desired by my mind and heart?
Be not hurt that I am slow to believe you,
    faith should lag in things so important.
I am pleased if my beauty has been noticed
    by Venus and pleased too that you thought
me the greatest prize and also that you placed
    first neither the honours of Juno
nor those of Pallas after you had been told
    about the great beauty of Helen.
I am courage then, I am a famous throne.
    If I did not love a heart like yours,
I would be made of iron; but iron I am not,
    believe me, though I resist loving
one I have decided can hardly be mine.
    Why should I try, with a plough's curved share,
to turn over the wet shores and follow hopes
    denied to me by the place itself?[8]
I am not skilled at stealing love and never –
    I call the gods as my witnesses –
have I cleverly played with my husband's trust.
    As I confide these words to a speechless page,

this letter performs an unaccustomed task.
    Happy are those who come to such deeds
with ease; I, not knowing the ways of the world,
    think the byways of guilt must be hard.
Fear is heavy: I am confused, all eyes stare
    at me. I have good reason for this;
I have heard our people murmur evil thoughts
    and Aethra brings some of this to me.[9]
You: either hide your love or cause it to stop.
    But why should you stop? You can pretend.
Maintain your act, but maintain it in secret.
    The absence of Menelaus makes
me freer now but not yet totally free;
    his business required a far journey,
he had good reason for a quick departure –
    or so it seemed to me at the time.
In fact it was I, when he could not decide,
    who said, 'Go soon, but quickly return!'
Pleased by this and convinced, he kissed me and said,
    'See to my business and my household,
care for the guest who has come to us from Troy.'
    I nearly laughed aloud, I struggled
with mirth; there was nothing I could say to him
    except the simple promise, 'I will.'
Though he has set his sails in a good wind bound
    for Crete, all things are not as you wish.
Though my lord is absent, still he protects me:
    you know, a king's hands have a long reach.
My beauty oppresses me, for as your kind
    praises me, the more he rightly fears.
This delightful glory also condemns me:
    sometimes I wish fame had passed me by.
Do not wonder that he has gone and left me
    here, he has learned to trust my virtue.
My face gives him cause to fear, my life calms him;
    my virtue is his security
while my beauty arouses his deepest fears.
    You argue that opportunity
tendered so freely ought not to be wasted;

a simple husband should profit us.
I am torn between desire and proper fear;
    I have not decided, I waver.
My lord is gone, your sleep is lonely; beauty
    attracts you to me as me to you.
The nights are endless, and we have met to speak;
    you – poor me – utter compelling words
and we together live beneath the same roof.
    Let me die if all does not conspire
to cause my downfall; but fear still restrains me.
    I wish that you could compel me with honour
to do what you have so vilely invited.
    You should have dismissed at once the qualms
of my rude heart. It can happen that profit
    will come to those who suffer evil;
I might have been forced to accept happiness.
    Let us resist this new love; a flame
freshly lit dies quickly if sprinkled with just
    a little water. A stranger's love
is not dependable, like him it wanders
    and when it seems most sure, it is gone.
I call Hypsipyle as witness, I call
    the Minoan virgin as witness,
both of them left to languish in wedding-beds.[10]
    Unfaithful Paris, it is said you
have abandoned Oenone whom you cherished
    as your wife for so many long years.[11]
You have not denied this. I have spent much time
    making careful inquiry of you.
If you tried to be a faithful lover, you
    would fail because you are unable.
As I write this letter, your Phrygian sailors
    are outfitting your ships; while you speak
to me anxiously of that night you desire,
    the winds blow that will take you away.
Hardly begun, you will leave pleasures still new;
    your love for me will go on the wind.
Should I come with you as you suggest and see
    for myself that Pergamum you praise

so highly?[12] Should I be wed to the grandson
    of mighty Laomedon? Be sure
I would not so ignore men's published words that
    I would let them fly over the earth
announcing my shame to all. What will Sparta
    or what would all of Achaia and
what would the people of Asia, your Troy, say?
    How would Priam and his wife and your
crowd of brothers with Dardanian wives see me?
    And you, how might you hope that I be
faithful, unaffected by your example?
    As every alien ship is beached
in Ilion's harbours, you would be plagued by fear.[13]
    How often your fear will prompt anger
to say, 'Adulteress,' forgetting your charge
    against me is also against you.
You will be the judge and the cause of my fault
    because you will have led me to sin.
I pray, before something so awful occurs,
    may earth be shovelled over my face.
But, you argue, I will have for my pleasure
    Ilion's great wealth and a rich life;
and I am to be given gifts surpassing
    even your extravagant pledges.
Most precious purple and fine gossamer cloth
    is to be mine and I will be rich
with a measure of gold in heaps. Forgive me,
    I must say it, your gifts are not worth
all that much to me. The land you scorn holds me.
    Who will come to me there on the shores
of Phrygia with nurture if I am hurt?
    When I am there, in your native land,
where shall I find brothers or a father's help?
    Lying Jason promised everything
to Medea, but she was then thrown out of
    Aeson's house. Aeëtes was not there
to welcome the maiden to her childhood home,
    nor was her mother Idyia nor
her sister Chalciope waiting for her.[14]

Though such is not quite what I fear, still
Medea too set out without any fear.
    Good hope is deceived by its omens.
Every ship that is pitched by the stormy waves
    left its harbour on a gentle sea.
And I am frightened by that torch, the bloodied
    torch borne by your mother in a dream
on the day before she began her labour.
    I quail at the words those holy men
put to this strange vision; I am told they saw
    this as a sign that Ilion would burn
with flames brought to it from Pelasgus.[15] And as
    Cytherea indulges you because
she triumphed and won two prizes for your choice,
    so now do I fear those other two
whose causes – if your bragging is true – were lost
    when you gave utterance to your judgement.[16]
If I were to follow you, I have no doubt
    that war would follow in my footsteps;
alas, love would pick its way through many swords.
    Did Hippodamia of Atrax
force the men of Haemonia to wage a war
    against the Centaurs?[17] Do you suppose
that Menelaus with my twin brothers and
    Tyndareus would be slow to take
action when driven by such righteous anger?
    For all your boasts and talk of valour,
your handsome face puts the lie to your speeches.
    Your body belongs to Venus more
than Mars.[18] Let the valiant man march to battle,
    Paris lives only that he might love.
Let Hector, whom you admire, fight in your place;
    your skills require another campaign.[19]
Such ability I could make use of if
    I had wisdom or something more bold.
But it will be used by any wise maiden,
    or I, forgetting my modesty,
will acquire wisdom and then, worn out by time,
    I will yield and surrender to you.

You ask that we discuss these things secretly,
   meeting face to face. I understand
quite well what it is that you desire and what
   you intend by having speech with me.
But you are too rushed, the harvest is still green;
   perhaps delay will befriend desire.
Enough of this. Let the written words that share
   my heart's secret cease their hidden task;
my hand is tired: what remains for words can be said
through my loyal companions, Clymene and Aethra.

NOTES

1. Taenarus was a high point in Laconia, the southernmost area of the Peloponnese. Sparta was situated inland and due north of this place. Certainly the area would be an appropriate landing-point for a ship coming from Troy.

2. This is a reference to Theseus, who was said to enjoy the protection of Neptune. The Theseus described by Helen – considerate, almost shy, of her virtue and maiden's condition and, finally, modestly repentant – is not the Theseus we encounter throughout antiquity. Of course, it is to Helen's credit that she remained virginal during and after her abduction by Theseus. See THESEUS in Appendix I: Principal Characters.

3. According to the myth of Leda and the swan to which Helen refers, Zeus became enamoured of Leda. Because she was already the wife of Tyndareus and presumably a woman of virtue and integrity, Zeus took the form of a swan and in this guise seduced her. Traditionally, Helen and her twin brothers, Castor and Polydeuces, were said to be the offspring of Zeus, though their paternity differs in various accounts.

4. Helen argues that because Jove (the Greek Zeus) came to Leda in disguise, her consent to the union did not compromise her integrity. On discovering the identity of her partner Leda presumably could only have described the affair as a happy – or perhaps fortunate – fault. In Helen's eyes now, it is nothing more and certainly could not have been anything less.

5. Helen points out that Jove is her father, while Paris is fifth in line of descent from Jove. Customarily, however, Paris is shown as seventh, through Dardanus, Erichthonius, Tros, Ilus, Laomedon and Priam.

6. It is important to note here that Helen is not so much rejecting the attentions of Paris as rejecting his offer of a new marriage. She is not at all

averse to the declaration by Paris of his love for her, but she avoids the implication that she must leave Menelaus. Clearly, the emphasis placed on material goods is significant to the development of the story. While Helen professes to want only love, for both Paris and Menelaus the presence of love is best demonstrated by the availability of great wealth.

7. The point made here is important to the love tradition. The love, separate from eroticism and material possessions, is adulterous and clandestine. At this point in the letter, Helen wishes it to remain non-erotic and non-sinful. Throughout this passage Helen reveals herself as the faithful and dutiful wife, sophisticated and wise in the practice of hospitality. Her easy admission that she finds Paris very attractive is an important clue to her state of mind. However, the time for choosing rich and attractive partners has passed.

8. That is, why should she attempt something so hopeless as trying to turn a furrow in wet sand and see it all come to nothing? If something like this cannot be done, so also something so hopeless as loving another when marriage has already been contracted must not be undertaken. Helen consistently argues her great innocence in the face of such worldly temptation.

9. Aethra was one of Helen's companions, probably a servant.

10. Hypsipyle, Queen of Lemnos and daughter of Thoas, met Argonauts when they landed on her island from the *Argo*. She later bore twin sons to Jason. (See letters VI and XII, and the entries for JASON and MEDEA in Appendix I: Principal Characters.)

The 'Minoan virgin' is a reference to Ariadne, daughter of Minos, King of Crete. She saved Theseus by betraying both her father and her homeland. (See letter X and the entries for ARIADNE and THESEUS in Appendix I: Principal Characters.)

Both Hypsipyle and Ariadne were seduced by foreign lovers, strangers to their shores, who made them grand promises and pledges of fidelity only to abandon them when the two women had given them everything.

11. Oenone, the fountain nymph, was the wife Paris left behind in Troy. (See letter V, and the entry for OENONE in Appendix I: Principal Characters.) It is obvious that Paris remained loyal to her only until such time as the goddess offered him something more desirable. Clearly, his ethical standards were less than exemplary.

12. Pergamum was the central fortification, the citadel, of Troy.

13. Ilion was an alternative name for Troy.

14. Aeson was the father of Jason, Aeëtes the father of Medea.

15. In this context, Pelasgus is another name for Greece.

16. Cytherea is another name for Venus. It derives from the fact that her

principal shrine and reputed birthplace was the island of Cythera. The two prizes won by Venus were, first, the golden apple and, second, the decision that she was indeed the most beautiful.

17. Hippodamia was the daughter of Oenomaus, King of Elis. Pelops, son of Tantalus and a Phrygian, won her in a chariot race with her father. He won the race after bribing one of Oenomaus' attendants to loosen the wheels of his master's chariot. Paris makes reference to Hippodamia in letter XVI where she is cited as an example of a woman who was won by a man, rather than voluntarily choosing him as her lover and companion. Hippodamia is also mentioned in the *Metamorphoses*, Book XII, as being the wife of Pirithous and the daughter of Adrastus. The battle between the Lapiths and the centaurs occurred at the wedding feast of Hippodamia and Pirithous. The point made here is that seduction and abduction, even outright rape, while not so uncommon, always carry the possibility of a terrible revenge.

18. Venus was the Roman goddess of love, Mars the Roman god of war.

19. Hector, the most eminent of the Trojan warriors, was the eldest son of Priam and thus the elder brother of Paris.

XVIII: Leander to Hero

Though Leander writes with all the foolhardy daring of an adolescent, he also displays a very thorough and sophisticated knowledge of mythology. But while he is remarkably astute in his ability to cite characters whose love ended in disaster, he seems quite unable to see himself as another in that long line. Leander, as the reader knows, will die because he is convinced that his strength and courage are invincible. That Leander and Hero both wish to keep their love affair secret only increases the certainty of his death because they effectively deny themselves the counsel of anyone wiser than they.

One might imagine that Leander and Hero wish to maintain this secrecy because they expect the opposition of their respective families. This possibility, however, is never developed except at the beginning of this letter where Leander merely refuses to allow his parents – and all of Abydos – to see him set out for Sestos. While there could well be compelling dynastic reasons to prohibit their liaison they are never made explicit; therefore we may conclude that these are two very young people whose initial experience of adult sexuality is something they do not wish to be known.

The eroticism of this letter emphasizes the youthful sexuality of Leander and is of an intensity we have not seen before in the letters. In this respect Ovid is making a new departure in the *Heroides*. Leander is a very young man for whom the experience of sexuality is almost overpowering. The simplest action – stripping himself and stepping into the sea, for instance – becomes a sensual experience that echoes the sexual experience. Towards the end of the letter Leander recognizes the risk he contemplates, yet even then he finds an almost perverse pleasure in imagining Hero caressing his broken body. Young love may be beautiful, but it is also irrational and dangerously uncontrolled.

If only the seas fell, one from Abydos
    would carry to a girl from Sestos
the greetings that he must send with another.[1]
    If the gods regard me with favour,
if they have care for my love, the eye that reads
    these words must read them reluctantly.
But the gods are unkind: why would they delay
    my pledges, why would they not permit
me to rush through waters so well known to me?
    You yourself can see: the skies blacker
than tar and the narrows torn up by the wind,
    no hull is willing to raise a sail.
One boatman only – he a man of courage,
    he who will rush this letter to you –
will set out from the harbour. I would have sailed
    with him, but as he throws off the lines
from his mooring, all of Abydos will watch.
    I would not escape my parents' gaze
as I did before; the love we have kept hid
    would too soon be known to everyone.
As I wrote these final words, I said: 'Go forth,
    happy letter, and before long she
will take you into her graceful hand. Perhaps
    you will be touched by her lips as she
hurries to break your seal with her snow-white teeth.'
    I muttered such words under my breath
while letting my right hand write out other words
    on the sheet before me. But how much
I wish that hand could swim rather than write and
    carry me on the waves I have known.
Better that hand for stroking the peaceful depths,
    though it serves now my feeling for you.
For seven long nights, it seems more than a year,
    the sea has been disturbed with hoarse cries.
If even once I have let sleep soothe my heart,
    may I be kept still longer from you.
I am sitting on a rock sadly gazing
    at your shore; my thoughts carry me off
to a place my body cannot reach. Indeed,

I see or think I can see lights set
in the very top of your tower. Three times
    I have laid my clothing on the sand,
three times, naked, I have entered the surf and
    as I swam with the boldness of youth
my head was covered over by the storm's force.
    Harshest of all the winds, why do you
make war against me? Boreas, it is I –
    perhaps you did not know – not the waves
against whom your fury is hurled. But if love
    were unknown to you, what would you do?
Are you able to deny that at one time
    even you were burned by Attic flames?[2]
How would it have been with you if when you sought
    joy, someone had closed to your passage
the air? Would you ever have permitted it?
    Spare me, release a more gentle breeze
and the child of Hippotes will give to you
    no harsh commands.[3] But I waste my prayers,
he hears them with murmuring and the waves he
    has summoned up in this vile tempest
are in no way abated by him. I wish
    that Daedalus could give me bold wings
though the shoreline of the Icarian Sea
    is near to this place.[4] I would suffer
Whatever the future brought if I who wait
    by the waves could have the gift of flight.
While both wind and wave deny my every wish,
    I remember the first times I came
secretly to your shores. Night had just fallen –
    that memory gives pleasure to me –
I slipped out of my father's doors intent on
    pursuing the ways of my new love.
I hardly paused, I stripped off my garments and
    as they fell so my fears also fell;
with strong arms I struck out against the water.
    Like a faithful servant, the moon lit
my path with a flickering glow as I swam.
    I lifted my eyes to her and prayed:

'Favour me, goddess of brilliance; let the rocks
    of Latmus rise up before your eyes.
Endymion, I'm sure, would not want you hard
    of heart. I beseech you, turn your face
to help me in my secret love. You, goddess,
    fell from the skies to find mortal love –
I pray that I can recite it truthfully –
    I seek one who is a goddess too.[5]
Without mentioning virtue that is divine,
    only the divine have charm like hers.
After the beauty of Venus and you, no
    other beauty is greater than hers.
You may doubt my words, only look for yourself.
    As every other star is less than
your brilliant flame when your silver light shines forth,
    so much is she more beautiful than
all others. Cynthia, if you can doubt this, then
    the brilliance of your light leaves you blind.'[6]
Words like these I spoke, or words not much different
    as I sped on through waters parting
easily before the stroke of my strong arms.
    The waves were brilliant with the moon's face
and the silent night became bright as the day.
    No voice, no call, came to me; no sound
could I hear but the soft rippling of the waves
    turned over by my rushing body.
Only the alcyons, with hearts faithful still,
    to the beloved Ceyx raised their sad song.[7]
But then my arms felt weakened where they are joined
    to the shoulder and with all my strength
I lifted myself to the crest of the waves.
    I saw, far off, a light: 'My love shines
in that distant flame; it is my love that is
    harboured there on that distant shoreline.'
With that, new strength flowed into my weary arms
    and the same wave was easier now.
Love helps me, warming my eager heart that I
    will not be chilled by the water's cold.
As I approach, the shoreline approaches me;

I come close and my joy increases.
When you can see me as I see you, I find
    new heart and new strength in my body.
I strain myself to give you pleasure, I lift
    my arms for you to see as I swim.
Your nurse can hardly stop you at the surf's rush.
    No one told me this, my eyes saw it:
though she held you back, she could not keep your feet
    from stepping out in the water's edge.
You take me in your arms' embrace and we share
    happy kisses – kisses, great gods, that
were well worth seeking across the sea's expanse –
    then you take from your shoulders clothing
to warm my shivering flesh and with your hands
    you wipe the sea from my dripping hair.
What remains to tell, only night knows and we
    and the tower that keeps our secret
and the light that opens a path through the tides.
    Like weeds growing in the Hellespont,
I cannot count the joys I found in that night.
    How little time we had for the theft
of that first love, and how much more care we took
    that time not pass us in idle waste.
Too soon, Aurora, Tithonus' bride, prepared
    to chase the darkness of night away
and Lucifer, preceding dawn, had risen.[8]
    Without order we rush our kisses
complaining because the night will not permit
    even a little delay. I wait
until your nurse shrilly forces me to go.
    I leave the tower and make my way
to the cold shore. Weeping, we part and I step
    into the virgin's sea looking back
as I swim into the tides.[9] Going to you
    I swam in strength and ease; leaving you
I swam exhausted, tired, like a man shipwrecked.
    I tell you, it seems now that I am
always gliding toward you but my return is
    across a steep slope of dead water.

Unwillingly, I come back to my own land;
    unwillingly, I wait in this town.
Why are our souls joined while the waves divide us?
    We are of one mind but of two lands.
Sestos should take me or Abydos you; your
    home is dear to me as mine to you.
Why am I disturbed when the sea is disturbed;
    why should a mere wind detain me here?
The graceful dolphins already know our love
    and I must be known to every fish.
By now my usual path through the waters
    is worn like a road pressed down by wheels.
I complained that this was the only way, now
    I complain that the winds prevent this.
Huge rollers foam and a moored boat is not safe
    in the wild sea of Athamas' child.
These waters must have been like this when they took
    from the drowned maiden the name they bear.
Sufficient is the notoriety that
    has come to this place for Helle's death;
though it lets me live, its evil name shames it.
    I envy Phrixus carried safely
by the ram with golden fleece over the storm
    yet I seek neither ram nor a ship
if I can but part the waves with my body.
    I lack nothing. If I can swim I
am both crew and ship, I have taken passage.
    My path is not set by Helice
or by Arctos, the Tyrrhian's guiding star;
    my love has no need of pilot stars.[10]
Another can sight on Andromeda, the
    bright Crown and the Bear of Parrhasis
gleaming in the frozen pole.[11] But as for me
    I have no concern for Perseus
and his loves or for Liber and Jove, to set
    out a treacherous path for my love.[12]
Another light, now, gleams brighter; it leads me
    in the dark, my love's path is not lost.
While my eyes are on such a beacon, I could

swim to Colchis or the farthest shores
of Pontus and that place where a ship of pine
   from Thessaly maintained its long course.[13]
By such light my swimming will exceed even
   young Palaemon and he who tasted
the unusual grass and found himself a god.[14]
   Many times my arms are wearied by
the endless stroke and can hardly go on through
   the endless waters. When I tell them,
'Your reward will not be poor, for you will have
   the neck of my lady to embrace,'
they find strength and reach for the prize like a horse
   just let out of the chute in Elis.[15]
I keep my eyes fixed on the love that burns me
   guided by you, worthy of the skies.
Though you too are destined for the starry skies,
   you must linger here until you guide
me to the gods above or tell me the way.
   You are on earth still but your lover
has only a miserable share in you;
   when the sea is stirred up by the storms
my heart also is stirred up. What good is it
   that the sea is narrow? It parts us.
Such a little span of water is no less
   an obstacle thrown across my way.
I almost wish all the world were between us:
   as we are closer to each other,
closer is the flame that burns me; I have hope,
   now, instead of her for whom I hope.
Reaching out my hand, I almost touch her hand;
   she is so near, but 'almost' starts tears.
How was catching for fleeting fruits and sucking
   at a vanishing stream different?[16]
Am I never, then, to clasp you unless the
   breaking wave gives leave? Will I never
be happy when the tempest blows? Though nothing
   is more fickle than wind and the sea,
must I consign hope to the wind and waters?
   But it is still the time of summer.

How will it be when the sea is assaulted
    by the Pleiad, Arctophylax and
Capella's flock?[17] Perhaps I am foolish and
    do not understand what will happen;
perhaps my foolish love will cause me to go.
    If you think I make a hollow threat
because I might not yet be ready to go,
    know – my pledge to you will not be late.
Let the tides be high for just a few nights more
    and I will try to make my crossing
without any regard for the breaking waves.
    In my happy adventure I will
be safe or the end of my troublesome love
    will be marked by my death in the sea.
I pray that my lifeless body be tossed up
    on that shingle and that my shattered
bones may find safe harbour on your distant shore.
    You will shed tears over my cold flesh;
you will not hesitate to caress my corpse
    with the words, 'I was his cause of death.'
This awareness of my impending death must
    frighten you and this letter I'm sure
displeases you. Enough of my complaining:
    only, I beg you, pray with me that
the sea's anger may end. I need a little
    break in the storm while I cross to you.
When I step out of the surf, let the storm rage
    again. You are the right dock for me;
no waters are safer than you for my keel.
    When I am there we will let Boreas
close the port in a place where delay is sweet.
    When I am there, I will not hurry
to swim away: I will take care, I will not
    shout accusations at the deaf waves;
I will never again complain that the sea
    has become too rough for me to swim.
Let both the tempest and your arms keep me there –
    two reasons shall prevent my escape.
When the storm subsides my arms will become oars;

be sure to keep the beacon burning.
Until then, may these words comfort you through the
   night;
most solemnly do I pray that I follow soon.

NOTES

1. Abydos is on the south-eastern side of the Hellespont, Sestos on the opposite side. The Hellespont, a strait in north-east Turkey joining the Sea of Marmara with the Aegean Sea, is now more commonly known as the Dardanelles. Because its channel is narrow in relation to the size of the two bodies of water which it joins, the flow between the two seas can be extremely dangerous, especially for a swimmer or a small boat.

2. Ovid tells in the *Metamorphoses*, VI, the myth of Boreas, the north wind, and Orithyia of Athens. Even in this story, Boreas is cruel and harsh. When he tries to win Orithyia by kindness and gentleness he feels rebuffed by her and by her father Erechtheus, even though Ovid notes that Boreas did not pursue his suit with much vigour. After this Boreas resorts to his usual tactics of persuasion, violent storms and anger, and in a storm carries Orithyia off to his icy domain.

3. Aeolus, ruler of the winds and the god who is superior to Boreas, was the child of Hippotes. Jove had once confined Boreas to the cave of Aeolus and the suggestion being made here by Leander is that it could happen again. The story is told by Ovid in Book I of the *Metamorphoses*.

4. Daedalus, the father of Icarus, was a master builder who went to Crete to build the labyrinth in which to confine the Minotaur. After the work was completed King Minos detained Daedalus and his son Icarus. To escape, Daedalus fashioned wings, made from wax and feathers, for himself and the boy. As they flew away from the island Icarus flew too near the sun, the wax melted, and the boy fell into the sea which now bears his name – the Icarian Sea – and died. Leander writes that even though Abydos is not far away from the place where Icarus died – the closeness is a bad omen – he would be willing to take any risk necessary to cross the Hellespont.

5. The moon observed the young Endymion asleep on Mount Latmus. So taken was she with the beauty of his masculine form that she caused him to sleep on forever so that she could gaze at him each time she passed overhead. In this context Leander's reference to the myth must be read as an ironic foreshadowing of his own death.

6. The Romans sometimes referred to Diana (the Greek Artemis) as Cynthia, after the hill of Cynthus on the island of Delos where she was said to have been born.

7. The alcyons were birds who lived on the sea, and it was thought that they nested on the surface of the water. Hence their presence was thought to calm the sea. Alcyone was the wife of King Ceyx, the son of Lucifer, the morning star which rises in the east just before dawn, but the ceyx was also a bird, probably the tern, that lives on the sea. The image of Alcyone is one of the faithful wife; at the death of Ceyx by drowning, Alcyone threw herself into the sea and she too was drowned. The story is told by Ovid in the *Metamorphoses*, XI, and is also found in Chaucer's *Legend of Good Women*. In another version, Alcyone was said to be the daughter of Atlas and Pleione, one of the Pleiades, and was seduced by Neptune. The point of convergence of both versions is that the woman was injured by the violence of the sea.

8. Aurora, goddess of the dawn, abducted. Tithonus, Priam's brother. By him she bore Memnon and Emathion, who became kings of Ethiopia and Arabia. Some accounts say that Tithonus also fathered Phaethon. In her great love Aurora petitioned the gods to confer immortality on Tithonus, but she carelessly neglected to ask that he should remain ageless. When he began to show his advancing years, she left him for other, younger lovers.

9. The 'virgin's sea' is the Hellespont, which was named for Helle, the sister of Phrixus; they were the children of Athamas and his first wife, Nephele. When they fled from their wicked stepmother Ino, Helle and Phrixus were carried on the back of a great ram with a golden fleece (it was this fleece which Jason later sought and eventually secured). As they travelled over the sea Helle lost her hold and fell into the strait that came to have her name.

10. Helice was the constellation Ursa Major, or the Great Bear. Arctos is the joint name for the two constellations Ursa Major and Ursa Minor.

11. The 'bright crown' is the Northern Crown, the Corona Borealis. This constellation was believed to have been the crown of stars given to Ariadne by Dionysus when they married.

The Bear of Parrhasis, another name for Ursa Major, is a reference to the myth of Callisto, who was changed into the constellation Ursa Major.

12. Perseus, the constellation, was named after the son of Zeus and Danaë. Perseus rescued Andromeda when her father had chained her to a rock in the hope of appeasing a sea-monster.

Liber was one of the names given by the Romans to the Greek god Dionysus. In conjunction with Jove, the suggestion here is one of reckless promiscuity. In earlier times, Liber was one of the Roman gods of fertility.

13. Colchis was the homeland of Medea and the place to which Jason went in search of the golden fleece. Pontus is Pontus Euxinus, or the Black Sea. The term 'pontus' can refer to any large area of ocean.

The reference to a ship of pine from Thessaly suggests the *Argo*, the ship on which Jason and the Argonauts sailed across the Aegean to Colchis in Asia Minor.

14. Palaemon was a god of the sea. Athamas, the father of Helle and Phrixus, fathered a son called Melicertes by his second wife, Ino. Ino finally went mad and leapt into the sea with this child in her arms. Like Ino, Melicertes became a deity of the sea and was re-named Palaemon. As a god, he was said to come with his mother to the aid of sailors in distress.

Glaucus was originally a fisherman who ate a herb which was unfamiliar to him and was transformed into a god.

15. The horse races that were run on Mount Olympus in Elis formed part of a religious festival.

16. This is an ironic reference to the myth of Tantalus and his punishment in the Underworld. The answer to the question posed by Leander is simple – there is no difference between his situation and that of Tantalus.

17. The Pleiad is a constellation of stars, the seven Pleiades. Its appearance on the horizon was associated with the onset of rainy (here, stormy) weather.

Arctophylax is the constellation Boötes, which is also known as the Bear-keeper.

Arctos was the name given to the constellations Ursa Major and Ursa Minor, hence their keeper would be Arctophylax.

Capella is a star found in the constellation Auriga, which is also known as the Charioteer. 'Capella's flock' is a reference to the other stars that surround Capella in the constellation.

Each of these astronomical references has an association with storms and turbulent seas.

XIX: Hero to Leander

It would seem that it is Hero's letter which prompts Leander to begin swimming the Hellespont. Although after the opening lines the letter repeatedly expresses her fears for his safety, it must be read as a strong incentive for Leander to set out. Hero even accuses him of being a man of leisure who is only occasionally concerned with love, and a little later she reproaches him for not taking advantage of a break in the weather. But before this complaint at his failure to swim the strait, Hero describes, in a way that strongly recalls the Fates who spin out the length of men's lives, the night-time vigil which she and her nurse keep. There is a palpable suggestion that the night will come when Leander, urged on by Hero's pleading, will swim to his death while she passes the time spinning yarn and chattering inanely to her nurse.

But Hero is not consistent. She no sooner chides Leander for what seems to be a new-found caution than she worries that he will take unnecessary risks. She wants Leander present with her but she fears the risk his presence entails. She finds herself caught on the horns of a dilemma and she is afraid she will lose him as he hurries to her side. Hero concludes with the hope that if Leander cannot set out at least he will be consoled by her letter. Ironically, it is more than likely that it will have quite the opposite effect.

Hero describes a dolphin which has been washed up dead on the shore. Suggesting as it does the myth of Dionysus and the pirates, it provides an insight into the disaster about to be enacted. But where Dionysus escaped their assault when the pirates were turned into dolphins, who were said to nurture and befriend the seafarer, this dolphin has been killed in the stormy sea and can certainly provide no security for Leander, as it might have done for Dionysus. Hero appears to be unaware of the myth and of the symbolic role this dolphin might possibly play in their lives. While the myth resonates in the letter, we know that Leander will not be saved. Hero sees the dolphin as an image of the sea's destructive power, and it is by this sign that Leander should be saved; but we know that he will not heed this warning. When Leander is lost at sea no dolphin will rescue him.

Hero is one of the naive heroines in the *Heroides*. She is quite knowledgeable about her own emotional state and she understands the reality of the love she feels. She does not, however, comprehend the way in which Leander experiences love and she quite fails to understand the impact which her letter is almost certain to have on him. In the conversation with her nurse which she recounts in such detail she appears almost silly, speaking without real thought. In the lines which follow she masterfully dissects the twinned experience of love and fear. But she is innocent of any understanding of the motivation for his actions. If it can be argued that it is this letter which precipitates Leander's attempt to swim the strait, then it must also be argued that it has become the unwitting instrument of his – and her – destruction.

Both Hero and Leander in their letters make reference to the story of Alcyone. This is important because the myth foreshadows the events which will come to pass. Like Ceyx, Leander will drown in the sea; like Alcyone, Hero – as we know from other sources – will drown herself when she learns of Leander's death.

> Come Leander, that I might enjoy in fact
>   the greeting your letter has brought me.
> All delays of joy are too long; forgive me,
>   I cannot wait patiently for love.
> We burn with the same blaze but I am weaker
>   than you, for men have a greater strength.
> Like our bodies, women's spirits too are frail;
>   any more delay and I will die.
> Men like you are now caught up in the chase or
>   now caring for a pleasant acreage,
> you spend long hours in your many affairs.
>   Either the market holds your interest,
> or the contests of the wrestling mat, or you
>   turn the neck of a fine, well-trained horse.

You snare a bird or hook a fish and relax
    at day's end with a cup of fine wine.
For me, denied these pastimes, even if I
    were not so enflamed, I could but love.
What remains, I do: I love you, my one joy,
    with more love than you give back to me.
I whisper about you to my old nurse, as
    I wonder why you have stayed away
or I look out over the sea and I scold
    the waves turned up by a hostile wind,
using words so much like the words you have used.
    And when the sea's mood is a little
less fierce, I fret that you should come but will not.
    In my complaint, tears begin to flow
from the eyes that love only you, and the old
    woman who knows my secret gently
wipes them away from my face with her frail hand.
    I search the shoreline for your footprints
as if wet sand could keep an old impression.
    Asking every man if anyone
has come from Abydos, or if anyone
    will soon leave for Abydos, I try
to learn more that I may better write to you.
    I should not tell how often I kiss
the garments you left by the water's edge as
    you prepared to swim the Hellespont.
Thus, when day's light is gone and night's more friendly
    hour hangs out the glimmering stars and
overcomes the daylight, I hurry to set
    on the roofline of our house the lamps
that will watch for you, the beacons that will guide
    you along the way you came before.
Then we two, women, twist our spindles and turn
    wool to yarn through the long hours of night.
And what do I say during such a long wait?
    My lips form only Leander's name.
'Tell me, nurse, has my delight stepped from his door,
    or is the house awake and watchful
so that he waits for fear of his family?

Now, perhaps, he removes his warm robe
and rubs precious oils, the fruit of Athena,
 into the strength of his arms and legs.'[1]
She nods and seems to agree, my kisses mean
 little, she dozes, her old head sinks.
A pause, then, 'He must be setting out, spreading
 the waters with the stroke of his arms.'
My spindle reaches the floor, I have finished
 a few more lengths of yarn and I ask
whether you have come half-way across the strait.
 I look out to sea. In a low voice
I pray that a kind breeze will hurry your trip.
 I hear strange noises and all the time
I am certain you have already arrived.
 Finally, most of my night has passed
in such deceits and sleep slips over my eyes.
 Perhaps, my unworthy lover, you,
though unwilling, spend the night with me, perhaps
 you came, though you did not wish to come.
It seems that you swim nearer to me, and now
 it seems your wet arms have touched my neck;
it seems I throw my warm cloak over your flesh
 and that at last I warm your body.
I could say more, but a modest tongue stops and
 says nothing while memory delights;
words spoken now would bring a blush to my face.
 But how swiftly these pleasures have passed;
they are not the truth because you always leave
 as our sleep comes to a sudden end.
Let our anxious love be tied up more tightly
 that joy may be more faithful and true.
Why have I spent so many cold nights alone,
 why are you so often far from me?
I know, the sea is not a swimmer's sea, but
 last night the wind became more gentle.
But you did not come. Why were you fearful of
 what was not? Why did so fine a night
pass by and you did not begin your voyage?
 I pray that you will soon have many

more chances to come, though this time was better
    because it came upon you sooner.
'But,' you might say, 'the surface of the peaceful
    depths changes swiftly.' You often came
in a shorter time when you hurried to me.
    If you had been caught here by the storm,
I am sure you would not complain and while you
    held me close no storm would injure you.
Indeed, at that time, I would joyfully hear
    the wind as it raged and I would pray
that the waters might never again be calm.
    What has happened now? You are become
more cautious of the tides, it seems that you fear
    the sea that once you held in contempt.
I remember one time you came when the surf
    was no less dangerous – or perhaps
only a little less – and I cried to you,
    'If you are always so reckless with
good luck, I fear that I in misery will
    one day shed tears for such great courage.'
But from where does this new fear come; to what place
    has that boldness you once displayed gone?
I ask you, where is that wonderful swimmer
    who often defied the winds and tides?
On the other hand, be as you are rather
    than as you were; make your way to me
when the sea is calm, be safe. Just be the same,
    just let us love as you write to me;
just let it be that this flame burning in us
    will never burn down to cold ashes.
I do not fear the gales that impede my vows
    so much as I fear that your love will
stray like a fitful wind or that I be found
    unworthy of love. I fear the risk
you take will outweigh the reason for that risk,
    and my value to you be too small.
At times I fear that the place of my birth might
    bring harm, that it will be said that I,
a maid from Thrace, must not be wife to a man

from Abydos. I could bear all things
if only you do not delay, held captive
    by the charms of another mistress;
with arms other than mine twined about your neck,
    a new love ending the love we know.
Better that I die than I be wounded by
    such as this, may I be caught by fate
before you accept such a burden of guilt.
    Not because you gave signs this pain would
be mine, nor because rumour worries me, I
    say this because I fear everything.
Has any lover ever been free of care?
    Fear for those who are gone is worsened
when the distance is great. Happy are those who
    by their presence know what is truthful
and thus cannot fear what they only suppose.
    Imagined injuries beset me,
what is real and what is true I do not know:
    both errors equally tear my heart.
If only you would come, if only I knew
    that storms or your father – no woman –
kept you there. But if it were a woman and
    I knew, be sure that grief would kill me.
If my death is your desire, then you must sin
    against me with no further delay.
My fears of such calamities are silly
    because you will not commit this deed.
You have not come because a spiteful storm beats
    you back to your shore. Poor me: this beach
is beaten by a great surf and blackest clouds
    wrap up the day in hiding. Perhaps
Helle's devoted mother came to the sea
    and grieves now with rushing tears the death
by drowning of her child or maybe
    the stepmother, become a goddess,
tears at the sea that has been given the name
    of the stepchild she hated so much.[2]
These waters, as they are today, are hardly
    kind to gentle maids. In these waters

195

Helle met death, from them comes my own trouble.
Neptune, recall the flames of your heart
and you will not let love be hampered by wind.[3]
If the fables of Amymone
or Tyro, ladies much praised for their beauty,
are attributed to you, or of
bright Alcyone, or Calyce, or of
the beautiful maiden, Medusa,
before vipers were twisted into her hair,
or golden-haired Laodice and
Celaeno who was taken up to the skies
or those others of whom I have read –
but surely, Neptune, these and many more like
them, as the songs of the poets go,
have at some time wrapped their soft embraces in
your embraces.[4] After all this, why
have you, you who have so many times enjoyed
the power of love, shut up with storms
the pathway we have learned to follow to love?
Spare us, rash one, engage your battles
far out upon the open seas. This water
between our lands is all too narrow.
One so mighty as you should harass great ships
or perhaps disturb an entire fleet;
it is shameful for the god of the great sea
to frighten one so young as he swims.
What you gain by such an act is less glory
than you would get troubling a still pond.
He is of noble birth and renowned family,
but the wily Ulysses whom you
cannot trust is nowhere a part of his line.[5]
Take pity on him and save us both.
He will swim, but the arms of Leander and
my hope hang together on that wave.
The flame of my lamp drops down then rises – look,
I write with it near my hand – it first
falls then flares up, I find in it good omens.
See, now, my nurse is sprinkling the flame;
she watches it closely. 'By tomorrow's light,'

she says, 'there will be one more of us.'
At that, she drinks the cup of wine. I beg you,
    make us more than we are, glide across
the sea that you conquer, you whom I have let
    come into the welcome of my heart.
Return to camp, you who have left love, your friend;
    why should I sleep in my bed's middle?
With nothing to fear, Venus will favour you;
    she who was born of the sea will smooth
out for you the pathways of the sea.[6] Often
    I think that I will step in the waves
but I know this strait is safer for men. Why
    was it that Phrixus and his sister
both rode over this place, but the maid alone
    left her name on these stormy waters?
Perhaps you fear that time will pass too quickly
    for your safe return or strength will fail
before the doubled labour is done. Let us
    then meet midway and exchange kisses
on the cresting waves before returning both
    of us to the towns from which we came.
Little enough, still it is more than nothing.
    I wish this shyness that hides our love
could end or that we gave up a kind of love
    that makes us fear the words men might say.
As it is now, our passion and our concern
    for what is said of us are at war.
Which of these I will follow cannot be said,
    one is proper, the other is joy.
As swiftly as Jason entered Colchis, he
    took the maiden away in his ship;
as swiftly as that lover from Troy arrived
    in Sparta, he rushed his prize away.[7]
But you, you found your love then left her behind;
    when ships cannot sail, you swim alone.
My young lover, though you conquer the waters
    still you must live in fear of the sea.
Ships carefully built can be easily sunk;
    can your two arms have more strength than oars?

Leander, you are eager to swim but that
    is what a sailor fears above all
because the sailor swims when his ship is wrecked.
    Poor me. I do not want to convince
you to come to me as I urge; may your strength
    withstand my pleading. But finally
you must come to me, throwing about my neck
    those arms weakened by the pounding sea.
But each time I look out over the blue waves
    my frightened breast is seized with a chill.
And a dream frightens me still, though I have made
    sacrifice to keep its threat away.
Just before dawn, when my lamp was burning low,
    a time when dreams most often are true,
my fingers opened, the yarn slipped to the floor,
    and I laid my head down, fast asleep.
How clearly I could see: a dolphin swimming
    in the stormy sea was cast up on
the dry sands and water and life itself left
    the miserable thing abandoned.[8]
I am afraid of whatever this might mean
    while you – do not laugh at these my dreams –
do not put your arms to sea unless it be
    that you can swim in a tranquil sea.
If you cannot save yourself, at least preserve
    this cherished maid whose safety is yours.
Now the surf begins to be weary, I hope
    this means that a calm will soon be here.
Part its gentle ways with every strength that you
    can summon to your aid, come to me.
Until the ocean's swells let the swimmer set out,
let my letter ease the awful hours of delay.

NOTES

1. Olive oil is produced by crushing and pressing the olive. The olive
tree is sacred to Athena in recognition of a myth concerning Athena
(commonly identified with Minerva by the Romans) and Poseidon (the

Roman Neptune), who competed for selection as the patron deity of Athens. Each presented valuable gifts to sway the choice: Poseidon caused a salt spring to flow on the Acropolis and Athena produced an olive tree. It was decided that this was the more useful gift, and the city was given to Athena. The Athenians, however, prudently maintained a shrine of Poseidon on the Acropolis.

2. For Nephele, the mother of Helle and Phrixus, see note 9, page 188. At last, Ino and Athamas were made insane by Hera and killed their own children. Ino finally leapt into the sea but was saved from death by being made a lesser deity, Leucothea or the White Goddess, who lived with the nereids. Clearly Ovid is echoing this tradition in Hero's brief reference to Ino. However, the allusion is heavy with irony because in point of fact Leander will not be saved by the ministrations of Leucothea.

3. Neptune, god of the sea, earthquakes and horses, was notorious for his many affairs and liaisons.

4. Amymone was one of the daughters of Danaus. When Danaus settled Argos he sent his daughters out in search of water. Amymone, however, allowed herself to be distracted and eventually gave chase to a deer. She threw her spear, but instead of striking the deer she struck a satyr who pursued her. At this, Neptune appeared, frightened off the satyr, and in his turn gave his attention to Amymone, whom he seduced.

Tyro, the daughter of Salmoneus and Alcidice, grew to maturity in the house of her uncle, Cretheus, who in time took her as his wife. However, she became enamoured of the river-god Enipeus, and Neptune exploited her by appearing to her in the form of Enipeus and seducing her. The story is referred to in the *Odyssey*, XI. 235–59, where Odysseus, on a sea-coast, summons up the ghosts of the dead with propitiatory sacrifice.

For the story of Alcyone, see note 7, page 188. In his letter (XVIII), Leander also makes reference to the story, though his reference is from a different point of view. Another story of Alcyone has her the daughter of Atlas and Pleione, one of the Pleiades. In this story Alcyone was seduced by Neptune. The point of convergence for the two stories is that in both, the woman was injured by the violence of the sea.

Calyce was the mother of Endymion. She was a daughter of Aeolus and hence associated in this passage with the sea and its storms. At this point, however, the textual tradition is confused. Dörrie (op. cit., see note 2, page xx) gives a number of variant readings (page 252), as does Showerman (op. cit., see note 3, page xx), page 268. Clearly, the point of the passage is that Ovid is enumerating a variety of amorous situations which have involved Neptune and the violence of the winds and the seas.

Medusa was once a beautiful girl who lay with Neptune in a place sacred to Athena. To punish the girl, either because Medusa had allowed herself to be seduced in Athena's shrine or because her great beauty caused Athena to be envious, Athena turned Medusa's hair into snakes and made her face so ugly that a mere glimpse of it turned men to stone.

Laodice was the daughter of Priam and Hecuba who, after the conquest of Troy, fell into a chasm and was never seen again.

Celaeno, the daughter of Atlas and Pleione, bore a child to Neptune. Celaeno was a sister to Alcyone, who had also been seduced by Neptune.

5. This allusion to Ulysses recalls the episode in the *Odyssey* of Ulysses and Polyphemus, the Cyclops (I. 68–79 and IX. 105–566). Polyphemus, who was blinded by Ulysses, was the son of Poseidon. Though Ulysses was clearly fighting for his life and the lives of his men against a horribly barbarous adversary, the deed earned for him the awful enmity of Poseidon. While trickery and deceit were a way of life for many of the characters of myth, Ulysses was particularly renowned for his cunning. In her letter (I), Penelope refers to this characteristic.

6. Venus (the Greek Aphrodite) was the goddess of love and the mother of Cupid, or Eros. She was born from the waves after Kronos had castrated his father Uranus and flung the genitalia into the sea.

7. In abbreviated form, this passage refers, first, to the expedition of Jason and the Argonauts to Colchis where they seized the golden fleece and, second, to the voyage of Paris to Sparta where he abducted Helen. To accomplish the theft of the golden fleece, Jason had the indispensable assistance of Medea. The treachery and deceit with which this was accomplished necessitated stealth as well as haste. Similarly, the allusion to Paris and Helen contains many of the same elements. It is noteworthy, however, that most accounts of both Medea and Helen have the women going quite willingly, if not eagerly, with their paramours, while Hero here seems to suggest that some coercion may have been involved. It is also noteworthy that at least in the story of Jason, the primary objective at the beginning of the voyage was not Medea but the golden fleece. From Hero's point of view, it would be natural to assume that both voyages were undertaken solely to accomplish an abduction.

8. The image of the dolphin suggests the myth of the Tyrrhenian pirates who kidnapped the youthful Dionysus as he travelled by ship from Icaria to Naxos. Suddenly the ship was stopped in its course with its sails still billowing before the wind. The sailors heard music and were astonished to see the ship suddenly entwined in ivy and grape-vines. Beasts next appeared on the ship's deck. Terrified, the crew leapt into the sea and were all changed into dolphins. Because the dolphins had once been human, they remained after that solicitous for all human beings.

The significance of the dolphin here is that a beast which is most at home in the water, and which is also concerned for the safety and well-being of men, could not survive. If the dolphin could not survive, then Leander certainly could not.

XX: Acontius to Cydippe

Acontius opens this letter by arguing that the oath recited – albeit unwittingly – by Cydippe is binding and should now be obeyed. While the letter has a legalistic ring to it, the reader must know that Acontius' argument does in fact turn the very notion of law on its head. Acontius is very frank about this when he refers to Love (i.e. Cupid, or Eros) as a lawyer who has taught him new tricks. In the eyes of Acontius, then, the law is a mass of trickery to be manipulated to his own advantage. If the law can be so manipulated, then the trickery he has used to win Cydippe is at least tolerable if not actually a good thing.

The idea of law has never been far from any of these letters, whether it be a code deduced from self-perception or a law imposed by statute. And certainly the suggestion that the beloved ought to be bound suggests not only being tied with ropes but also the idea of a bond or a surety given to guarantee the performance of some act. The letters of the *Heroides* (with the probable exception of XIII: Laodamia to Protesilaus) are concerned with a great variety of deceits that tailor objective facts to subjective desires. In each of these letters there is some failure of imagination to effect a correspondence between the mind and the reality it hopes for.

Part of the discontinuity between the mind of Acontius and the world about him is manifest in the way in which he perceived Cydippe. Though he is greatly attracted to her feminine beauty, he also describes her as a hunted quarry, something to be captured in a trap, or snared, or even brought to ground by weapons. Later, however, he lays the blame for all this at the feet of Cydippe, whose beauty has inflamed his passion. In other words, Cydippe has no one but herself to reproach for the misery she is now experiencing. In just a few lines Acontius has made his victim the villain of the piece.

But no sooner does he assert his overbearing masculine strength before which Cydippe is certainly helpless than he insists that he is a slave in her presence; that he is helpless, reduced to tears, quite overcome by her great strength. His only fear is that she might injure her delicate hand as she attacks him. Finally, Acontius blames the man to whom Cydippe has already been properly betrothed by her father.

At one point in the letter Acontius does admit that perhaps he has some responsibility in the matter. However, his response to that awareness is not that he should allow Cydippe to forswear her oath. Quite the contrary; he asserts that he is more than willing to bear the guilt for her misery as long as she can be his. If a penalty must be exacted for a broken oath, he hopes that he can be the surrogate victim.

So blinded by passion is Acontius that nothing can possibly sway him. He has made certain choices in the hope of attaining his goal and he will not deviate. Every moral and legal consideration is set aside so that the only morality he acknowledges is the morality which will result in his gratification. For Acontius, love is indeed blind to everything except its own satisfaction.

Do not be afraid! Reading this will not cause
    you to swear another lover's oath.
It is enough that you were pledged to me once;
    read on to the end and as it ends
so may the faintness that besets you pass on.
    That you should feel any pain, pains me.
Why blush before you venture into these words?
    I do suppose your cheeks have reddened
now as they did in Diana's holy place.
    What I want from you is not a crime
but the bond of marriage and the faith you pledged:
    my love is the love of one betrothed
and not the love of a common deceiver.
    Recall the words brought to your pure hands
by the fruit which I picked and threw before you.
    What you promised then, maiden, I wish
you, rather than the goddess, will remember.

My desire is no less strong. Sharpened,
the flames of my love are stronger and passion –
    never a small thing – is large, nurtured
by delay and the hope you have given me.
    Hope you gave because my eager heart
put all its hope in you. Do not deny this;
    the goddess herself is my witness.
Present as she was there in her holy shrine,
    she took note of your words and she seemed –
by the movement of her hair – to accept them.
    I will let you claim to be deceived,
deceived even by my tricks, but you must see
    those tricks as evidence of my love.
What other reason for tricks except that I
    should by them be made as one with you?
What you complain about will join you with me.
    Neither by nature nor by training
could I have such wiles; it is you, maiden, who
    has caused me to discover these skills.
If by this act I have gained anything, it
    was Love, such a clever one, who tied
you to me with a few words written by me.[1]
    He wrote the bond of our betrothal;
Love became a lawyer and taught me new tricks.
    Call this act 'craft' and let me be called
'clever' just as long as the desire to have
    what one loves can be called cleverness.
This is the second time I write pleading words;
    and again you have cause for complaint.
If you are injured by my love, I admit
    that I will injure you forever
and I will always work to win you over
    even though you fight my advances.
Other men have taken maidens with the sword;
    is this my secret letter a crime?
May the gods put into my hands more fetters
    that I can bind you up more tightly
so that at last the pledge you have given leaves
    you with nothing that might be freedom.

There are a thousand tricks still at hand; waiting
  to begin my climb I only sweat,
my eagerness for you leaves nothing untried.
  Perhaps you cannot be won; at least
the winning will have been attempted by me.
  Now it is in the hands of the gods;
however, I am sure you will be taken.
  Perhaps you will miss some of the traps
set for you by Love, but you cannot escape
  all the snares which he has set for you
in greater number than you can imagine.
  If craft will not suffice, I will use
weapons so that you can be seized and carried
  far away in my longing embrace.
I will not scold Paris nor any other
  who became a man that he might have
what every man should have. But I say no more.
  Perhaps death is a just punishment
for one who steals you, still death is lesser than
  the pain of never possessing you.
Had you been one of lesser beauty you would
  be sought more modestly. By your charm
I am driven to such boldness. All of this
  has been caused by you: you and your eyes,
burning brighter than the stars in the sky and
  the reason for my burning love, and
your golden hair, your throat of ivory and
  your hands which I pray touch my neck and
your pretty face, demure but not common and
  your feet, hardly a match for Thetis.[2]
I would be happier still if I had such
  knowledge that I could praise other charms
but I am certain that in its many parts
  your body has such beauty as these.
Before beauty like this, it should not seem strange
  that I have sought your pledge of marriage.
Finally, then, only admit that you are caught
  and I will let you say you were caught
by deceit. I can bear the weight of my guilt

just allow the bearer his reward.
Should such an accusation lack its payment?
    Telamon received Hesione,
and Briseis was taken by Achilles –
    each recognized her victor as lord.[3]
You may scold, you may be angry as you wish,
    only let me enjoy your passion.
As I cause your rage, so too will I bring ease;
    give me just a brief chance to soothe you.
Allow me, please, to weep before your face and
    let me shape words to go with my tears;
allow me to reach out my hands to your feet
    like a slave fearful of a lashing.
You do not know your own strength, just summon me.
    Why am I accused when I am not present?
Call me before you, be an angry mistress.
    With your own commanding hand you may
tear my hair, and with your fingers bruise my cheeks.
    I will submit to anything and
my only fear is that your delicate hand
    will be injured in striking at me.
But do not bind me up in shackles or chains,
    my only bond is my love for you.
When your anger has been satisfied in full
    you will say, 'His love for me still lives.'
When you see me bear all of this you will say,
    'A slave so fine can become my slave.'
In misery now, I am accused without
    my presence; my case, though good, is lost
because there is no one to appear for me.
    And furthermore, no matter how much
my words injured you, it is not only me
    of whom you should utter your complaint.
The Delian does not deserve betrayal
    by you. If you cannot be faithful
to me, at least be faithful to the goddess.
    She was there and she certainly saw
you blush as you stepped into my snare; your words
    reside in her remembering ear.[4]

May the omens you see now be without cause.
    There is nothing more savage than she
when she sees – what I hope she will never see –
    her deity scorned and insulted.
I call as my witness Calydon's wild boar:
    he is savage but not so savage
as that mother whose anger was turned against
    her own son.[5] Actaeon, too, I call
as witness: once he was thought to be a beast
    by those with whom he had hunted beasts.[6]
And last, I call to testify that haughty
    mother, turned to rock, who to this day
stands, weeping, on the soil of Mygdonia.[7]
    Cydippe, it is my sad burden
to tell you the truth, though it may seem to you
    self-serving of me to speak like this.
You must know why you are often ill as you
    approach the day set for your marriage.
The goddess causes this, she would not permit
    your oath to be forsworn, she wishes
that you be kept safe by keeping your faith safe.
    Every time you would break your oath, she
steps in to prevent your fault. Do not invite
    the virgin's cruel bow, you can still
make peace with her, if only you will permit.
    Do not waste your body with fevers,
preserve the beauty of your limbs for my joy;
    preserve that face that was born to light
my love, preserve the blush that slowly rises
    to colour cheeks that are white as snow.
If my enemy or anyone would keep
    you from my arms, may they suffer as
I have suffered when you have been ill. Whether
    you marry or whether you are ill,
my torture is the same; I cannot say now
    which of these dreadful things I want least.
There are times when I am stunned with grief that I
    might cause you pain and that my deceits
might be the cause of your hurt. Let the burden

of that broken oath be mine, I pray,
let the awful penalty fall on my head:
    I pray only that she may be safe.
But I do not wish to be kept ignorant
    of your condition. I lurk about
before your closed door, stealthily I follow
    both your chamber-maid and serving-boy,
asking them if sleep or perhaps a light meal
    has worked some change in your dismal health.
Poor me, I am not the one to carry out
    the wishes of your physicians;
I cannot sit beside your couch caressing
    your hands. Miserable me, when I
am far away from you, perhaps another
    one I would not want is by your side.
Yes, it must be he who holds your hands, he who
    sits by you in your sickness. He is hated
both by me and by all the gods in heaven.
    While his finger feels your beating pulse,
he holds your fair arms. Then he touches your breast
    and perhaps he even kisses you.
For giving to you a service such as this
    the price that is paid is far too great!
Who allows you to reap this crop before me?
    Who opened another's fields to you?
Those breasts are mine; the kisses you take are mine.
    Do not touch the body pledged to me.
Wicked man, take your hands from her, she is mine;
    you risk the charge of adultery.
Find another among those who are not claimed;
    I tell you, these assets have a lord.
You may not believe what I say. Read the words
    of our agreement and if you think
it false, then let her read out the words for you.
    Leave the room that is another's, leave,
I tell you. Why stand beside another's bed?
    Though you possess another contract,
one just like mine, do not think your position
    in the affair is equal to mine.

Though her father promised her to you, it was
    she who gave herself by pledge to me.
Though he is her father, surely she is more
    herself than he can ever be. While
he promised her, she gave herself with an oath;
    his witnesses men, hers a goddess.
He has a fear of breaking his word; her fear
    is that she perjure herself. Can you not see
which of these two must be the more serious?
    Even though you might try to compare
the two dangers, observe their situation:
    her health is shattered and he is well.
And we – you and I – are met though we have come
    to this struggle with different intent.
Our hopes and our fears both are quite unequal;
    your claim is made without risk to you,
while for me, rejection would be worse than death
    because I came to this already
loving her while you can only hope that you
    will one day come to have love for her.
If equity were your first concern, or if
    you had any care for what is right,
you would have stepped back and given my passion
    your permission to stand in first place.
But his heart, Cydippe, still remains unmoved;
    how then am I to close this letter?
He has caused your wasting illness, it is he
    who puts you in Diana's peril.
If you are wise, you will close your doors to him;
    because of him you face these hazards.
I wish that he who caused such an awful plight
    might himself perish rather than you.
Deny him, refuse your love to one condemned
    by the goddess and I will be safe.
Forget your fear! Respect the place of your pledge
    and you will receive good health because
it is not by oxen slain in sacrifice
    that the holy ones above are pleased,
but rather fidelity to bonds given

by us even without a witness.
To find good health, some maidens are quite willing
    to endure the pain of steel and fire;
others seek a dismal solace in bitter
    potions brewed from the juices of plants.
You need none of these: keep your pledge and avoid
    false oaths, you will save yourself and me.
The fault you have already committed will
    be absolved by your ignorance for
surely the contract you recited had slipped
    from your mind. But now you have been warned
both by this my letter and by the sickness
    you suffer as you elude the vow.
But even if you escaped these perils, would
    you, when you labour to deliver,
call on her, seeking help from those radiant hands?
    She will hear your cries: remembering
what she has heard before she will ask which man
    has brought you to such pain. You will pledge
a gift in return for her assistance but
    she knows your word is not honest. Then
you will swear an oath; still the goddess will know
    that you can deceive even the gods.[8]
It is not for myself that I am concerned –
    I carry a greater load of care –
for you alone my mind is greatly troubled.
    Why is it that when you are at risk
your fearful parents weep though they do not know
    your sin? Tell your mother everything.
Cydippe, do not blush because of your deeds.
    Only tell her the way that first you
were known to me while she offered sacrifice
    to the bearer of the quiver.[9] Tell
her how, when I first saw you – if you noticed –
    I stood, unmoving, gazing at your
beauty; tell her how, while I stared eagerly –
    a sure sign of love's insanity –
my cloak slipped from my back and fell to the ground
    and somehow then an apple with sly

words cleverly scratched across its skin rolled out;
    tell her then how those words were read out
before the deity of Diana and
    the goddess was witness to your pledge.
Perhaps, even after this, she will not see
    the gravity of these words; repeat
for her the words that you once read out. 'Marry,
    I beg you,' she will say, 'him to whom
the kindly gods joined you. He whom you have sworn
    to marry shall be my son-in-law.
Let him become our choice, whoever he is,
    for he is the choice of Diana.'
If your mother truly is your mother then
    words like these will be that mother's word.
But be sure that she makes careful inquiry
    of me, from where I come, my manner;
then she will know the goddess had only you
    and your house as her foremost concern.
Cea, an isle bounded by the Aegean
    and once inhabited by the famed
Corycian nymphs, is the land of my birth.[10]
    And if your people have high regard
for an aristocratic name, it cannot
    be said that I am descended from
men of low reputation. We too are rich
    both in wealth and in our worthy name.
But even if none of that existed, I
    am bound to you all the same by love.
Even without your oath, you would always hope
    to have for a husband one like me.
But you have spoken your oath and though I were
    something other, still you should have me.
These words Phoebe, she who wields the darts, told me
    in a dream to write in a letter.[11]
Awake, it was Love that caused me to write you
    these words. I am already wounded
by the arrows of the one; you must take care
    that the other's darts do not hurt you.
The health of each of us is bound together:

take pity on me and on yourself;
why would you delay in giving help to both
    of us at the same time? If you can do this,
on that day when the fanfare sounds and Delos
    is drenched with the blood of sacrifice,
a golden image of that lucky apple
    will be offered to the goddess and
the reason for its sacrifice will be set
    out in the words of two little lines:
'By this copy of the apple Acontius
    swears, what once was written now is done.'
Enough: that your frail body not be wearied more
by a letter too long, let me close with 'Farewell.'

NOTES

1. This is a reference to Cupid (the Greek Eros), the god of love and the
son of Venus. Cupid was normally depicted carrying a bow and arrows with
which he caused men and women to fall in love.

2. Thetis was a minor goddess of the sea who figured in many myths. She
was chosen to marry a human, Peleus, the Thessalian king. To take her in
marriage, however, it was necessary for Peleus first to subdue her because she
had the capability to change her appearance at will. Peleus, however,
overcame this obstacle and finally married her. All the gods and goddesses, as
well as many eminent mortals, were invited to the wedding feast. But an
invitation was not extended to Eris (or Strife). Angered, she threw into the
party a golden apple with an inscription, 'For the fairest'. The goddesses
Hera, Athena and Aphrodite each assumed the apple was meant for her. As
Eris had planned, a quarrel between the three and their partisans broke out.
It was decided that the three goddesses and the apple should be taken to
Paris, son of Priam, where he was tending his flocks on Mount Ida. In what
is known as the Judgement of Paris, he chose Venus, thereby accepting the
bribe she offered him – of Helen for his bride – and the Trojan War ensued.
By Peleus, Thetis was the mother of Achilles. To render him immortal,
she dipped the infant into the river Styx. All of his body became invulnerable,
except for the heel by which she held him. In battle before the walls of Troy,
Achilles finally died because Paris managed to strike him in the heel with a
poisoned arrow.
The reference to Thetis recalls the fact that she was reputed to be a great

beauty. This, coupled with her ability to change her appearance, obviously enhanced her attraction. The effect of the reference here is to evoke for the reader a rich pattern of allusion which Ovid in fact never elaborates. Thetis figures in the *Metamorphoses*, XI, XII and XIII.

3. Telamon, one of the Argonauts, was also a participant in the Calydonian boar hunt. The most important episode in the story of Telamon, however, concerns his presence with his friend Heracles in the Greek forces at Troy. Telamon was the first of the Greeks to enter the conquered city. For this marvellous feat, he was awarded as booty the maiden Hesione.

The story of Achilles and Briseis is told earlier (letter III). See ACHILLES and BRISEIS in Appendix I: Principal Characters.

4. The goddess Diana (the Greek Artemis) had her principal shrine at Delos and hence was often called 'the Delian'. The virginal Diana was the patroness of all things that were untamed, as well as of birth and generation. Her identity is well outlined in Catullus' *Hymn to Diana* (XXXIV, 'Dianae sumus in fide . . .'). Ben Jonson described her as 'Queen and huntress, chaste and fair'. Women in childbirth had a particular devotion to Diana.

5. Calydon was the primary city of Aetolia. During the reign of King Oeneus it was the practice to make sacrifice to the gods from the first fruits of the harvest. Inadvertently, one year Diana was not included in the ritual. Greatly angered by this oversight, the goddess sent a huge boar to harass the populace. This beast so terrified the residents of Calydon by ruining crops and killing both men and their livestock that the people of the area would not venture into their fields when the time came for the spring planting. In desperation Oeneus sought help from the neighbouring cities and offered the skin of the boar as trophy to the hunter who drew the first blood. Among the hunters was a woman, Atalanta. Her presence caused several of the men to withdraw because they refused to hunt with a woman. The son of Oeneus, Meleager, forced them to rejoin the hunt. According to some accounts Atalanta made the first strike, but it is generally agreed that Meleager killed the animal and the pelt was then awarded to him. Because he was already in love with Atalanta, Meleager in turn gave the pelt to her as her rightful prize. At once, the other hunters renewed their objection to the role of a woman in the hunt and Meleager found himself and his city at war with his neighbours, the Curetes. The forces of Calydon were victorious as long as they were led by Meleager. However, Meleager accidentally killed several of the brothers of Althaea, his mother, and she in her anger and grief cursed him. Meleager then refused to fight. The Curetes attacked the city and Meleager was finally persuaded to take his place at the head of his city's troops. The attack was turned back, but Meleager was killed. This account is in the *Iliad*, IX.543–99.

In another version of the story, to be found in the *Metamorphoses*,

VIII.268–546, the victorious Meleager gives the boar skin to Atalanta. At this juncture the brothers of Althaea stole it from her and Meleager killed them in revenge. At this murder his mother became enraged and remembered the log whose consumption by fire, it had been prophesied, would cause Meleager's death. She took the log from its hiding place, threw it into a roaring fire, and Meleager quickly died in great agony. Althaea, stricken then with remorse, killed herself, as did Meleager's wife, Cleopatra. The sisters of Meleager and the other women of the household mourned his death extravagantly until Diana took her final revenge by turning them all into a kind of guinea fowl, known as *meleagris*.

6. As a young man, Actaeon was taught the art of hunting. In some way he managed to offend the goddess of the hunt, Diana, probably because while in the woods he discovered the goddess bathing in a mountain pool. So that he could not boast of this, Diana changed him into a stag and he was attacked and killed by his own pack of dogs.

7. According to Showerman (op. cit., see note 3, page xx), page 282, this is a reference to 'A "weeping Niobe" rock ... in Mygdonia, a province of Phrygia'. Niobe was the mother of many sons of whom she was unusually and overbearingly proud. She insulted the goddess Leto (the Roman Latona) with her claim to have more and better children than the goddess herself. Leto then asked her children, Phoebus Apollo and Diana, to avenge the insult. This they did by killing at least some of Niobe's children. Unable to stop weeping, Niobe was turned to stone. The story is told in a number of sources, but especially in the *Iliad*, XXIV.605–17, and in the *Metamorphoses*, VI.146–312.

8. Diana was often called on by women in childbirth as they sought a swift and easy end to their labour. Acontius clearly argues that if Cydippe persists in denying the oath that was witnessed by Diana, she will not only be incurring the enmity of the goddess – as evidenced by the strange illness besetting her – but will also be forced to forgo the assistance of the goddess at a time when assistance will be greatly needed and very much desired.

9. A reference to Diana and her shrine in which the affair of the apple took place. Diana was usually depicted carrying a hunting bow and a quiver of arrows.

10. The Corycian nymphs, who once lived on the island of Acontius' birth, were the daughters of Plistos, and they finally came to inhabit the Corycian Cave on Mount Parnassus, a place that was sacred to the god Pan, as well as to all the nymphs. The Corycian Cave is mentioned by Ovid in the *Metamorphoses*, I.320ff., as the place of safety to which Deucalion and his wife Pyrrha came by boat when the gods flooded all the earth.

11. Phoebe was, originally, one of the Titans. In later accounts, she was identified with the moon and with Artemis, the sister of Phoebus Apollo.

XXI: Cydippe to Acontius

Cydippe writes her letter to Acontius within the context already set by him: an oath has been read out before the goddess and Cydippe has been entrapped by Acontius in a struggle between him and another suitor. But Cydippe makes a shift in emphasis that denies the very validity of such an oath — a nice point of law — and then she recognizes the fact that two men are suddenly in contention for her hand. At the outset Cydippe does not seem to object to the fact that she has been betrothed to a man chosen by her father but not by her. As the letter progresses, however, we realize that she is more and more attracted to Acontius, the strange man who played a most unusual trick on her in the shrine of Diana at Delos.

Though Acontius certainly attributes her sickness to the anger of a goddess scorned, it is obvious in Cydippe's letter that she, while preserving the myth, is also deeply conscious of the reality underlying it. Her illness is one of emotional origin; she is trapped between two men and as yet she has chosen neither, but she comes to find that the attraction of love is more compelling than that of duty and familial piety as characterized by the unnamed suitor provided by her father.

Cydippe's brief reference to the tale of Atalanta seems to focus on the fact that Atalanta was overcome by a trick involving a golden apple. The myth, however, has a greater significance in the story of Cydippe. When her father began seeking prospective husbands, Atalanta insisted on maintaining her own standards of choice, a course that Cydippe has not followed in the case of the unnamed suitor. Atalanta wished to preserve her maiden status while at the same time keeping the goodwill of her father. The golden apples of Hippomenes finally tricked Atalanta into a marriage agreeable to her father.

As the letter progresses it is clear that the unwelcome attentions of Acontius become more attractive to her. In her girlish simplicity

HEROIDES

Cydippe accepted the man provided by her father. However, given time and an incentive to reconsider her situation, she finds that her choice turns to Acontius.

Yet Cydippe takes great pains to attack the specious argument by which Acontius maintains the existence of a binding oath. This is a finely drawn discussion of what we might call informed consent. For Cydippe, reading aloud the words of the oath did not constitute a binding contract because the utterance was devoid of that consent which can derive only from an informed mind. The *ersatz* legalisms of Acontius are very properly countered by a well-reasoned and psychologically accurate statement on the nature of a contract. Here we find no trickery, no Cupid done up as a lawyer, but only a very cool and dispassionate statement of a basic tenet of the law.

And finally, Cydippe does the unkindest thing of all. She reduces the argument of Acontius to the absurd by urging him not to limit his acquisitive ambition to her but to seek wealth and kingdoms elsewhere. At the hands of this enfeebled girl Acontius (his name suggests sharpness or acuity) has been rendered merely silly.

In the end Cydippe has demolished the arguments of Acontius, but then she freely and without compulsion chooses him to be her husband. With this paradoxical choice Ovid closes the *Heroides*.

> In fear, I read your letter, careful that not
>   even a whisper escaped my lips
> for fear that I might again utter an oath
>   by some god or goddess. I suppose
> you might try a second time to entrap me,
>   though you admit one pledge was enough.
> I should not have read, but harshness would only
>   have angered more the cruel goddess.
> I do all that I can do; I burn incense
>   before Diana. She smiles on you
> more than is right and, as you say, she provides
>   for you her unremitting anger:
> Hippolytus himself was not treated so.[1]
>   The virgin goddess would have done well
> to indulge the years of a virgin like me;

216

years I think she wishes to be few.[2]
The weariness hangs about me for reasons
    I do not know. Tired, I find no help
from doctors. My limbs are shrunken, I am pale;
    see me now, hardly able to write,
hardly able to lift myself on my arm.
    And now I have another fear, that
someone besides my nurse whom I have trusted
    with my dreadful secret will know that
we are now sending letters to each other.
    She sits outside my door and when she is asked
how I fare, replies, 'Asleep.' Safely, I write.
    Soon enough, I require more than sleep
to be believed, I linger too long and those
    she cannot prevent come to my room.
She coughs, giving the agreed sign. I hurry
    to hide the page, my words unfinished,
the letter I began is hidden in my
    shivering bosom. Removed from that place
again, it wearies my fingers. See the weak
    letters, what labour you are for me.
May I die if you are worth such an effort;
    I am more kind than you should deserve.
Now then, is it because of you that my health
    is frail, is it because of you that
I suffer the penalty of your deceit?
    Is this a payment for the beauty
that you have claimed to hold in such high esteem?
    Must I be hurt because I have pleased?
Had you thought me grotesque – I wish that you had –
    you would not have noticed my body
and now it would have no need for assistance.
    But I was praised, and now I cry out;
now you two struggle, bringing me to despair
    and my beauty is my gravest wound.[3]
You will not give him the first place just as he
    will never take second place for you;
you confound his prayers as he confounds yours.
    All the while I am a little boat

driven by Boreas out to sea while the waves
     and the tides return it to that day
my dear parents desire. Then a terrible
     anguish strikes me and at the time set
for marriage pitiless Persephone knocks
     at my door, long before her right time.[4]
I am ashamed and fearful, though not guilty,
     that I might seem to have earned the wrath
of the gods. One argues that my illness came
     by chance, another that my betrothed
is spurned by the gods, and – so you do not think
     you are free of such gossip – that you
have caused my illness by some artful poison.
     The source is hidden, but my illness
is plain enough for all to see. You two men
     provoke strife, dispel peace and hurt me.
Tell me, what would you do out of hatred when
     your love for me is so destructive?
Do not deceive me as you have already.
     If you abuse one you claim to love,
I will have good reason to love your rival.
     Save me, shameful man, wish for me death.
Either you no longer have any care for
     the maid you hoped to have because you
permit your unbending will to injure her,
     letting her sink to a shameful death,
or if instead you seek the good graces of
     that cruel goddess to assist me,
she has given you nothing that you can boast
     of when you address your pleas to me.
Either you fail to please Diana and thus
     you have failed to consider my plight
or you are unable to please her and thus
     Diana fails to consider you.
Now I wish that I had not known – at least then –
     Aegean waters and their isle, Delos.
When I went to that place, we hoisted our sails
     on a troublesome sea; we set out
on our voyage at an inauspicious time.

How my feet stepped out, how my feet left
my door, how eagerly my feet stepped onto
  the bright deck. Then twice the canvas sails
came about in a hostile wind. How stupid:
  that wind favoured me, it brought me back,
it tried to prevent this great unhappiness.
  If only it had not changed. But winds
are always fickle and it is foolish to
  complain because they suddenly change.
Excited by the distinction of that place,
  I hurried to visit Delos but
the boat in which I rode seemed without spirit.
  How many times I scolded the oars
for laziness, how many times I complained
  that the wind was saved from more canvas.
Myconos passed, then Tenos, and then Andros
  and Delos stood bright before my eyes.
When land was sighted, I said, 'Why do you fly
  away as we approach? Do you still
float on the sea as you did in ancient times?'[5]
  My feet stepped on the land; nearly dusk,
the sun would soon unharness his radiant team.
  When the sun stirred his horses to work,
my mother arranged my fine hair, setting gems
  on my fingers and gold in my hair,
and with her own hands she draped the splendid robes
  over my shoulders. We went at once
and offered our greetings to the deities
  for whom the isle is a holy place.
We made an offering of golden incense
  and wine and while my mother poured out
the blood of worship on the altar stones and
  heaped up slices of steaming flesh on
the altar's smoky flames, my ambitious nurse
  took me up the path to the temple
and we wandered about in the holy grounds.
  Now I stroll in the porches, and now
I marvel at rich gifts brought by kings and at
  statues placed all about; I marvel

at the high altar made of horns and I see
    the tree that eased the goddess's pain.[6]
I saw everything I could, but memory
    fails me now and my feelings will not
permit me to write about all the wonders
    I was able to see in that place.
Perhaps, as I was looking about, you looked
    at me, Acontius, and to you
my innocence must have seemed an easy prey.
    I turn my steps back to the temple
of Diana with its soaring flight of steps –
    surely no place is safer than this –
when an apple is thrown in front of my feet,
    an apple with this verse – again, I
nearly pledged an oath to you – my faithful nurse
    stooped to catch it, she was startled and
she said, 'Read it.' I read your deceitful lines,
    O great poet. At the word 'marriage',
I was abashed, distracted, and felt the blood
    rush to my face. I turned my eyes down,
in shyness my eyes were drawn down to my breasts,
    the eyes whose aid you sought for yourself.
Pitiful man, are you happy? What glory
    has come to you, whose praise have you won
by playing tricks like these on such a young girl?
    I did not come with shield and axe like
some Penthesilea on the soil of Troy,
    nor did I give you a great sword-belt
of fine Amazon gold like Hippolyte.[7]
    Why rejoice that your words tricked me, a
simple girl, who was taken by your deceit?
    Cydippe was caught by an apple,
an apple caught the daughter of Schoeneus,
    you are a second Hippomenes.[8]
It would have been better for you – if indeed
    that boy truly had you trapped, the boy
who you tell me has those torches – if you did
    as good men do, not try to cheat hope
by deceit but win me by persuasion.[9] Then

you would have gained a prize as precious
to you as surely it is precious to me
        and I would then be free of your tricks.
Why, when you sought me, did you fail to announce
        what you have that I might want to win
your love? Instead of this, why did you use force
        rather than words to win my love as
I weighed your case? What good are such careful oaths;
        why should one's tongue call on a goddess
to be its witness? I tell you now, it is
        the mind that makes an oath; and no oath ever
has been uttered by me to benefit you.
        Only intention gives form to words.
Only counsel and the soul's careful reason
        can shape an oath, for without judgement
to set limits to the deed, no oath is said
        to have force or even existence.
If I chose to pledge you my hand, then demand
        the rights of the promised marriage-bed.
But if you have nothing but words without will,
        you have nothing but words without force.
I never swore, I read out words in the form
        of an oath. That is not the way you
should be chosen by me to be my husband.
        Deceive other young girls, send letters
after sending them apples. If this can be,
        take for yourself the wealth of the rich;
let kings pledge their thrones to you; let anything
        that gives you any pleasure be yours.
If your writing has such a god-like force then
        you must be greater than Diana.
However, after all these bold words, after
        refusing you, after my plea that
my promise is defective, I must admit:
        I fear Leto's violent offspring,
and I suppose that my illness comes from her.[10]
        Why is it, do you think, whenever
the holy ritual of wedlock is prepared,
        the limbs of the chosen bride collapse

221

in weariness? Three times, now, Hymen has come
    to the altars erected for me
and three times has he fled, his back turned upon
    the doorway of my wedding-chamber.
The torches that have blazed up so many times
    at his easy touch will hardly rise
again; the torch he waves is hardly lighted.

    Many times, the sweet scent of his hair
has gathered about us and the bright saffron
    of his cape has made our house splendid.
When he sets his foot on the threshold and finds
    nothing here but tears and mortal fear —
so much that has nothing to do with his ways —
    then with his hand he tears the laurel
from his head, throws it down and wipes the sweet oil
    from his shining hair. He is ashamed
to stand, joyful, in a crowd of mourners and
    the blush of colour in his mantle
soon passes to his cheeks. But I, how wretched:
    my arms are dry from my fever and
the blankets that cover me seem too heavy.

    I see my parents weep beside me;
instead of a wedding-torch my bed is lit
    up by the dismal torch of dying.
Goddess, who takes such delight in that quiver
    so richly decorated, give me
the healing help of your brother.[11] You would be
    disgraced, then, if your brother brought health
to me dispersing this dread disease while you
    alone remain the cause of my death.
Is it possible, goddess, that once you washed
    in some pool and I, not knowing, saw
you naked at your bath?[12] Or have I ignored
    your altars, forgetting you among
the gods and goddesses of heaven above?[13]

    Perhaps at some time my mother gave
offence to your mother.[14] But I have not sinned,
    except that I spoke a false oath and
I was able to read some unlucky verse.

You, if your love for me is no lie,
prepare an offering of incense, and let
the hands which have injured me bring help.
If you are so angry that one pledged to you
is not yet yours, why are your actions
such that she can never be yours? While I live
your hope is all; why should the cruel
goddess take away both my life and your hope?
Do not think that he to whom I am
betrothed caresses my fevered limbs. Rather,
he sits by my bed, a virgin's bed.
Somehow, he seems to question me, for his tears
suddenly come out of hiding and
his praise is less, he kisses me less, he calls
me his in words that are less certain.
I cannot be surprised, by many signs I
reveal myself: when he comes I turn
in silence to my right side; I pretend sleep
and I remove his hand from my flesh.
His quiet body heaves with sighs; he endures
the annoyance he does not merit.
Poor me, that you can be glad at such a state;
poor me, I reveal myself to you.
If anger were to come to me it is you
who deserves it, you who spread the net.
You ask permission to visit my sickroom;
from a great distance, you can hurt me.
I wondered at your name, 'Acontius'. Yours is
a sharp point that wounds from far away.
I have not yet recovered from such a wound
because your letter — a dart — pierced me.[15]
But why would you come to me? I am just a
poor body, the prize won by your skill.
My flesh is wasted and it hangs from my bones,
my colour is not tinted with blood —
that apple, I remember, was colourless —
my face is white, without any red.
New marble has such a brightness and
equally white is silver set out

on the banquet table, pale because it has
    been touched with the chill of iced water.
If you saw me as I am, you would say that
    you had not laid eyes on me before,
and you would say, 'I have never used my skills
    to win for me a maiden like that.'
Seeing me, you would return to me my pledge,
    afraid that perhaps I might be yours;
you would hope most sincerely that the goddess
    would willingly forget all of it.
Perhaps, on seeing me now, you might again
    require a pledge, but this time a pledge
phrased in words for me to read quite opposite
    to the words of what I pledged before.
Still, I wish that you could sit here by my side,
    as you have asked, so that you might see
the sickly limbs of the bride promised to you.
    But if your will were harder than steel,
Acontius, still you would ask that my pledge be
    forgiven. Know that the god who speaks
at Delphi is being asked to tell us what
    is required to make me strong again.
It is whispered that on the testimony
    of his sister he has some complaint,
that a pledge once made has not been carried out.
    So the god has said, so his prophet,
the oracle.[16] Indeed, what your heart desires
    must surely be the will of the gods.
How have you found such favour? Perhaps you found
    some new text by which even the gods
can be netted. And since you have snared the gods
    I must obey them and cheerfully
let my captive hands carry out your prayers.
    With my eyes turned to the ground in shame,
I have told my mother of the oath my tongue
    was forced to swear. What remains will be
your concern; even this letter, which is more
    than women of virtue should write, has
not hesitated to address you. I tire

myself with this pen; my feeble hand
now objects to do its work. There is nothing more –
since I hope to join you soon – to add but 'Farewell.'

NOTES

1. The story of Hippolytus is told more fully in letter IV. See also
HIPPOLYTUS in Appendix I: Principal Characters.

2. In this passage the goddess to whom Cydippe refers is Diana (the Greek
Artemis) in whose shrine she inadvertently and unwittingly read the oath
that prompted this letter and that of Acontius.

3. The two in contention are Acontius and the unnamed suitor to whom
the hand of Cydippe has already been given by her father.

4. Persephone (the Roman Proserpina) was a goddess of the Underworld.
The only child of Zeus and Demeter, she was kidnapped from a garden on
earth by Hades, presumably with the permission of Zeus but without the
permission of her mother. Eventually, it was decided that she should spend
one third of the year in the Underworld with her husband and two thirds of
the year on earth with her mother. Her annual return to earth occurred in
the spring and coincided with the sprouting of the seeds which had lain
dormant all winter. Although Persephone was identified with the fertility of
the land in the spring, she was also associated with death and burial. These
two aspects of Persephone should not be seen as contradictory so much as
mutually fulfilling. The story of Persephone is found in many different
sources: in the *Odyssey* (X.492–510, XI.213–27 and XI.632–5); in the 'Homer-
ic Hymn to Demeter'; in Ovid, *Metamorphoses* (V.341–571); and in Claudian,
'The Rape of Proserpine'.

5. The islands of Myconos, Tenos and Andros lay along the route to the
island of Delos. There was a tradition that in early times Delos had floated
on the surface of the sea until it became fixed in the place it occupies now. In
antiquity Delos was the site of shrines to Apollo and Artemis, and also a very
prominent centre for maritime trade.

6. Leto became pregnant by Zeus. She wandered across the earth searching
for a place to give birth, but no place was willing to have her because, it was
said, all were fearful of the burden that would come to the birthplace of a
child of Zeus. More likely, however, all feared that those who sheltered Leto
would also win the enmity of Hera, who hated Leto. There are various
accounts of Leto's delivery, but the reference here is to the story that she
found shelter under a palm tree on Delos where she gave birth to Apollo.
The story of Leto is to be found in the *Homeric Hymns*, 'To Delian Apollo',

as well as in Hesiod, the *Theogony*, and Homer. The story is told in great detail by Ovid in the *Metamorphoses*, VI.157–381.

7. Penthesilea, an Amazon queen, killed her friend Hippolyte, also an Amazon queen, in an accident. She went to Priam seeking purification and forgiveness. According to some accounts, this was given in exchange for her promise to help Priam in his conduct of the war with the invading Greek armies. Soon, she became one of the most formidable of Priam's warriors, killing many Greeks in battle. Finally, however, she was killed by Achilles. For Cydippe to assert that she is unlike Penthesilea is an understatement on her part.

When Hercules was assigned his seven labours, the sixth was that he should win the belt of Hippolyte and, presumably, Hippolyte herself. When the contest was over, Hercules gave Hippolyte in marriage to Theseus in gratitude for the latter's assistance.

8. Schoeneus was a little-known king in Boeotia. He is chiefly known as the father of Atalanta. Disappointed when his new-born child was not a boy, Schoeneus abandoned her in a forest. However, a bear suckled her and the infant was eventually found by hunters who raised her to maturity. Atalanta came to love the hunt above all other things and resolved to remain a virgin so that she might go on enjoying the sport. She soon became famous and her father, regretting his earlier rejection of the infant, invited her to his court where he immediately set about finding her a suitable husband. She devised a scheme whereby all suitors were received but she contrived to remain unmarried. Each suitor had to run a race against her. If the suitor won he was to have her hand in marriage, but if he lost he was to be beheaded at once. The suitors were given every opportunity to win the race, with the odds being so skewed that the suitors ran naked while Atalanta ran in full armour. Because of her very great beauty there was no shortage of male candidates, but her prowess on the track was such that none could vanquish her and save his life. However, one young man, Hippomenes, sought the help of the goddess Aphrodite, probably because this particular goddess had quite a low regard for either male or female virginity. Hippomenes entered the race with three apples made of gold. Early in the race he dropped the first before Atalanta and she stooped to pick it up, but she quickly made up the lost distance. Again, the young man dropped a golden apple, and a second time Atalanta paused to pick it up. Nearly at the end of the course, Hippomenes threw the third apple far off to the side and Atalanta, her curiosity unabated, left the course to find it. This final delay ensured Hippomenes' victory and he received the hand of Atalanta. The story is told in Ovid, *Metamorphoses*, X.560–704.

9. Cupid was sometimes depicted with at least one torch symbolizing the ardour of carnal love and desire.

10. Cydippe is here formulating an important legal principle. A contract is more than the words in which the contract is stated. To be valid, the contract must have been entered into willingly and without duress by either party. In fact it is generally held that a contract exacted under duress, or even with insufficient deliberation, is not valid and can be cancelled. Nevertheless, in such instances the burden of proof is heavy. The fact that Cydippe has uttered the words of an oath without forethought and without consideration must be weighed against the fact that a witness, hearing the words, could reasonably expect that they were uttered knowingly and willingly.

Diana is the daughter of Leto.

11. Again, this refers to Diana and Apollo, the children of Leto or Latona. Among his many qualities Apollo was credited with the healing arts. He was invoked in illness, but especially in any mysterious illness which did not respond to the usual medical regimen. Ancient literature has many accounts of Apollo, but he is especially prominent in the *Odyssey* (VIII.226-8 and XV.243-53) and in the *Metamorphoses* (VI.204-66, VI.382-400 and XI.153-71).

12. This suggests the myth of Actaeon: see note 6, page 214.

13. The altar which has been ignored is probably a reference to Oeneus, who caused the advent of the Calydonian boar by neglecting to pay proper homage to Diana.

14. The offence given by the mother of Cydippe to the mother of Diana is a reference to the myth of Niobe and her boast to Leto about her children: see note 7, page 214.

15. The name 'Acontius' is derived from the Greek word for dart. The same word occurs in Latin as *acontias*, a kind of meteor that looks like a dart in flight. Both usages are significant to an understanding of this passage.

16. This is Apollo, the brother of Diana. The wishes of the god were communicated to the suppliants at Delphi through the words of the Delphic Oracle.

Principal Characters

ACHILLES was the son of the goddess Thetis and the Phthian king, Peleus. After being deserted by his mother the infant was raised to manhood by the wise centaur, Chiron. Under Chiron's tutelage Achilles learned all the manly arts and, nourished on the entrails of wild animals, grew up endowed with great strength and courage. The young man returned to his father's court where he met Menoetius, who had recently come to Phthia with his young son Patroclus, seeking shelter in the house of Peleus. Peleus gave Patroclus to Achilles as his companion and, according to some accounts, the two soon became lovers.

After Helen had been abducted by Paris, Achilles and Patroclus joined the Greek forces on their way to Troy under the command of Agamemnon. On their arrival they found the city well fortified and virtually impregnable. The Greek forces then began to lay waste the surrounding cities and towns, of which Lyrnessus was one. This action occupied the Greeks for a period of almost nine years before they were able to begin the siege of Troy.

After the sack of Lyrnessus Achilles took Briseis with him as his concubine. Meanwhile, Agamemnon had taken as his concubine the young girl Chryseis, who was the daughter of Chryses, a local priest. Because his daughter had been abducted by the Greek forces, Chryses enlisted the help of the gods to recover her, and a plague was sent to ravage the Greek forces. When Agamemnon, in council with the Greek leaders, learned that, of all the booty he had taken on this expedition, he was being asked to return Chryseis to her father's house, he rebelled and threatened to abandon the Greek forces. Achilles chided him for being willing to give up any amount of treasure in order that he might keep the girl; Agamemnon countered by saying that if Briseis were to be given to him, he would reluctantly relinquish Chyrseis to her father. The decision was made, and Achilles summarily lost Briseis. The quarrel of Achilles and Agamemnon was notable because each argued that the other was foolish in the extreme to value a barbarian concubine so highly while in fact each man had fallen in love with the girl he had abducted and was then blind to her origins.

This event marked the onset of Achilles' wrath, which figures in the opening lines of the *Iliad*. Achilles sulked in his tent, refusing to go into battle until the plight of the Greeks became so desperate that they had no alternative but to try to placate him. In desperation Agamemnon sent old Phoenix, the son of Amyntor, with Ulysses and Ajax, the son of Telamon, to offer not only the return of Briseis, but also a very substantial amount of treasure if only Achilles would consent to rejoin the battle. Still angry, Achilles refused their offer. Then Patroclus begged permission to wear the armour of Achilles into battle because he saw all too clearly that the Trojan forces, demonstrating their superiority, were threatening to burn the Greek ships. Achilles gave his consent. Unfortunately Patroclus, after fighting with great distinction, was killed in battle by Hector, one of the sons of Priam.

With the death of Patroclus, Achilles' rage knew no bounds. He joined the battle and single-handedly turned back the Trojan attack. Many Trojan men were killed as Achilles sought revenge for the death of Patroclus. Finally the Trojans were driven back within their walls and only Hector was left on the plain to meet the charge of Achilles. With the help of Pallas Athena, Achilles killed Hector and stripped the body, refusing to permit the Trojans to take it for burial. Finally, Priam came to him after dark, alone, and with the greatest humility begged to be given the corpse of his son. On the advice of his mother, Thetis, Achilles relented. Achilles himself was killed by Paris at the walls of Troy.

ACONTIUS is a character found primarily in the *Priapea* (XVI.5), a collection of erotic stories circulating in Rome at the time of Ovid. According to this account Cydippe had gone to the temple of Diana at Delos where a young man, Acontius, rolled an apple across the pavement before her with an inscription scratched on its surface. Unable to resist her curiosity, Cydippe stooped to pick up the apple and, noticing the inscription, read the words aloud: 'I swear by this place that is sacred to Diana to marry Acontius.' By making the statement she had in fact sworn an oath, albeit unwittingly, and set in motion the turmoil which is the topic of letters XX and XXI.

AENEAS was the son of Anchises, a Dardanian king, and the goddess Aphrodite. When the Trojan War broke out he and the Dardanian troops were brought into the Trojan army and he took command of them under Hector. By the time of Virgil the Homeric story of Aeneas was altered to include the prophecy that Aeneas would become the founder of Rome. Aeneas is described as escaping from Troy leading his infant son, Ascanius, and carrying his aged father and the statues of their household gods on his back. As they fled from the burning city Aeneas' wife, Creusa, became separated from them and was lost. Aeneas had no idea where he must go to establish his new city; they travelled from place to place, experiencing terrible hardships, until they were told by their household gods that they should seek the country from which Dardanus, their ancestor, had come. That country was Italy.

After many adventures, Aeneas and his ships reached Carthage in Northern Africa where, at the instigation of Cupid, Dido fell in love with him almost as soon as he disembarked. Aeneas would have been quite happy to remain in Carthage for the rest of his life. With great reluctance, however, he finally recalled his divine mission, gathered his men, and set sail. In time Aeneas and his men reached the coastal town of Cumae, near Naples, south-east of the present site of Rome, where they settled. Silvius, the son of Aeneas by Lavinia, founded the city of Alba Longa, while the establishment of Rome itself would await a descendant of Aeneas, Romulus, many generations later. Aeneas figures in the *Iliad* and in the *Metamorphoses of Ovid* (XIII.623–726, XIV.72–157 and XIV.441–622). Virgil's *Aeneid* is devoted entirely to his adventures.

ARIADNE was a daughter of Minos, King of Crete, and his wife, Pasiphaë. Ariadne had many brothers and sisters but probably her most renowned sibling was her sister Phaedra, who eventually married Theseus, to whom Ariadne writes the tenth letter of the *Heroides*. The brothers of Ariadne all became powerful kings of various lands and cities subject to the rule of Minos. As a daughter of Minos and Pasiphaë, Ariadne was descended from Zeus and Europa on her father's side and from Helios, god of the sun, and Perseus on her mother's side.

BRISEIS was the daughter of Briseus, King of Lyrnessus. When the Greek forces were gathering at Troy they systematically attacked and defeated the surrounding cities that were allies of the Trojans. Achilles and his men attacked Lyrnessus and in the battle the king and his sons, Mynes and Epistrophus, were killed, as was the husband of Briseis. Of the family only Briseis survived and she was captured by Achilles who made her his concubine. The first book of the *Iliad* is largely devoted to the quarrel of Agamemnon and Achilles which followed the sack of Lyrnessus; Agamemnon's concubine, Chryseis, had been taken from him and in her place he had been given Briseis. Letter III in the *Heroides* is written by Briseis as she waits for Achilles to reclaim her as his own.

CANACE was the daughter of Aeolus. The name Aeolus is commonly given to the god of the winds, but a Thessalian king also had the same name. This latter Aeolus seems to have sired ten sons and seven daughters by Enarete, his wife. Among these offspring were Canace and Macareus. Aeolus discovered that Canace was guilty of incest with Macareus, and, after killing them both, he himself committed suicide.

In some sources Aeolus the king is also identified as the keeper of the winds, and it would seem that Ovid wrote the eleventh letter of the *Heroides* following that tradition. It is significant that in this letter Canace has clearly been commanded to kill herself; though incest was hardly unusual among the gods, Aeolus – whether he was human or divine – attached to the act the stigma it bore in the Roman world. It is possible that Aeolus took such grave exception to his children's incestuous relationship because he feared that incest was solely an Olympian prerogative. Ironically, the name Macareus is derived from a word meaning 'happy'.

CYDIPPE: See ACONTIUS.

DEIANIRA was one of the daughters of Oeneus, King of Calydon, and his wife, Althaea. She became the wife of Hercules. Though Deianira had a number of brothers and sisters, the best-known of her siblings was her brother Meleager who organized the Calydonian boar hunt, one of the great adventures of the Greek myths.

DEMOPHOON was the son of Theseus, the Athenian king, and Phaedra. Demophoon and his brother Acamas took part in the siege of Troy, and it was on his return voyage from the city that Demophoon met Phyllis. Accounts of the two brothers are sometimes confused, so that the tale of the affair with Phyllis is also told of Acamas. However, most accounts agree that the man who seduced Phyllis and promised to return to become her husband in fact left Thrace with no intention of every returning. It would seem that the lives of Demophoon and Acamas are completely overshadowed in ancient literature by those of their parents and little is know of the brothers apart from this incident.

DIDO, who was also known as Elissa, and her brother Pygmalion, were born in the city of Tyre. In time Pygmalion succeeded their father, Belus, as king and Dido was married to their uncle, Sychaeus. Pygmalion, however, learned that Sychaeus was a much richer man than he seemed, and in an attempt to obtain that wealth he killed his uncle. The ghost of Sychaeus came to Dido, told her of the murder, and urged her to leave the city as quickly as possible. She left in haste and made her way to the area of Libya, in North Africa, where she bought from the inhabitants enough land on which to found a city. When fleeing the ruins of Troy, Aeneas came to Carthage where he and Dido became lovers.

The presence of Aeneas was welcome to Dido because she had been increasingly pressed to receive the attentions of Iarbas, a neighbouring king. Though Aeneas and Dido were very much in love, Aeneas was unable to lose sight of his divine mission – to establish a new city somewhere in Italy on the banks of a river. The story of Dido figures prominently in Virgil's *Aeneid* (I.335–756, IV.1–705 and VI.450–76).

HELEN was the daughter of Zeus and Leda. Leda was the wife of Tyndareus, but Zeus coveted her great beauty and seduced her after taking the form of a swan. Leda was also the mother of Clytemnestra who became the wife of Agamemnon, and of twin sons, Castor and Polydeuces, known as the Dioscuri. Though accounts disagree on the paternity of these children, it is most commonly asserted that Helen and Polydeuces were the offspring of Zeus, while Clytemnestra and Castor were the offspring of Tyndareus.

At about the age of twelve Helen was abducted by Theseus who desired her not so much for her great beauty as for the fact that she was of the lineage of Zeus. There is a myth, though it is not very widespread, that Iphigenia was the result of this abduction. The Dioscuri immediately raised an army and rescued their sister.

Not long after, Tyndareus decided that Helen should be married. Because of Helen's celebrated beauty, suitors came from far and wide to seek her hand. Tyndareus realized that with so many suitors from all the rich and powerful cities of Greece there was a real possibility that war would break out among those who would necessarily be disappointed. He sought the advice of Ulysses who shrewdly suggested that Tyndareus should exact from each of them an oath that they would always defend the couple against adversity. All the suitors willingly consented, not knowing that this oath would bind them together as allies in the Trojan War.

After being given to Menelaus of Sparta as his bride, Helen conceived and bore a daugher, Hermione. Later, Paris was promised by Aphrodite that he would be given Helen as his wife and came to Sparta to press his claim to her. Her subsequent seduction by Paris who carried her off to Troy marked the beginning of the Trojan War.

Helen figures prominently as a character in Euripides' *Helen*, *Electra* and *The Trojan Women*. She also is to be found in both the *Iliad* (III) and the *Odyssey* (IV and XV).

HERCULES (or Heracles, to the Greeks) was one of the most popular figures of Greek mythology. He was the son of Zeus and Alcmene, the wife of Amphitryon. Alcmene's brothers had been murdered by pirates and she refused to lie with her husband until their deaths had been avenged. Amphitryon successfully attacked and defeated the pirates in their stronghold, and after the victory he returned immediately to Thebes to claim his marital rights. However, on the night before his return Zeus, having disguised himself as Amphitryon, went to Alcmene's bed. In the proper time Alcmene was delivered of twin boys, Hercules and Iphicles. The birth was attended by the goddess Hera, who was greatly angered at the behaviour of her husband. Throughout the infancy and boyhood of Hercules there was often evidence of divine intervention. Amphitryon suspected that one of the boys was his own while the other was the son of Zeus, but he was unable to decide which of the two was in fact his own child. Finally the problem was solved when Hera caused two snakes to approach the infants. Iphicles was terrified and promptly began to cry and scream. Hercules, on the other hand, very coolly strangled both snakes with his hands. At this Amphitryon could no longer doubt which of the two was of human and which was of divine paternity. As Hercules grew to manhood his exploits of courage and strength were the subject of many stories.

The twelve labours of Hercules were imposed on him by King Eurystheus when Hercules had gone to him seeking to be cleansed of the guilt of killing his own children while in a fit of madness sent him by Hera. After the completion of these labours Hercules decided that he would give his wife, Megara, to Iolaus; later he married Deianira, but after his marriage he learned that King Eurytus of Oechalia, who had trained him as an archer, was offering his daughter Iole to any man who might prove himself a better archer than Eurytus himself. Hercules entered the contest and quite easily proved himself the champion. Eurytus, however, refused to keep his part of the bargain. In time Hercules raised an army against Oechalia and after defeating the city found himself in love with Iole. Deianira's revenge finally brought about the death of Hercules.

HERMIONE was the daughter of Helen and Menelaus. At the time of Helen's departure with Paris, Hermione was about nine years of age. When the Greek forces began to mobilize shortly after this, Hermione was promised to Orestes who was in all probability still a boy, not very much older than Hermione herself. Later, while the Greeks were besieging Troy, Menelaus offered and gave Hermione – now a young woman – to one of the Greek generals, Neoptolemus (also known as Pyrrhus), the son of Achilles. The sequence of events here is important. Though Hermione was first promised to Orestes and only later to Pyrrhus, she was in actual fact first given to Pyrrhus. Her account in letter VIII of her protests to Pyrrhus refer to the fact that she regards herself as certainly betrothed, though perhaps not yet married to Orestes. She and Orestes were quickly married after Orestes murdered Pyrrhus.

HERO: See LEANDER.

HIPPOLYTUS was the son of Theseus, King of Athens, and his mistress, the amazon Hippolyte. Theseus was later betrothed to Phaedra, the daughter of King Minos of Crete, but Phaedra fell in love with the young Hippolytus, who had been made King of Troezen by his father. Hippolytus, however, rejected the love of the older woman because he had been pledged to Diana, the virgin goddess. In her fury, Phaedra hanged herself and in a suicide note to Thescus alleged that she had been raped by Hippolytus. Theseus, enraged, not only banished his son but brought down upon him the curse of Poseidon. As Hippolytus was driving along the seashore a bull of monstrous proportions came from the sea and frightened the young man's horses. Hippolytus was thrown from his chariot and killed by the runaway team. After the death of Hippolytus, Theseus learned the truth from Diana herself. The story of Hippolytus is told by Ovid in the *Metamorphoses*, XV.497–546. In this account Hippolytus journeyed down to Hades after his death. There he was rescued by a son of Phoebus Apollo (probably Asclepius) who restored the young man to life. Eventually Hippolytus was smuggled out of the Underworld by Diana who fabricated a disguise for him. Looking for a place where he might live safely she rejected both Delos and Crete and finally took him to Italy where he reigned in Aricia as king. In that area Hippolytus was later honoured as the minor god Virbius, and at Troezen he was revered by young women about to marry.

HYPERMESTRA was one of the fifty daughters of Danaus, the son of Belus. Belus was king of the vast lands drained by the Nile as well as of those territories which had become subject to Egypt. Danaus' twin brother, Aegyptus, had fifty sons. In time Belus divided his kingdom between Danaus and Aegyptus, giving Libya, or the African territories, to Danaus, and Arabia, or the territories to the east, to Aegyptus. Aegyptus suggested to Danaus that his daughters should be betrothed to his own sons. Danaus, with good reason, suspected that Aegyptus was using this as a ploy to destroy him and seize for himself all the lands once ruled by their father, and in her letter Hypermestra subscribes to this theory.

Danaus, accompanied by his daughters, then set out for Argos which he claimed by virtue of his descent from Io. Eventually the sons of Aegyptus arrived to press their suit for marriage with the daughters of Danaus. Danaus, whether willingly or not, consented to the marriage of his daughters, known as the Danaides, to their cousins. But after the wedding when all in the palace had eaten and drunk heavily Danaus gave each of his daughters a knife with the command that their new husbands were to be killed as they sought their marital rights. While Ovid suggests in this letter that Hypermestra spared the life of Lynceus because she found herself suddenly in love with her cousin, a more ancient account says that she refrained from killing him as a reward because he had not taken her virginity. However, the fact that the entire party had eaten and drunk to excess before going to the bridal chambers may well have been sufficient cause for this purported consideration of Lynceus. It is significant that while Hypermestra heard the sounds of men dying, none of the victims was able to raise an alarm. She helped Lynceus escape from her father's house before dawn.

Hypermestra was imprisoned by Danaus as a punishment. Before long she was tried for this crime of disobedience but the court acquitted her of the charge. By virtue of the fact that she alone of all her sisters disobeyed her father and spared her new husband, Hypermestra actually resolved the dilemma in which she found herself. She had Lynceus as her husband, and it was now impossible for Aegyptus to implement his plan to depose Danaus. In fact in one account Danaus is finally reconciled with Hypermestra and her husband.

The story of Hypermestra and Lynceus is also to be found in Apollodorus, *Bibliotheke*. An epic poem, the *Danaides*, and the last two plays of an Aeschylean trilogy beginning with the *Supplices*, are no longer extant. The story seems to have been very widely known in antiquity.

HYPSIPYLE, Queen of Lemnos, was the daughter of Thoas. On their voyage in search of the golden fleece the Argonauts came to Lemnos where they remained to enjoy the hospitality of Hypsipyle. During this time Hypsipyle became pregnant by Jason and after his departure gave birth to his twin sons. Before the arrival of the Argonauts the women of Lemnos had revolted against their men and had eventually killed every man on the island. The suggestion in the myth is that the Argonauts were welcomed to Lemnos with more than customary hospitality. The story of Hypsipyle is contained in Apollonius of Rhodes, *Argonautica* (I.609–909).

JASON, the eldest son of Aeson, was the grandson of Aeolus, god of the winds. His mother is variously named in different accounts. Because Aeson's younger brother had unjustly usurped the Thessalian kingdom of Iolcus, Aeson and his wife – who had every reason to fear for their lives – arranged that when their first child was born the rumour was to be spread that the infant had died at birth. After the birth they hastened to send him to Chiron, the centaur, who raised him to manhood. Jason's uncle, Pelias, the unlawful king of Iolcus, held an annual festival to honour his father, Poseidon. Pelias took great pains in this festival to honour all the gods except Hera. Jason, when he reached the age of twenty-one, determined that he would attend this festival and win back the kingdom that should properly have been his. In coming down from the mountainside where he had spent his youth and early manhood he reached a river. On the bank he found an elderly woman who sought his help to make a crossing, and he carried her to the opposite shore. In the river he lost one sandal but did not stop to find it. When he reached the opposite bank he put the old woman down and hurried on to the city wearing only one sandal.

Pelias, the usurper, had been told years before by an oracle that he would meet his death at the hands of a man descended from Aeolus, a man who would come to him wearing only one sandal. Most accounts of the story agree that the old woman was actually the goddess Hera, the enemy of Pelias, in disguise. Because she had been consistently slighted by Pelias she was preparing to take revenge. Hera's goal in the matter was to bring into the picture Medea who, she thought, would be able to overthrow and destroy Pelias. Medea, however, would have had very little reason to concern herself with the affairs of Iolcus and the fortunes of its ruling dynasty. To engage her interest, Hera determined to make use of the bold and handsome young Jason.

Upon Jason's arrival in Iolcus, Pelias was told that a man with only one sandal had entered the city. Terrified, he hurried to the square and there found Jason. Pelias asked his name. Not only did Jason give Pelias his name, but he also told him that he was there to lay claim to the throne, whether in his father's name or his own. Pelias urgently sought a solution to this problem; he seems not to have entertained the possibility of killing Jason, perhaps because there were in the city many people who could be expected to be partisans of Aeson and his family. The solution Pelias adopted was to ask Jason for his advice about what should be done if someone had threatened to kill him. Jason answered that he would order that person first to bring back the golden fleece.

Another and more plausible version is that of Pindar who tells us that Jason entered the city and immediately met with two of his uncles and their sons. After he told them of his plans to claim the throne for its rightful heirs they encouraged him to present his demand to Pelias. Jason attempted to strike a bargain by offering to allow Pelias to keep the flocks and the land that he had unlawfully seized, while Aeson and his heirs would be given royal power. Pelias, however, cleverly invented a story about a very disturbing dream he had had which had been interpreted to mean that the gods of the Underworld were displeased because the body of Phrixus had been left unburied in Colchis. According to Pelias, the only way to placate the gods was to return the body to Thessaly and bring with it the golden fleece. Pelias begged Jason to do this and further promised that when Jason had accomplished this twofold task he would be given the kingdom.

Whatever the exact circumstances, Jason accepted with great eagerness because he desired adventure and glory. He sent messengers throughout Greece inviting young men from all the cities to join him. A ship was built for him and his men and was named the *Argo* after its builder, Argus. Pelias sent them on their way with every sign of favour and gratitude because he was quite certain that he would never again see either the ship or its crew.

The adventures of Jason and the Argonauts are many and they are found in a variety of sources. It can be said, however, that Jason's success in his quest was furthered more by his glib tongue and his ability to win women to himself than by any heroic qualities; this is confirmed by both Hypsipyle (letter VI) and Medea (letter XII). In all their adventures Jason and his crew were preserved by Hera from harm so that, finally, Medea would be brought back to Iolcus. This was the single-minded intention of Hera – not merely that Pelias be driven from the throne, but that he be utterly destroyed.

Finally Jason and the Argonauts with Medea returned to Iolcus and with the aid of Medea's craft Pelias was killed. With Pelias dead, Hera appears to have lost all interest in Jason. In spite of the success of his quest Jason seems never to have actually reigned in Iolcus. The principal source for the story of Jason is in Apollonius of Rhodes, *Argonautica*, and is also to be found in Euripides' *Medea* and in the *Metamorphoses* of Ovid (VII.1–397).

LAODAMIA was one of the daughters of Acastus, King of Iolcus, who in his youth had sailed with the Argonauts. She became the wife of Protesilaus, King of Phylace. After the death of Protesilaus at Troy Laodamia mourned so deeply that Protesilaus was permitted to return to her for a mere three hours. When Protesilaus went back to the realm of the dead Laodamia committed suicide in order that she would never again be parted from him. Wordsworth used this myth in his poem 'Laodamia'. There is a very brief reference to Laodamia in Homer, *Iliad* (II.695–710). There is also a reference to her in Apollodorus, *Epitome* (III.30), and in Hyginus, *Fabulae* (103–4).

LEANDER (and Hero to whom Leander addresses letter XVIII), who drowned while attempting to swim the Hellespont to reach Hero, does not figure in any extant text before the time of Virgil, who refers to the story in the *Georgics* (III.258–63). In Virgil's text the tale is clearly presented with the presumption that the reader will know it in its entirety since it is summarized without mention of the names of the two lovers. Ovid makes reference to the myth of Hero in the *Amores* (II.xvi.31f.). In the fifth century AD Musaeus Grammaticus composed in Greek a *Hero and Leander* which was widely read in late antiquity. The story was the source for Christopher Marlowe's *Hero and Leander* which was published in 1598 after its author's death. In 1810 Byron swam the Hellespont, crossing from Abydos to Sestos, and in 1813 he published the poem *The Bride of Abydos*. Keats devoted a sonnet – 'On a Leander Which Miss Reynolds, My Kind Friend, Gave Me' – to what would seem to be a graphic representation of Leander swimming through the stormy sea. The legend has also been the subject of paintings by Rubens and Turner. According to the story, Hero drowned herself in the Hellespont after learning that Leander had drowned.

LYNCEUS: See HYPERMESTRA.

MACAREUS: See CANACE.

MEDEA was one of the daughters of Aeëtes, King of Colchis, and either Idyia, one of the Oceanides, or Hecate, the daughter of Perses. As a young woman Medea was renowned for her very great beauty. She became a priestess of Hecate, one of the goddesses associated with the Underworld. Because of her training in witchcraft and sorcery she was adept at casting spells in the practice of magic. She was also famous – or notorious – for her skills in the use of medicinal and poisonous herbs.

The goddess Hera had conceived an all-consuming hatred for the Greek king Pelias of Iolcus, because he had either refused or neglected to give her proper worship. For some reason Hera herself was unable to punish the king so she devised an extremely elaborate scheme that would bring Medea to Greece to accomplish his ruin. The scheme, briefly, caused the Argonauts to set out for Colchis at the command of Pelias. While the apparent reason for their voyage was that they should bring back to Iolcus the golden fleece, it was actually Hera's primary intention that they should return to Greece with Medea. That so complex a campaign was devised to achieve a relatively simple end necessarily led to many complications. However, we must remember that it is in the complication that we find the delightful story.

When Jason and the Argonauts reached Colchis they were met by Aeëtes and his family. Through Hera's influence, Jason fell in love with Medea at their first meeting. After Jason had promised to marry her, Medea with her charms and spells gave him control of the dragon that guarded the golden fleece so that he could seize the fleece, kill Aeëtes and flee from Colchis. According to some versions of the story she also helped Jason to kill her brother Absyrtus, whose corpse they dismembered and threw from the deck of their departing ship so that the people of Colchis would gather up the parts of the body for burial before they continued their pursuit of the pair.

While Jason had been promised by Pelias that the throne of Iolcus would be his when he delivered the golden fleece, the Argonauts doubted that this would in fact prove to be true. Medea, however, saved the day by going to Pelias in disguise and promising to restore his youth. This was to be accomplished by inducing the daughters of Pelias to kill their father, dismember his body and boil the flesh. Medea assured them that after this had been done their father would be completely rejuvenated. All too eagerly they acquiesced and it was only after the body had been boiled as Medea directed that they realized – in horror – that they had been deceived.

Eventually Jason and Medea left Iolcus and went to Corinth where they inherited the throne once held by Medea's father, Aeëtes. They remained in Corinth for about ten years during which time Medea bore Jason either two or three sons. The Corinthians welcomed the rule of Jason but they hated and feared Medea, whom they perceived to be a barbarian and a sorceress. It quickly became obvious to the people, as it had now become obvious to Jason, that Medea would have no scruples in gaining her wicked ends, and he recognized his own danger. In the past he and Medea had shared the same or similar objectives; now, however, they were living a life of peace and stability, with little need for violent intervention, and in this context Medea and her proclivities for evil were not only embarrassing but also dangerous. Finally, Jason was offered the hand in marriage of Creusa, the daughter of King Creon. Because Creusa was Greek and Medea a barbarian, Jason, with Creon's aid, decided to banish Medea and marry Creusa.

Medea, on learning of this, devised a horrible revenge. Feigning acquiescence in Jason's plan, she prepared a splendid robe as a wedding gift for Creusa. The fabric of the garment, however, was impregnated with a deadly and painful poison. When Creusa wrapped herself in it, her body began to burn and though she threw herself into a cistern of water she very quickly died in agony. Medea escaped the wrath of Jason and the Corinthians by being carried off to the skies in a chariot drawn by a team of dragons.

While Medea was reputed to be a thoroughly evil person, she is presented by Ovid as one who has also been deeply hurt. While no attempt is made to hide the truly vicious side of her personality, she reveals herself here as a woman of at least some feeling. In the *Metamorphoses* (VII.1–397) Ovid tells a somewhat different story: he characterizes Medea as a sorceress quite devoid of any nobility, and certainly as anything but a tragic heroine. In the *Metamorphoses* she is utterly evil, destructive and inhuman; in the *Heroides* her portrait is somewhat softened.

OENONE was the daughter of the river-god Cebren. Her home was on the slopes of Mount Ida, where she met and fell in love with the youthful Paris. She was married to Paris but eventually he left her behind in Troy so that he might journey to Sparta to claim Helen, the wife of Menelaus, who had been promised to him by Venus. Her story is told by Apollodorus in his work *On the Gods*.

ORESTES was one of the sons of Agamemnon and Clytemnestra. Though he had many adventures, the most notable derives from the fact that his mother and her lover, Aegisthus, killed Agamemnon. This murder was committed because Agamemnon had sacrificed Iphigenia, his daughter by Clytemnestra, in order that the goddess Artemis might be appeased and the Greek fleet allowed to sail to Troy. In some accounts the girl was actually spared at the last minute, although it would seem that the bystanders did not perceive this turn of events and word of her death eventually reached Clytemnestra. Clytemnestra, with the aid of Aegisthus, murdered Agamemnon in retaliation and eventually she and Aegisthus were married.

On learning of the death of his father and the recent marriage of his mother and her lover, Orestes set out to plot their murder. This was accomplished with the help of his sister Electra and his close friend Pylades. For this act, justifiable though it might well have been, Orestes was haunted by the Erinyes, or Furies. The story is told in the trilogy of plays by Aeschylus, the *Oresteia*, but it is only mentioned briefly by Homer.

The episode of Hermione, however, occurred before Orestes killed his mother and her lover.

PARIS was the son of Priam, King of Troy, and his wife Hecuba, and he was the younger brother of Hector, the renowned Trojan warrior. During her pregnancy Hecuba had a dream in which she had given birth to a blazing log of wood which caused the city of Troy to be engulfed in flames. In great agitation, Priam consulted his prophets and soothsayers and was advised most emphatically that the infant about to be born would cause the downfall and ultimate destruction of Troy; because of such potential danger, it should be killed at birth.

After the birth Priam took the infant to a shepherd with instructions that the boy be exposed on the slopes of Mount Ida. This command was carried out. Several days later, however, the shepherd returned to verify the baby's death and found that, far from being dead, the child was not only alive but was also being suckled by a bear. The shepherd, perhaps not realizing the significance of the baby's survival, took it to his hut and raised it as his own. The infant grew to be a youth of great strength and most remarkable beauty.

At one time Paris was tending his flocks when a band of brigands attempted to steal the animals in his care. Single-handedly the boy fought off the robbers and saved both the flock and the other shepherds who were there with him. For this he was given the name Alexander, which means 'defender of men'.

One day servants from Priam's house came to take away the finest bull in the herd. They explained to the boy that Priam was holding funeral games to honour a dead son and the bull was to be the prize for the victorious athlete. Because Paris did not wish to lose this particular bull but could hardly refuse the king's command, he gave the bull to the servants and then followed them into the city hoping that he might enter the games and receive the prize. Paris competed with many young men of noble birth and position and it quickly became obvious that he was an athlete of unusual quality.

In the course of the games he defeated both Deiphobus and Ilioneus, sons of Priam and his own brothers, and certainly the very best examples of Trojan virtue and strength. Deiphobus became angry that someone with no name and no background was winning all the contests and he drew his sword and pursued the stranger who took refuge at the shrine of Apollo. It was there that Cassandra recognized Paris as her own brother. After this he was welcomed into the family of Priam and soon after married Oenone. In letter V of the *Heroides* there is a strong suggestion that Oenone and Paris were at least lovers, if not husband and wife, before his recognition as the son of Priam. At the time he was restored to his proper place in Troy, there seems to have been no indication that the prophecy of the fall of Troy at the hands of Paris was recalled. After the death of Paris, Deiphobus became the husband of Helen. Deiphobus was killed by Menelaus as the Greek king searched through the ruins of Troy for his wife.

Meanwhile Peleus and the goddess Thetis (who would one day be the parents of Achilles) were celebrating their nuptials. All the gods and goddesses had been invited to the occasion except Eris, known also as Strife. Eris took her revenge on the married couple by throwing into the assembled company a golden apple inscribed 'For the fairest'. When the inscription was read out, three goddesses – Aphrodite, Hera and Athena (known to the Romans as Venus, Juno and Minerva) – immediately claimed the bauble. Clearly Zeus did not wish to see the wedding feast disrupted by a quarrel so he decreed that the three were to go to Mount Ida and show themselves to the most beautiful man in the world, Paris, who would be well qualified to judge their claims to the title.

The three goddesses, escorted by Hermes, appeared before Paris. The situation was explained to the young man and at once the three goddesses began to ply him with favours and bribes. Hera promised that by choosing her he would become monarch of all the earth. Athena pledged that if he chose her he would always be victorious in war. Aphrodite, however, promised a gift that was not so grand but probably much more suited to the personality and proclivities of Paris. She promised him the love of the most beautiful woman in the world, Helen, who was now the wife of Menelaus. Confronted with such a choice, Paris lost hardly a moment in announcing that Aphrodite must be the most beautiful of the three.

Paris returned to the city and the palace of Priam to announce his imminent departure for Sparta. When the family, and in particular Cassandra and Oenone, learned of the plans for his voyage they were greatly disturbed. Paris, however, did not listen to their concerns and went about his affairs, making preparation to sail at the earliest opportunity.

Arriving in Sparta he was received by Menelaus with the greatest hospitality and, when Menelaus was called away to Crete, Paris and Helen together set sail for Troy. The abduction of Helen marked the beginning of the long and bitter Trojan War, which eventually led to the death of Paris.

The story of Paris figures prominently in the *Iliad*, particularly in books III.15–382, VI.312–64, VI.503–29, VII.347–64, XI.368–83 and XXII.355–60.

PENELOPE was the daughter of Icarius, a king of Sparta. Though her father urged her to remain in Sparta even after her marriage to Ulysses, she went with her husband to his kingdom on the island of Ithaca. One son, Telemachus, was born of this marriage. When the Greek forces were called to fight in the Trojan War, she remained at home with her infant son to preserve the possessions of her absent husband. In time her name became identified with the images of the faithful wife. When the Greek troops had all returned to their homes Ulysses and his men were still abroad. As soon as it became apparent that Penelope's husband was not managing his own affairs in Ithaca she found herself surrounded by suitors, all of whom were anxious for her hand and the rich properties that would come with such a marriage. She resisted, insisting that it was her obligation first to weave a shroud for Ulysses' father, Laertes. By day she would ostentatiously work at the loom but by night she would undo the day's work. In the meantime the suitors were virtually living in her house waiting for her decision. Eventually they learned of her deception and gave her no choice but to finish the work without delay. At this point Ulysses returned, slaughtered the suitors, and reclaimed his kingdom and his household.

Penelope figures prominently in those sections of the *Odyssey* devoted to the kingdom and homeland of Ulysses. The accounts of her activities as the wife of Ulysses are to be found in the *Odyssey*, particularly in Books I, XIX and XXI.

PHAEDRA was the daughter of Minos, King of Crete, and his wife, Pasiphaë. She was also the sister of Ariadne. Eventually she became the wife of Theseus and thereby stepmother to Hippolytus. At the time of Phaedra's marriage to Theseus, Hippolytus was a very young man. When Hippolytus rejected her overt advances because he had already pledged himself to the cult of Diana, she hanged herself and left a suicide note for Theseus in which she told him that his son had attempted to rape her.

The story of Phaedra is told in Euripides' play *Hippolytus*, as well as in the *Metamorphoses* of Ovid (XV.497–546).

PHAON is the name given to the lover of Sappho in letter XV of the *Heroides*. This character is unknown in ancient literature except in conjunction with Sappho. There is very good reason to believe that he is a fiction invented in later years. Some attention, however, should be given to the information about Phaon which is here provided. In the opening lines of this letter Sappho makes reference to the fact that he is in Sicily, somewhere near the volcanic Mount Aetna. This could very well be an attempt by Ovid to link Phaon with the girlhood sojourn of Sappho in Sicily, though the apparent disparity in their ages would make it quite unlikely that Sappho as a girl could have known Phaon when she was living in Sicily. We can infer, though we know little else, that Phaon has not merely gone away from her, but has in fact gone a very great distance, almost across the breadth of the Mediterranean world.

PHYLLIS was the daughter of a Thracian king. When the Greek forces were returning to Greece from Troy, Demophoon's ship was driven ashore in a storm. As a result, Demophoon and Phyllis met and fell in love, and as a pledge of her fidelity she gave him her virginity. Her father's kingdom was offered to Demophoon, but the young man declined to accept it. He left Thrace and vowed to come back in a short while for Phyllis. Eventually Phyllis realized that he had no intention of ever returning for her and in her despair she hanged herself. On her grave an almond tree took root and flourished. Though very little is known of Phyllis, Ovid does suggest that her properties included at least parts of what had once been the kingdom ruled by Lycurgus. Apart from the name and the barest description of the seduction and abandonment, there is very little about Phyllis in ancient literature beyond what is to be found in the *Heroides*.

PROTESILAUS was King of Phylace, a city in Thessaly. He was the son of Iphiclus and Diomedia. Not long after he married Laodamia he set out for the shores of Troy with forty ships. An oracle had warned the Greeks that the first man to set foot on Trojan soil would also be the first to die. It would seem that the prospect of such a fate should have prevented a Greek landing. However, the ships were met by forces under the command of Hector and Cycnus, an ally of Troy. Protesilaus impetuously leapt from his ship as he led an attacking band of Greek troops. A skirmish immediately broke out between the Greeks and the Trojans and Protesilaus killed several Trojans, but before long he himself was killed. With that first Greek death many others soon followed. Though there is mention of the death of Protesilaus and of Laodamia in the *Iliad* (II.695–710), there is little beyond the passing reference to the fact of his death and her grief. There is a very brief reference to Protesilaus in Herodotus, *Histories* (VII.33 and IX.116–20). There is also mention of the story in the *Cypria*.

SAPPHO, the lyric poet, was born about 612 BC. Very little is known of her life, and the date and place of her death are not recorded. It is probable that she spent her childhood in Sicily and it is certain that she spent her adult life on Lesbos, an island which lies off the coast of Asia Minor. In Mytilene, a city on Lesbos, she established herself as a lyric poet and became the leader of a cult, composed mostly of young girls, which honoured Aphrodite and the Muses. She lived among these cult members, lavishing great affection on various of them, writing poems both about them and dedicated to them. As they came of age and were married, Sappho also composed wedding songs for them. Sappho became the wife of Cercylas and bore him a daughter, Cleis. She had one brother, Charaxus, who caused her severe disappointment because he wasted his virtue and his estate on a prostitute, Rhodopis.

Beyond these few details, nothing is known of her life and death. The account of her death which is suggested by Ovid in the fifteenth letter of the *Heroides* seems to be entirely fictional, as is the story of her infatuation with the young boatman, Phaon. The tale, however, has persisted and has come to be one of the great legends of unrequited or frustrated love.

THESEUS was the son of Aegeus, an Athenian king who as a young man found that he was unable to conceive children. He went to the Delphic oracle to seek advice and was told that he should not open the neck of his wineskin until he had returned to Athens. Not understanding the meaning of this, Aegeus stopped at the court of Pittheus, known throughout that part of the world as a very wise man, on the way home. Aegeus recited the oracle and confessed to his great confusion. Pittheus saw its significance at once but said nothing of it to Aegeus. At a banquet that evening he saw to it that Aegeus became very intoxicated before being led to the bedchamber of Pittheus' daughter, Aethra. As Aegeus was about to depart the next morning he placed sandals and a sword beneath a large stone, telling Aethra that if she should happen to conceive as a result of the previous night's union and bear a son strong enough to move the rock, she was to send the boy to him with the sword and the sandals. Aegeus then set off for Athens, quite unaware that after he had fallen into a drunken stupor the god Poseidon had also entered the bedchamber and had spent the remainder of the night with Aethra. In due time Aethra was delivered of a very handsome and strong son who was named Theseus. When he was old enough he moved the stone and, taking the sandals and the sword, set out for Athens.

Because the boy wished to emulate the heroic tales of Hercules he insisted on travelling to Athens by land because the road was frequented by notoriously dangerous robbers. When Theseus reached Athens he was greeted most warmly by Aegeus, who did not recognize the boy as his son. Medea, however, had already come to Athens with the promise that she could bear sons for Aegeus. She recognized the boy at once as a dangerous rival to her own son and to her position at the court of Aegeus. She prepared a cup of poisoned wine which she caused Aegeus to offer the young guest. At the last minute the king recognized the sword fastened to the boy's belt and as he hurried to embrace his son he knocked the cup of wine to the floor.

The presence of a son to inherit the kingdom caused the king's brother, Pallas, and his sons to begin a rebellion. Single-handedly, Theseus killed many of the followers of Pallas and finally forced Pallas and his sons to flee. Some years before, King Minos of Crete had attacked Athens at a time when the inhabitants were weakened by disease. The Athenians were unable to mount a defence and had finally made peace with Minos by agreeing to send a tribute in every ninth year of seven boys and seven girls to be fed to the Minotaur. Theseus volunteered to join the group. On the voyage from Athens to Crete there were many adventures, not unlike the adventures of Hercules.

When he reached Crete, Theseus caught the eye of Ariadne, daughter of Minos and Pasiphaë. She knew all too well that if he were able to enter the labyrinth and kill the Minotaur he would still be unable to find his way out of the maze. Accordingly she gave him a ball of string which he was to unwind as he searched the labyrinth for the Minotaur. He entered the underground maze, found and killed the Minotaur, and made his way back to the surface. Because Ariadne had betrayed her father by befriending Theseus she was obliged to leave Crete as he set out for Athens. Among many different accounts of the subsequent fate of Ariadne, the most likely is that Theseus abandoned her on an unpopulated and barren island, Dia, now known as Naxos. She was rescued either by Dionysus or by his priest, Oenarus.

ULYSSES (the Greek Odysseus) was the son of Laertes, King of Ithaca, and Anticleia. Because Ulysses was so devious it was sometimes suggested that he might really be the son of Sisyphus, and not of Laertes. Like most of the prominent young men of that time Ulysses also was one of the suitors of Helen, the daughter of Tyndareus, the Spartan king. Tyndareus feared that when Helen finally made her choice of husband, violence and war would break out among those rejected. Ulysses promised to solve this problem for Tyndareus if in turn Tyndareus would secure for Ulysses the hand of Penelope, Tyndareus' niece. Gratefully, Tyndareus agreed to the plan and Ulysses advised him to require of each and every suitor the vow to defend Helen's husband against all hazards that might befall as a result of his marriage to Helen. This was done, and in time Helen married Menelaus and Penelope married Ulysses. When Helen was later abducted from the palace of Menelaus and messengers were sent to each of the former suitors to remind them of their vow, Ulysses reluctantly left his kingdom, his wife and his infant son to follow Menelaus and Agamemnon to war. After the fall of Troy the Greek forces found their way back to Greece. Ulysses and his men, however, remained absent. His palace quickly came to be filled with many suitors all seeking the hand of Penelope and while they pressed their respective suits they consumed the wealth, the flocks and the storehouses of Ulysses.

From all sides, Penelope was pressured to accept the hand of one of these men, not only because Ithaca needed a king to take change of its affairs, but also because it did not seem appropriate that she and her son should live without the guidance and protection of a man. Of course, as her marriage would provide a king for the country and a master for her house, the man selected would also become extremely rich and powerful.

Most of the stories of Ulysses revolve around his ability to deceive his foes in a variety of ways. For this he came to be known as wily, and his name became synonymous with trickery. Needless to say, this trait won for him very many powerful and spiteful enemies.

The sources for the life of Ulysses are very rich, but the most obvious and accessible are Homer's *Odyssey* and *Iliad*, and the *Metamorphoses* of Ovid.

Index of Names

Abderus, 86
Absyrtus, 114, 238
Abydos, 179f., 184, 187, 192, 195, 238
Acamas, 231
Acarnania, 144
Acastus, 118, 237
Achaia, 154, 163, 174
Achelous, 82, 87, 157, 164
Achilles, 4, 7, *letter III*: 19–27, 66ff., 70f.,
    73, 75, 206, 212f., 226, 228ff., 233, 241
Acontius, xiv, xvii, *letter XX*: 202–14,
    letter XXI: 215 27, 229
Acropolis, 199
Actaeon, 207, 214, 227
Actium, 139, 144f.
Adonis, 37
Adrastus, 178
Aeacus, 69f., 73
Aeëtes, 50ff., 106f., 114, 174, 177, 238f.
Aegean Sea, 65, 75, 152, 161f., 187, 189,
    211
Aegeus, 13, 32, 36f., 94f., 159, 244f.
Aegina, 73
Aegisthus, 68, 70, 74, 240
Aegyptus, 234f.
Aeneas, *letter VII*: 56–66, 163, 229ff.
Aeneid, 56, 230f.
Aeolus, 54, 85, 91, 95ff., 98ff., 102, 187,
    199, 230f., 235f.
Aerope, 163
Aeschylus, 17, 66, 68, 235, 240
Aeson, 49f., 52, 54, 106, 110, 174, 177,
    235f.
Aethra, 16, 94, 156, 172, 176f., 245
Aetna, Mount, 133, 141, 243
Aetolia, 213
Africa, 230f.

Agamemnon, 20ff., 23, 25ff., 45, 66ff.,
    73f., 164, 228ff., 232, 240, 246
Agrius, 82, 88
Ajax, 24f., 26, 229
Alba Longa, 230
Alcaeus, 86, 134, 142
Alcides, 80f., 86
Alcidice, 199
Alcimede, 51, 54
Alcmene, 84, 232f.
Alcyone, 188, 191, 196, 199f.
Alexander (Alexandros), 165, 240
Allecto, 15, 18
Althaea, 26, 213f., 231
Amazon, 30
Ambracia, 139, 144
Amor, 29, 63, 161
Amores, xvf., 237
Amphitryon, 78, 84f., 232f.
Amymone, 196, 199
Amyntor, 21, 25, 85, 229
Anactoria, 134, 141
Anatolia, 162
Anchises, 63, 65, 155, 163, 229
Androgeos, 92, 95
Andromache, 43, 46, 66, 69, 73,
    117
Andromeda, 134, 142, 184, 188
Andros, 219, 225
Anna, 64
Antaeus, 79, 86
Antenor, 43, 45
Anticleia, 245
Antigone, 123
Antilochus, 3, 7
Antinous, 6, 8
Antiope, 38

247

INDEX

READ MORE IN PENGUIN

In every corner of the world, on every subject under the sun, Penguin represents quality and variety – the very best in publishing today.

For complete information about books available from Penguin – including Puffins, Penguin Classics and Arkana – and how to order them, write to us at the appropriate address below. Please note that for copyright reasons the selection of books varies from country to country.

In the United Kingdom: Please write to *Dept. EP, Penguin Books Ltd, Bath Road, Harmondsworth, West Drayton, Middlesex UB7 0DA*

In the United States: Please write to *Consumer Services, Penguin Putnam Inc., 405 Murray Hill Parkway, East Rutherford, New Jersey 07073-2136.* VISA and MasterCard holders call 1-800-631-8571 to order Penguin titles

In Canada: Please write to *Penguin Books Canada Ltd, 10 Alcorn Avenue, Suite 300, Toronto, Ontario M4V 3B2*

In Australia: Please write to *Penguin Books Australia Ltd, 487 Maroondah Highway, Ringwood, Victoria 3134*

In New Zealand: Please write to *Penguin Books (NZ) Ltd, Private Bag 102902, North Shore Mail Centre, Auckland 10*

In India: Please write to *Penguin Books India Pvt Ltd, 11 Community Centre, Panchsheel Park, New Delhi 110017*

In the Netherlands: Please write to *Penguin Books Netherlands bv, Postbus 3507, NL-1001 AH Amsterdam*

In Germany: Please write to *Penguin Books Deutschland GmbH, Metzlerstrasse 26, 60594 Frankfurt am Main*

In Spain: Please write to *Penguin Books S. A., Bravo Murillo 19, 1°B, 28015 Madrid*

In Italy: Please write to *Penguin Italia s.r.l., Via Vittorio Emanuele 45/a, 20094 Corsico, Milano*

In France: Please write to *Penguin France, 12, Rue Prosper Ferradou, 31700 Blagnac*

In Japan: Please write to *Penguin Books Japan Ltd, Iidabashi KM-Bldg, 2-23-9 Koraku, Bunkyo-Ku, Tokyo 112-0004*

In South Africa: Please write to *Penguin Books South Africa (Pty) Ltd, P.O. Box 751093, Gardenview, 2047 Johannesburg*